1.50

MAJ

IBIZA AND TENERIFE

A Rock Climbing Guide
by
Chris Craggs

CICERONE PRESS
MILNTHORPE, CUMBRIA

© Chris Craggs 1995
ISBN 1 85284 189 3
A catalogue record for this book is available from the British Library

Acknowledgements

This book is dedicated to all the people with whom I have climbed with on these superb islands over the past six years: John and Oliver Addy, Mike Appleton, Colin Binks, Dave Gregory, Rory Gregory, Willie Jeffey, Mike Riddings, Jim Rubery, and Dave Spencer. Special thanks go to Pete (POD) O'Donovan who, in a hectic week, proved to be a very effective one-man checking machine, devouring many of Majorca's harder routes with relish. Also thanks to all the talented climbers who have offered advice about the grades of the harder routes, especially Andy Barker, Roger Briggs, Gary Gibson, George Haydon, Paul Harrison, Tony Mitchell, Dave Musgrove, Mike Owen, and Karl Smith. And to Dave Gregory whose hawk-eyed proof-reading has pulled out most of my more glaring grammatical gaffes. Special thanks as ever to my 'other half', Sherri Davy, who always handles the mundane tasks of organising flights, accommodation, car hire, shopping, etc. and still finds the energy to do plenty of belaying and a few routes. Thanks also to Harrison Photovideo, London Road, Sheffield who have always handled my photographic needs faultlessly, to Premier Car Hire of Harlow for many years of good service and to Cicerone Press who have supported the idea of this volume from its inception.

A special thanks must go to the small nucleus of climbers on each island without whose talents and hard work these places would not be worth a visit by the serious sport climber.

Where we have gone others will follow, and they will wonder why it took them so long to catch on.

ADVICE TO READERS

Readers are advised that whilst every effort is taken by the author to ensure the accuracy of this guidebook, changes can occur which may affect the contents. New fences and stiles appear, waymarking alters, there may be new buildings or eradication of old buildings. It is advisable to check locally on transport, accommodation, shops, etc. but even rights of way can be altered, paths can be eradicated by landslip, forest clearances or changes of ownership. The publisher would welcome notes of any such changes.

Front Cover: *Pete (POD) O'Donovan on the perfectly named*
NA C'AL LES SEYCHELLES, 7a (E5 6b), Tijuana

CONTENTS

ROCK CLIMBS IN MAJORCA

ROCK CLIMBS IN IBIZA

ROCK CLIMBS IN TENERIFE

MAJORCA - CRAG LOCATIONS

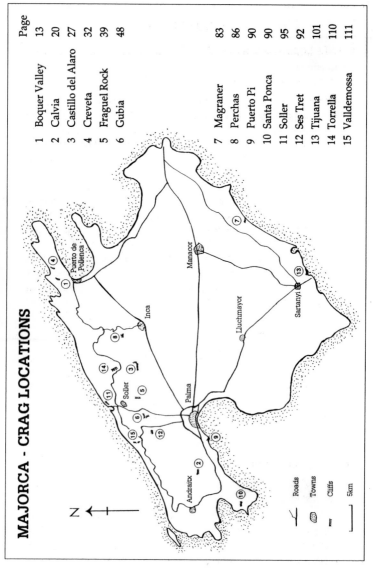

Majorca

INTRODUCTION

I first visited Majorca in 1988 after a series of excellent winter holidays in and around the Costa Blanca. As always when visiting somewhere new, I had some reservations: chiefly because information on the climbing was hard to come by and I had heard that the weather could be less reliable than on the mainland. It was therefore with some trepidation that we booked a trip, but then again nothing ventured... Flying in over the Sierra del Norte on that first afternoon dispelled all the doubts, and as we have got to know the island so our feelings for the place have continued to grow. It is a truly stunning place, worth one visit by anybody, and a lot of visits by most others. Whether you want a few easy routes to spice up a restful beach holiday or you want to climb classics in superb surroundings or to spend a week climbing routes in the upper 7s, Majorca has lots to offer.

On that first trip to Majorca in the winter of 1988 I was impressed by several things. As expected, the weather was pleasantly mild and the island was quiet, having its annual breather from the invading hordes. More surprising was the stunning beauty of much of the island, and perhaps of most significance was the amount of undeveloped rock scattered around the place.

In the back of my original 1990 guide to the Costa Blanca I included a brief thirty pages on Majorca as a simple introduction to it. Since that guide was published there has been considerable development, and I stand firmly by my 1990 prediction that "...there is little doubt that Majorca will become a major European centre for sports climbing in the years ahead". Indeed it is not inconceivable that Majorca will become **the** premier European centre for winter rock climbing, such is the wealth of rock, the ease of access from the UK and Germany, and the good weather.

Majorca (referred to locally as Mallorca) remains the premier foreign holiday destination for Britons abroad. Even given the emergence of Greece and Turkey and other more exotic summer venues, Majorca stills sees in excess of 7 million visitors a year. The chief attractions are the unending summer sunshine, fine beaches and crystal clear seas. To service this summer influx there is a massive infrastructure with the 'Costa de Concrete' stretching around the Bahia de Palma from Santa Ponca to

El Arenal, and with various soulless outliers scattered up the eastern edge of the island. There are also much more traditional resort towns typified by the beautiful Puerto Pollenca on the north of the island, and Soller to the west.

The flights, the accommodation, the weather and the rock are already organised, the rest is up to you!

GETTING THERE

There are more flights to Majorca from the UK than to any other holiday destination, and they leave from all national airports. Prices vary from knock down (less then £50 return) at quiet times to rather inflated (say £150+) during the school holidays. All inclusive packages can be good value, though self-catering accommodation of all classes abounds. Shop around! If all else fails it is worth considering taking a scheduled flight with Iberian Airlines, though this can be rather pricey. They fly direct from Heathrow, or from Manchester via Barcelona. At quiet times they do special 'two for the price of one' deals. Telephone London: 0171 8300011, Manchester: 0161 4366444, Glasgow: 0141 2486581.

TRANSPORT

A car is pretty much a necessity. Although the island has a reasonable transportation system a number of the cliffs are remote, and the distances involved between the various centres make for difficult commuting. It would be possible to stay at Gubia or Fraguel Rock and cope without a vehicle (once you were established) but then there are the problems of shopping, water and security. For car hire I have always used Premier Car Hire who are based in Harlow. They offer a range of vehicles with prices starting at about £85 a week in the winter. Telephone 01279 641040 for a current brochure. A rep will meet you at the airport (don't forget your driving licence) and the car is normally delivered with a full tank of petrol. You leave it as empty as you dare at the end of the holiday. I have had a request from Premier to ask climbers not to park too close to the cliffs. One car was returned with a do-it-yourself sun roof!

A BASE

Quite where you stay on the island depends in part upon the kind of holiday you envisage. Both Puerto Pollenca and Soller are exceptionally pleasant but they are a touch remote from the mainstream climbing areas. However they are ideally situated for exploring the northern mountains and coasts and make perfect bases for family holidays. On the other hand the modern resorts, for example Magaluf or Palma Nova, have some positive points:

they are quiet in the winter, accommodation is plentiful and most of the climbing is within a 20 to 30 minute drive. If you want comfortable, cheap accommodation, with easy shopping and some low-key nightlife you could do worse!

It is probably best to avoid resorts such as Porto Cristo and Calla Millor on the eastern edge of the island unless you enjoy driving. If you book a package with accommodation allocated on arrival, beware; Murphy's Law ensures that you will end up as far from your favourite cliff as is geographically possible!

A good percentage of the accommodation on the island is owned by British people and it is usually possible to sort something out before you leave home. The Sunday papers and magazines like *Dalton's Weekly* or *Private Villas* have plenty of places to rent, usually with UK contact numbers. Another alternative is simply to turn up and look for signs saying 'apartments to rent' in any of the resorts. Prices can be as low as £10 a night for basic accommodation for four (cheaper than camping back home or even than camping in Spain). Again, the key is to shop around.

SEASON

It goes without saying that the best time to visit Majorca is in the depths of the northern winter; the climate then is usually pleasantly mild and the whole place is quiet. Unfortunately good weather is not guaranteed, but you would be unlucky not to get an adequate time on the rock any time between October and April. Despite this I once heard of a team of Scots who had a week's holiday on Majorca: it rained every day and they all got flu! Their experience was exceptional.

If family commitments and other circumstances conspire to force you to visit the island during the hotter months of the year, all is not lost. With a bit of foresight there is enough rock that faces out of the sun at different times of the day, so some good sport should be available. The mountains are high enough to escape the worst of the heat, and of course the beaches are always available once it becomes just too hot.

THE GUIDEBOOK

This is the fourth guidebook I have written to foreign rock climbing destinations and the production of these guides has undergone a gradual evolution. Wherever possible I have tried to take on board the comments people have made on the previous books, and the overriding aim of this guide is to provide as much information as possible. It strikes me that if people buy a guide, the more information it contains the better! To this end

9

I have included full descriptions with Spanish and UK grades for as many climbs as possible, pitch lengths, star ratings, and as much peripheral information as has been available.

The cliffs in the guide are broadly of two types. The first and largest number are the traditional, well publicised cliffs on which I have been able to accumulate detailed information from a variety of sources. The second class are cliffs (often recently developed) for which solid facts and even the route names have been harder to come by. The information on these has come from an amalgamation of personal experience, searches of the Spanish magazines, conversations with both British and local climbers, and a variety of rough topos. The first set of cliffs has been covered in full, whereas the second has been described using a combination of topo format and brief description. Where names have been unavailable I have simply numbered the routes. I hope this provides an adequate basis for locating the cliffs and routes.

I have pondered long and hard as to whether to include UK grades or just stick to the French (Spanish!) grade, but once again the precept of providing the maximum amount of information has held sway. Part of the reason for this is the fact that many (though not all) of the routes on Majorca are graded rather stiffly when compared to their mainland counterparts; this can be up to one and a half grades' difference. It means that some Gubia routes graded *6a+* would get *6c* on the mainland and *6c+* at Buoux. Also there is the slight 'fly in the ointment' that grade anomalies are more marked on some cliffs than others. In the end I have decided to use the currently accepted Majorcan grades and to include UK grades wherever possible. Please feel free to ignore the latter (or the former!). If you find the Spanish grades rather (or very) tough, it is not because you are having an off day; don't get too demoralised!

The grades given are in the form:

6b (E4 6a) indicating confirmed Spanish and UK grades, or *7a?* indicating suspected Spanish grades.

For routes with just a *?* you can fill in your own grades!

Any comments on new routes, grading anomalies, descriptions, etc. are always welcome and can reach me via Cicerone Press.

The cliffs are scattered around the island in a fairly haphazard way, so I have described them in alphabetical order as this seems as logical as any other approach. The map should aid location, with the descriptions in each chapter pin-pointing the cliffs. They are described in the following order.

Crag	Aspect	No. of Routes	Comments
Boquer Valley	All	30	Generally short superb setting
Calvia	S	20	Mid-grade face climbing
Castillo del Alaro	SE	20	Mostly hard, great outlook
Creveta	SW	20	Sharp mid-grade classics
Fraguel Rock	E	45	Tough tufas
Gubia	All	100	The best on the island. Classics
Magraner	SE	30	Pleasant mid grade
Perchas	N	13	Very steep tufas
Puerto Pi	W		Bouldering
Santa Ponca	N	7	Short and sharp
Ses Tret	N	18	Steep and shady
Soller	W	25	Short & easy,+ long & hard
Tijuana	S	30	Majestic, though generally tough
Torrella	NW	12	A couple of great classics
Valldemossa	W	25	Varied roadside crag

THE CLIMBING

All the cliffs in this book are composed of high quality limestone, though the variety of climbing on one kind of rock is quite amazing. From the dripping chandeliers and dribbling wax tufas of Fraguel to the grey sheets of Calvia and the tilted quarried walls of Ses Tret; From the gloomy cave of Las Perchas to the stunningly-situated Creveta, there is climbing here to suit every mood and style. With only two low grade exceptions (Gubia

Normal and Shark's Fin Original) all the climbs are protected by *insitu* fixed bolt protection. Belays on all the routes described are fixed with *insitu* karabiners, maillions or steel rings. All that is needed is a collection of quick-draws - up to a dozen on the longer climbs - and a rope. A 50m rope is an absolute minimum with 60m a better bet. In any event many of the pitches are long enough to require a spare rope to allow an easy descent. If you do not fancy sport climbing then the amount of quality rock scattered around the island, both as mountain crags and sea cliffs, means that you should be able to go off and do your own thing. The chances are you will not see a soul.

Whatever you prefer: enjoy your visit.

A PLEA

Despite the massive scale of the tourist industry on the island, much of Majorca away from the coast remains amazingly unspoilt. This applies explicitly to many of the climbing areas; please treat them and the local inhabitants with due respect. More specifically (and I shouldn't need to say this), don't leave litter, be careful with fires, don't block access routes, avoid crossing cultivated land and don't taint water supplies. If you cannot organise your bodily functions to use the resort facilities, get WELL away from footpaths and the climbing areas. A group trowel might not be a bad idea. If in doubt treat the place like your back garden at home, and you won't go too far wrong.

A WARNING

Crime on Majorca does not appear to occur on the same scale as parts of the mainland where the popular parking areas are regularly 'checked out'. Despite this it makes good sense not to leave any valuables in your car. As an extra precaution I always make a point of leaving the doors unlocked, the empty glove box open, the boot empty and the parcel shelf out of the car so as to discourage speculative break-ins; it makes sense to avoid any holiday hassles.

THE BOQUER VALLEY

Character

A superb wild valley running out to the sea from just north of the beautiful town of Puerto Pollenca, from where it can easily be reached. There is a wealth of rock in the valley and up to the present day the development of the considerable potential of the area has been rather sporadic, concentrated mainly on the boulder field at the entrance to the valley and the prominent 'shark's fin' above these. The path that runs out through the valley towards the sea is an immensely popular walk and is much used by 'twitchers' in search of rare Mediterranean species. The northern side of the valley is bound by the Cavall Bernat ridge, a fine rocky scramble which is Majorca's best known answer to Crib Goch. It is exceptionally exposed on its 'other side' where it overlooks the dramatic setting of the small resort of Cala San Vincent.

Access

The entrance to the Boquer Valley is easily reached from Puerto Pollensa via the prominent tan-coloured castellated farmhouse on the hill behind the town. Drive through Puerto Pollenca towards Formentor until the farmhouse can be seen on the left. Running up towards this is an avenue of trees and just past these a left turn leads into the 'Urbanisation Boquer', a grid-iron road laid out with the street lights in place but no houses as yet (early 1994). Drive to the top left corner of this, then follow the track up past the front door of the farm (cats galore!). Go through the gate on the left, then bear right to reach the good track that runs up through the valley. In less than 10 minutes from the car the first of the boulders is reached; they are big enough to ensure that you are unlikely to miss them.

The routes are described as they are passed walking up the valley, on the boulders first and then on the ridge above the boulders. See map to aid location. As I have been unable to find names for most of the routes I have simply numbered them with the prefix 'B'. Arriving at the boulders, the first one to the left of the track has a low wall and entrance built under it offering a possible bivouac site for the terminally destitute. To the right of the track, opposite this potential doss, is a longer boulder with a very steep north face.

B1 7a? 10m

The underside of the boulder is protected by a selection of ancient bolts. The rather newer bolt on the top suggests that the route may be used for top rope training.

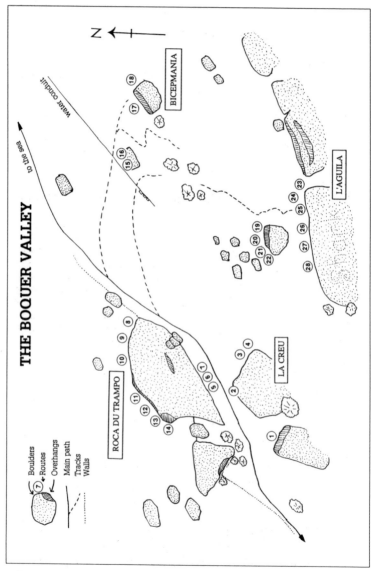

THE BOQUER VALLEY

N ←

to the sea

Water conduit

BICEPMANIA

L'AGUILA

LA CREU

ROCA DU TRAMPO

Boulders
Routes
Overhangs
Main path
Tracks
Walls

Continuing a short distance further the path passes through a narrowing, almost a ravine, between two high boulders. The one on the right side of the track has three routes on it, this boulder is called **La Creu**.

B2 4 (VS 4c) 20m
At the narrowest point of the ravine the rib on the right is approached steeply and then followed on the left or right to the easier upper section. Rather sparingly bolted at present, take a few slings and/or nuts.

Around to the left is a steep north-east-facing wall with two worthwhile routes towards its left side.

B3 ** 5 (E1 5b) 15m
The right-hand line, pleasantly steep and sustained.

B4 ** 5+ (E2 5c) 15m
The left line is slightly steeper, rather more sustained, and just as pleasant.

On the opposite (left when walking up the valley) side of the path through the 'ravine' is the southern side of the biggest boulder in the area (**Roca du Trampo**). On this major monolith is a good and varied selection of ten routes to suit most tastes, though what is arguably the finest face remains undeveloped at present. The attractive sharp arête that faces you as you approach the boulder looks as if it should be a classic VS; carry a rack. The first three bolted routes are located in the left-hand side wall of the ravine, to the right of the sharp arête mentioned above. These are short offerings though they are not without interest. They share a conspicuous and substantial mutual belay, and offer a pleasant introduction to the attractions of sport climbing.

B5 3 (Severe 4b) 7m
The red groove and its right rib lead to a move out right.

B6 4 (VS 5a) 7m
The wall just to the right leads directly to the chains.

B7 4 (VS 5a) 7m
The wall just right again trending leftwards to the chains.

Continuing through the ravine there is some scope on the same wall, notably a tough-looking roof and an easy-looking blocky staircase. The side wall of the boulder then swings round to face north, above a pleasant grassy field which is reached by climbing, with great care, over the stone wall. The rock here gets the sun late in the day, or provides cool shade at other times.

B8 ** 6b+ (E4 6a) 18m
The steeply leaning flake system immediately to the right of the stone wall offers a fine piece of thuggery. Above the termination of the flake continue rightwards up the still steep wall.

B9 * 7b (E5 6b) 18m**
The recently rebolted wall (paired old and new bolts) to the right is thin, sharp and technical. It leads with talent and tenacity directly to the belay of the previous route.

B10 * 7b+ (E6 6b) 18m
The drilled wall to the right starts from a block and at the moment it awaits the attention of the rebolting crew. Once they have given the route an overhaul it will be worth ** or even ***.

The attractive right side of this face is home to three new offerings. They all look well worthwhile though unfortunately I have not done any of them. Grades and stars are speculative.

B11 ** 6c 20m
The first of the new routes pulls over a small overlap then climbs the fine wall to the right of a grey streak to finish over the overhang just below the top of the wall.

B12 ** 6a 20m
The next route to the right looks slightly more amenable. It trends right up a vague scoop and crack line before heading away to the left to a pull over the capping overhang.

B13 ** 6b 20m
Just left of the right arête is a route trending slightly to the left until it almost joins the previous route, then back to the right; finish over the bulges above.

To the right the cliff swings round to form a fine west-facing wall. The excellent-looking central and right sides of this remain undeveloped, though there is a line of closely spaced bolts up the monumentally impressive leaning prow that bounds the left side of the wall:

B14 ? 20m
I hope this one is an aid route, though a recent topo graded it 8a.

The next routes to be described are to be found on the other (uphill) side of the main path. On exiting from the 'canyon' there are several tracks that branch off diagonally to the right and run up the hillside. At the point where the paths cross a water conduit with some small troughs is a diminutive boulder with two 'one bolt wonders' that both lead rapidly to a single bolt lower-off.

B15 4 (VS 5a) 4m
The wall a short distance right of the arête.

B16 4 (VS 5a) 4m
The arête on its right side.

Continuing in the same direction is a much more impressive boulder, easily recognised by its leaning valley face and sharply pointed summit. There are two worthwhile routes here. This is **Bicepmania Boulder**.

B17 ** 6b (E4 6a) 15m
Climb easily into a hollow in the left side of the overhanging face then climb through the roof and on up the tilted arête, using occasional holds around to the left until it is possible to lean across to the right to reach the chains. Steep!

B18 ** 5 (HVS 5a) 15m
Around to the left is a fine wall facing out to sea. Climb steeply onto a ledge at the foot of the face then continue straight up its centre on excellent rock to a lower-off just below the top of the wall.

The final boulder that contains routes is the egg-shaped one capped with conspicuous plants and standing in front of the right side of the 'shark's fin' of rock that towers over this area. Various vague paths lead through the exotic (and sharp) scrub to the boulder. The routes are described from left to right and it is worth pointing out that the upper sections of the first three climbs, though not too difficult, are not overly bolted.

B19 * 6a (E2 5c) 14m
The left-hand route starts (for most mortals) from a pile of stones and trends left through the bevy of bulges to easier angled rock above. The lower section is hard work.

B20 * 5+ (E1 5c) 14m
Gain a good flake then trend slightly leftwards through the bulges to reach the foot of the thin crack in the upper slab. Climb direct from here.

B21 * 5 (HVS 5b) 14m
Climb steeply past mouldering threads (best backed up with your own if you are carrying a sling) to gain access to the more amenable face above. Romp on up the thin crack line.

B22 6a+ (E3 6a) 9m
The right arête of the front face leads steeply to a swing right to chains at the top of the groove on the right. The groove itself contains no bolts, though once the chains are clipped it make a good candidate for a quick technical top roping session.

The final routes described are all found on the line of cliffs that tower over the right side of the valley. There are six climbs here at present; all are worth doing and all are located on the prominent 'shark's fin' locally known as **L'Aguila**. I have also had a report of a traditional route called *SOBRASADA 5-(VS-ish)* which climbs "the corner groove on the left-side of the central buttress, crossing from right to left where it narrows". I have not been able to identify this with certainty though it may be the chimney system that splits the left side of the buttress to the left of the 'shark's fin'.

The routes on the 'shark's fin' are described from left to right. These are:

B23 ** 5 (E1 5b) 20m
Start at the left edge of the face by an old bolt and pull rightwards onto the slab. Trend left up the gradually steepening face on superb rock following the line of speckled bolts to a tricky bulging section. This is most easily tackled from left to right above which a couple of more ticklish moves lead to easier terrain and a rather tatty belay. Leave a karabiner or abseil carefully from the *in situ* slings.

B24 THE SHARK'S FIN * 5 (HVS) 68m**
The original route up this section of cliff is a venerable classic, following a continuously interesting line. The traditional grade of *VS* is a bit niggardly, with the *HVS* tag just being deserved by the initial crack and one tricky move on the final pitch. The first pitch is now fully bolted though a few wires and slings may be required for the rest of the route.
1. 22m   5   (5a)   Climb onto the slab from the left (by an old bolt head) and traverse right to the foot of the crack. This is steeper than it looks and is also quite slippery. It eases after 12m then easier climbing leads to the belay on the previous route.
2. 24m   4   (4b)   Traverse to the right and make an awkward move out right below a bulging wall to gain the base of an easier groove line. Climb this past fixed gear at one possible stance to a better one at the top of the groove.
3. 22m   4   (4c)   Climb the slab trending slightly rightwards until it rears up and a tricky little wall is climbed past an antiquated bolt runner to a belay in a notch on the crest of the ridge. Enjoy the view before thinking about the:

Descent: Either abseil back down the line of the climb or, perhaps safer, traverse the crest of the ridge eastwards for a short distance to the better belays at the top of the *DIRECT ROUTE* and abseil back down this.

B25 THE SHARK'S FIN DIRECT *** 5 (HVS) 65m

A great route, as undeviating as the name suggests, on stunning rock and fully bolted. Well worth the trip to the valley to do.
1. 20m 5+ (5a) Climb onto the slab from the left (by an old bolt head) and traverse right to the foot of the crack of the regular route. Lean right to clip the first bolt to the right then climb the wall, awkwardly at first but generally on good holds, to where the angle drops back and a twin bolt belay and comfortable stance are found.
2. 20m 4 (4c) Climb straight up the slab to a steepening which is tackled by moving right then back left to reach the rib above. Up this to a small stance and very substantial belay.
3. 25m 4+ (5a) Climb straight up the slab to reach the left edge of a vegetated break (loose block in the grass on the right - beware) then continue up the fine sustained 'shark's skin' slab above to a stance astride the very crest of the ridge. Abseil descent.

B26 SECONDA, STELLA A DESTRA ** 7c (E6 6b) 15m

Start at the large painted name and climb the bulging wall on very sharp holds. Oh the agony and the ecstasy!

B27 ** 6b (E4 6a) 20m

Towards the right side of the front face are two bolt lines; the left-hand one has the newer bolts. A tough start leads to a shallow ramp that leads up leftwards until it is possible to trend back to the right to the lower-off.

B28 ** 6a (E3 5c) 20m

The right-hand line has rather older bolts. Climb easily to white ledges then continue up the steep sustained wall above on a collection of razors, knife edges and broken glass.

CALVIA

Character

An excellent small cliff of perfect grey limestone tucked away in a narrow valley in the lightly wooded rolling hills, a short distance inland from Palma Nova. The cliff faces south and so makes an ideal venue throughout the winter and offers an excellent introduction to the climbing on Majorca. The sheltered position of the crag means that it can get oppressively hot in the summer when an early start with a midday break for the beach may be called for. Generally speaking the climbs are not too steep and they are well protected by frequent and substantial bolts; climbing here is chiefly concerned with enjoyment. A competent party can tick all the routes hereabouts in a couple of visits, though in reality that is not what the place is about. To use an Americanism: kick back and enjoy.

From the ground the upward view of many of the climbs can be rather daunting because of the compact nature of the rock. Fortunately, once you rub noses with the raw material it becomes apparent that it is covered in a mosaic of tiny flakes and solution pockets making for elegant though often rather fingery face-dancing. Many of the routes have their names painted in neat black lettering at their foot, thus aiding identification. Without exception all climbs here can be done to the lowering points and back to the ground on a single 50m rope.

Access

From the centre of Palma follow the main coastal motorway eastwards towards the port of Andratx for 13 kilometres to a junction signed Palma Nova (towards the sea) and Calvia (inland). Turn uphill here and follow the road as it winds up away from the coast to reach the old town of Calvia after 6 kilometres. The town contains an impressive church and a number of very pleasant bars, though the latter are perhaps best left until later in the day. In the centre of the village take a right turn that is signed to the oddly titled town of Establishments. (Geographers may have noticed that a branch road runs past the local school and cuts out the need to travel through the centre of the town; this variation can be used as a faster route home.) The narrow road is followed for 2.5 kilometres until the stone wall on the right side of the road ends at a right-hand bend. It is possible to park on the right side of the road just a little further on at a small projecting lay-by or around the corner on the right. The number of cars here is normally a good indicator of how busy the crag will be.

Leave no valuables in the car.

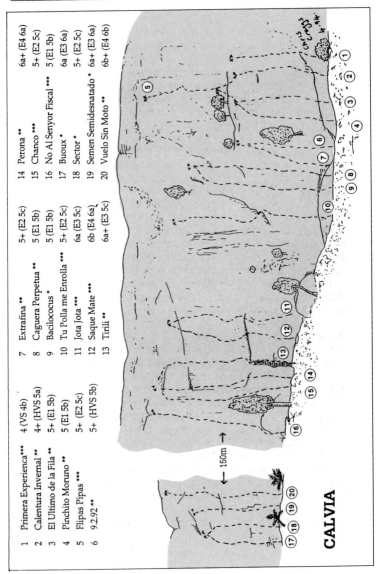

1 Primera Experienca ***
2 Calentura Invernal **
3 El Ultimo de la Fila **
4 Pinchito Moruno **
5 Flipas Pipas ***
6 9.2.92 **

4 (VS 4b)
4+ (HVS 5a)
5+ (E1 5b)
5 (E1 5b)
5+ (E2 5c)
5+ (HVS 5b)

7 Extrafina **
8 Caguera Perpetua **
9 Bacilococus *
10 Tu Polla me Enrolla ***
11 Jota Jota ***
12 Saque Mate ***
13 Tiriii **

5+ (E2 5c)
5 (E1 5b)
5 (E1 5b)
5+ (E2 5c)
6a (E3 5c)
6b (E4 6a)
6a+ (E3 5c)

14 Perona **
15 Chanco ***
16 No Al Senyor Fiscal ***
17 Buoux *
18 Sector *
19 Semen Semidesnatado *
20 Vuelo Sin Moto **

6a+ (E4 6a)
5+ (E2 5c)
5 (E1 5b)
6a (E3 6a)
5+ (E2 5c)
6a+ (E3 6a)
6b+ (E4 6b)

150m

CALVIA

*Willie Jeffrey enjoying some 'winter heat' on CALENTURA INVERNAL
4+ (HVS 5a) Calvia*

Return to the bend and enter the field (on the left coming from Calvia) at a rickety gate. The warning signs indicate that the area is not to be used for hunting, and is not a 'keep out' sign. Follow the track up to the right for 100m and then bear left along terraces making for the prominent valley that lies dead ahead. The main cliff is a rough 10 minute scramble up this and it is hidden until the very last moment; one wonders how the locals ever found it in the first place.

Opposite the point where the path to the crag leaves the main track there is a small crag, partly hidden in the trees on the opposite side of the valley. To approach this please keep off any cultivated land. There are four climbs here: three short and tough and well chiselled pitches on the left side based around an arch, and an innocuous-looking slab that rises behind a large pine tree and is a worthwhile * 5+ *(E2 5c)*.

SECTOR PRINCIPAL

This is the main section of the cliff, containing 16 climbs, all of which are well worth doing. These are described from right to left as this is the normal approach route. To the right of the first route is a slabby area of rock that could provide a few lower grade climbs.

PRIMERA EXPERIENCA *** 4 (VS 4b) 18m

This is the well named bolt line at the very right edge of the main section of the cliff, passing just left of a large bush at 8m. It provides a great pitch with excellent holds and exemplary protection. A tricky couple of moves at half-height from a massive hold provide the main entertainment. A perfect introduction to the cliff and the style of climbing. Now you should realise why you came to Majorca.

CALENTURA INVERNAL ** 4+ (HVS 5a) 18m

The name means 'winter heat'; how apt. Start below a substantial thread at 5m and follow the sustained rib and wall on generally excellent holds to the lower-off. There are plenty of rumours circulating to the effect that this pitch might be worth *E1 5b*; what do you think?

EL ULTIMO DE LA FILA ** 5+ (E1 5b) 18m

The central line on this section of wall gives excellent climbing, well worth doing, and offering pleasant climbing with a titillating couple of moves. Start from a ledge at 3m and head straight up the wall to a small red bulge that is passed slightly right then back left before sprinting smartly to the belays.

PINCHITO MORUNO ** 5 (E1 5b) 18m

Follow the line of bolts immediately to the right of the big tree that grows miraculously out of solid rock. Predominantly large holds lead to a shallow scoop, entering and leaving which requires just a touch of technical application. Just a little higher good holds lead out right to the belay of the previous climb.

The wall above the three previous climbs has a bolt ladder up its centre. This provides a rather tougher extension to the climbs below and is the delectable:

FLIPAS PIPAS *** 5+ (E2 5c) 18m
Large holds are followed to a 'blank' scoop which is crossed leftwards by a couple of slippery and technical moves to reach the belays just above. Excellent sport.

9.2.92 ** 5+ (HVS 5b) 18m
Immediately to the left of the big tree is a bolt line that is followed directly to the crux moves; an awkward bulge just above the final bolt. Lower off the same belay as *EXTRAFINA*.

EXTRAFINA ** 5+ (E2 5c) 18m
A line of bolts (the second one to the left of the big tree and just left of a tufa topped with a flower garden) trends slightly rightwards and passes below a patch of vegetation before reaching ledges and the belay of the previous climb. A sustained and fingery pitch that is a whisker tougher than it looks from below.

CAGUERA PERPETUA ** 5 (E1 5b) 20m
Ten metres to the left of the prominent tree growing from the rock is a steep slab with two bolt lines running straight up it. This route follows the right-hand line which gives fine sustained climbing with an abundance of *in situ* protection. Great fun.

BACILOCOCUS * 5 (E1 5b) 21m
The left-hand line starts at a small scratched arrow by a right-facing white flake. Climb straight up the slab towards a conspicuous flake system 20m off the ground. On reaching this move up and right to cross over to the lowering point of the previous climb.

TU POLLA ME ENROLLA *** 5+ (E2 5c) 25m
A superb pitch up the steepening wall immediately to the right of a prominent area of grey flowstone high on the cliff. The lower wall is quite tricky and leads to a diagonal steepening. Cross this leftwards and then head up the steep wall using a series of large wart-like protuberances to reach a

gradual easing in the angle above. Continue up the sustained wall with moderately spaced bolts to the lower-off. Superb.

To the left the base of the cliff rises up and a huge fallen flake is reached. The collection of climbs above this area is hardest on the cliff due to the steeper nature of the rock. Fortunately the bolt protection remains as good as ever. The next two routes start from on top of the flake.

JOTA JOTA *** 6a (E3 5c) 24m
One of the finest pitches on the cliff, giving sustained and involved climbing that is never desperate but is always interesting. If you find it easy award yourself an *E2 5c* instead of the given grade.

Step off the flake and climb the easy slab to steeper rock. Pull over the overlap leftwards on hidden holds (providing you can locate them) then head directly up the steep wall by complexed and sustained climbing, all very absorbing.

SAQUE MATE *** 6b (E4 6a) 24m
Another great climb, though a fingery little critter. From the flake climb the unprotected but straightforward slab to the steep rock to a bolt just to the left of yellow marks, or follow the previous climb to its second bolt and then step left. Cross the bulge by a tough sequence on small finger holds then continue straight up the wall on spaced sharp holds. Fortunately the frequency of the bolts allows you to concentrate on the technicalities of the climbing rather than having to worry about the prospect of imminent death.

The next feature to the left is a shallow corner crack formed by a right-facing flake. Starting here is:

TIRILI ** 6a+ (E3 5c) 22m
Climb the corner to the bulge and cross it awkwardly rightwards to gain a blunt, hanging rib. From here head up the steep wall on good holds to a second bulge which is passed to the right of the bolt line by a strenuous sequence of moves. Continue up the still steep face before strength evaporates and it becomes possible to head left to the belays.

Between the right-facing flake and a large tree there are two climbs that start up a smooth-looking slab and then climb steeper rock above.

PERONA ** 6a+ (E4 6a) 22m
Up the right side of the slab by thin move to reach the steeper wall. Step right, almost onto the previous climb, then trend slightly leftwards on small holds to a final steepening which is crossed with difficulty to better holds and then a lower-off as for the previous climb.

CHANCO *** 5+ (E2 5c) 22m

A fine pitch, steep, sustained and unlikely. Climb the left-hand line on the slab, passing the first bolt with difficulty to reach easier rock and then a good pocket containing an interesting collection of herbage. The steep wall above is sustained and requires occasional blind moves until relief arrives in the form of some large holds. Swing right to the lower-off of the previous two climbs.

NO AL SENYOR FISCAL *** 5 (E1 5b) 20m

The last route on the main section of the cliff is well worth seeking out and gives climbing that is no pushover but that is easier than it looks. Start 3m left of the big tree and climb a flake to the left of the initial bolt until it is possible to swing right to gain the line of the route. This gives superb sustained climbing. Clip in and relax; welcome to the cruise!

A couple of hundred metres further up the valley, on the same side as the main cliff, is a dome-shaped buttress known as the SECTOR BUOUX This section of rock has four worthwhile pitches that are useful when you have 'ticked' the main cliff, or if it proves to be a bit too busy. The grades here appear to be even more astray than on the rest of the crag. The area is most easily reached by following a vague path along the dried-up stream bed until the buttress appears on the right, though a vague track from the left edge of the main cliff can also be used. To the right of the routes described below is a clean slab that could provide half a dozen lower grade routes with just a little expenditure of time and energy. The routes are described from LEFT to RIGHT.

The first climb starts at the left edge of the front face of the buttress below three hollows in the rock 3m off the ground.

BUOUX * 6a (E3 6a) 14m

Climb into the scoops then step right and continue by sustained fingery and blind moves straight up the face until it is possible to swing right to the large but solitary belay bolt.

SECTOR * 5+ (E2 5c) 14m

Start between two clumps of bushes at a flat block on the ground directly below a red roof at 50ft. Climb the centre of the face on good but spaced holds until a long reach gains good holds in the hollow below the red roof. Swing left to the belay of the last climb.

SEMEN SEMIDESNATADO * 6a+ (E3 6a) 14m

Start to the right of the bushes and climb a floral slab to steeper rock. This is climbed up a red streak on small but generally good finger holds to a belay in the right side of the hollow.

VUELO SIN MOTO ** 6b+ (E4 6b) 20m
The rightmost line climbs the slab and then continues up the steep and technical wall passing just to the left of a prominent orange streak to gain a shake out at a large flaky pocket. A final difficult sequence leads from here up and right to the belay. The hardest pitch in the valley.

CASTILLO DEL ALARO

Character
The cliffs that almost completely encircle the impressive mountain (822m) behind the small town of Alaro are amongst the most extensive on Majorca, though development has been minimal up to the present date. There are enough climbs here for one or two visits at the moment, always depending on the grade you climb at, though most of the best routes here are pretty tough. These are crowded towards the left edge of the cliff where the rock is not high, and coincidentally this is also the closest point to the car park! Extending rightwards from the developed area the south-facing cliffs rise ever higher. According to a very rudimentary topo from the climbing shop in Palma there is a small collection of 'trad' routes here at the moment, up to four pitches in length. At the point where the cliff swings round to face east the rock is in the order of 250m high and it is manifestly magnificent. Climbers looking for a bit of traditional adventure climbing could do worse than to direct their attentions here. The cliffs at the Castillo del Alaro (and on Soncadena, 816m, directly across the valley) are approaching the scale of the Falaise d'Escales in the Verdon but their development is in its infancy; they will doubtless become major destinations in the fullness of time.

The climbs are numbered and described from right to left as they are passed walking up towards the entrance to the cliff top castle.
Note: On the regular approach and before the minor road begins to rise steeply it loops round a small valley that contains a couple of prominent large boulders, the bigger of which is egg-shaped. There are about ten short routes here, all bolt-protected and generally fairly hard. A good number of the routes utilise chipped or drilled holds. The boulders may be suitable for a short day, or to collect a few quick ticks on the way back down from the main cliffs, though the routes are not very inspiring.

Access
From the town of Alaro follow the road northwards towards Orient. In a couple of kilometres signs are seen for the Castillo del Alaro; follow these! The road that runs up the mountain starts off tarmaced but then becomes

unmetalled and rather rough. A considerate approach towards your car's underbody is probably a good idea. An impressive taverna is passed at about half-height (well worth checking out on the way back down) and the road continues to wind its way up the hill until it pops over a col to arrive at an extensive parking area in the trees. From here a well made path heads up rightwards towards the only gap in the cliffs about 10 minutes' hike away. Shortly before the main climbing area is reached the path jinks rightwards through a gateway and on the left here a huge boulder has a bolt line running up a scoop on its front face. The route looks quite worthwhile.

The buildings on the hill top are about another 10 minutes' walk from the climbing. They include a bar, restaurant, and cheap rooms and they form a very popular destination for weekend walkers who troop up the path in their hundreds. The walkers are always politely intrigued by the climbers though if you are not too keen on performing in a public arena it might be best to avoid weekend visits to the cliffs.

The Climbs

The first route described climbs a clean slab 50m after the last bend on the approach path to the castle and just to the right of a large tree growing at the foot of the slab, close to the path. On the right are two lines up to the right edge of the grey slab, the direct version is *SNOW BOARD* * 5 (HVS 5a), whilst the loop out to the right is a less worthwhile *FIDO DIDO* 5+ (HVS 5b). Fifty metres further right again is another slabby section of rock with three climbs, a slab direct *VAGON ROLL 5 (HVS 5a)*, its right edge *LAS MALLAS DE CRISTO 5 (HVS 5a)* and a short wall on the right *HOLA QUE TAL? 6a (E2 5c)*.

Returning to the slab above the path:

A1 *** 5+ (E1 5b) 28m
The pleasant slab leads to steeper rock and then a series of bulges which are passed using undercuts to reach a flake. From here swing briefly right into a groove and then back left to a steep pull to gain the belays. A fine sustained pitch.

To the left of the tree is an easy slab leading to a line of overhangs 10m up the face. Two short and rather inconsequential 'quick ticks' climb through these. The ledge at the base of the climbs is most easily reached by a short scramble from the left where a red ladder is painted on the rock. It is possible to belay on the first bolt runner.

A2 SOBRASSADA * 4 (VS 5a) 14m
Climb through the centre of the bulges by a right-trending groove. An exceptionally well bolted pitch and a safe introduction to 'sport' climbing.

CASTILLO DEL ALARO

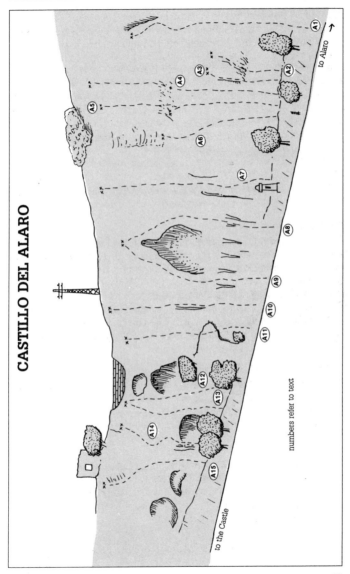

numbers refer to text

to Alaro

to the Castle

A3 FRIT * 5+ (E1 5c) 14m
A line up the left edge of the bulges following a vague crack line to a couple of taxing layback moves to reach the belays.

Directly above the slab with the ladder painted on it is a steep orange wall where there are three routes of rather more substance than those just to the right, and also a 'half route' for those looking for something a little gentler.

A4 NO RES *** 7a+ (E5 6b) 23m
The right-hand line is good and hard. It contains several blind moves and some mighty sharp rock.

A5 MATA GUIRIS *** 7a+ (E5 6b) 25m
The central line is another tough cookie with the crux passing the bulge and the top wall proving to be on worryingly 'crunchy' rock.

A5.5 ** 5+ (E1 5b) 16m
Climbing the previous route as far as the bulge just below its crux proves to be pleasantly sustained. When things turn tough it is possible to lower off using the substantial twin rings.

A6 AFERRA EL TUL ** 6b (E4 6a) 20m
The left-hand of the trio trends leftwards up the wall. The lower wall gives pleasant sustained climbing to a rest below a bulge. Passing this proves to be the crux with a difficult pull on poor holds being required to gain the easy angled hollow above. A worthwhile climb.

To the left is a bush on the slab and left again is an odd brick construction that may be of religious significance. On the wall behind the construction is:

A7 ZATROPECK *** 7b (E6 6b) 25m
A line between the prominent grey tufas is marked by old bolt heads and more recent bolts.

To the left of the construction is a large orange recess 10m up. Two tough routes climb either edge of this, making strenuous use of tufas and not quite uniting at their lower-offs just above the niche. These are:

A8 MUERTA YA *** 7c 25m
The right-hand line, *and*

A9 FROAM PARTY *** 7b+ 25m
the left-hand line.

A10 AMIGOS PARA SIEMPRE *** 7c (E6 6c) 25m
To the left of the orange recess is a wall with two more routes. This first one climbs a prominent thin tufa and continues up the steep pockets and bulging orange head wall to a move right to a lower-off in a niche.

Left again and directly under the electric cables is:

A11 ESTEBAN ** 7b (E5 6b) 23m
Climb easily over a right-facing flake then continue up the steep wall by fingery moves on a motley assortment of sharp pockets.

Further to the left is the final collection of routes hidden in a hollow by a collection of bushes and situated directly below part of the castle walls. There are four worthwhile climbs in this nicely secluded setting. These do not appear to have names. The rightmost line starting from the bay is:

A12 ** 6a (E2 5b) 16m
The juggy bulging rib is protected by white bolts. It is followed steeply on generous holds, trending generally leftwards. Muscle-bound gorillas will doubtless denounce the route as *VS 4c*.

A13 ** 6b+ (E3 6a) 15m
The bulging white rock to the left is climbed directly. The 'blank' section is overcome by judicious use of the cunning local idea of a drilled mono-doigt (if you can find it). Steep jug pulling up the rib above remains.

A14 *** 6c (E4 6a) 15m
Gain and climb the right trending orange tufas to the left of the cave 5m up, until these fizzle out. From here powerful moves can be made left across the bulging rib to regain the line which continues with sustained 'interest'.

A15 ** 6c (E4 6a)
The final route offers more steep climbing starting from the cave at the left edge of this section of the cliff, and trending leftwards up the steep wall into the final groove.

There are three other developed sections of cliff that lie about 10 minutes' walk to the right from the apex of the last bend on the approach to the above section of the cliff. Here there are (at present) about 25 routes varying in grade from 5+ to 8a and development continues. The most impressive sector is the ZONA CHORRERAS on the far right, recognised by its impressive tufa systems. The 7 bolt ladders here are from left to right: a project, HOB NOPSI 6c+, BUG 7a, TO PA TI 7a+, CLONACION 7a+, PILAR 7b and another project.

CREVETA

Character

A relatively recently developed cliff that has a lot to offer: a broad range of grades, perfect if somewhat rough rock, plentiful protection, and an idyllic outlook. In some ways the crag is complementary to the popular Calvia which is situated towards the other corner of the island, though the setting of Creveta is rather grander. The climbing tends to be less than vertical and much of it is on very sharp holds; a couple of days here requires a high pain resistance or skin like a pachyderm. A stiff pair of boots and good footwork may pay dividends. The cliff faces south-west and so is in the sun from about 1:00pm onwards. It is worth organising your day around this event, always taking due regard to the time of year and prevailing temperatures. Much of the vegetation around the foot of the cliff is very wiry; take care if lightly clad or you may well get lacerated.

Access

The cliff is reached in about 15 minutes from the first mirador (view point) on the road that eventually runs out to reach the Formentor lighthouse. From the town of Puerto Pollensa follow the road that runs north-east out towards the peninsula of Formentor. Soon after leaving the built-up area (from where the cliff can be seen if you know where to look) the road climbs rapidly via a couple of long zigzags and then as it levels out there is an extensive and usually busy parking area on the left for the mirador. A quick walk out to the end of this offers an excellent photo-opportunity. When done clicking, walk back towards Puerto Pollensa following a partly buried pipeline that runs away at a tangent from the road. Two hundred metres down this, and just before a warning sign, a very vague track heads uphill to pass beneath a series of rocky bluffs and arrive at a col with a large cairn. More direct routes usually end up in wiry vegetation and blocky outcrops. Cross the ridge at the lowest point of the col (on the left) and then either i) descend awkward slabs and terraces right then left for 50m until a cairned track is picked up heading horizontally in a south-west direction (to the left looking out), or ii) descend for 10m then follow a sloping terrace leftwards to a tricky descent right under the cliff face. Follow vague tracks and occasional cairns for a couple of hundred metres until just round the headland, at which point both Puerto Pollensa and the cliff come into view. The routes are described from left to right.

Sherri Davy on the final pitch of the classical SHARK'S FIN DIRECT, 5 (HVS 5a), high above the Boquer Valley

Note: 1
> On the way from the parking area to the col described above an earlier col is seen. DO NOT try to descend here. If you are not sure why, feel free to take a look over it.

Note: 2
> Returning to the car by continuing round below the cliff, or descending direct to Puerto Pollensa is not recommended unless you have full body armour and a machete!

Shortly before the developed cliff is reached there is an extensive and high cliff with a long north-facing corner. The corner itself looks like a traditional classic and its right wall has two steep bolt lines; no grades known, though they look harder than most of the other climbs on the cliff.

The first two routes described start to the right of a 10m high flake, on top of a pile of white blocks and below a smart grey slab forming the left side of the continuous section of the cliff face.

COORDINA COORDINADOR *** 4+ (VS 4c) 20m
Starting below the centre of the slab climb the tricky initial section slightly leftwards to a steeper area which is passed on an excellent selection of holds to reach a lower-off above the highest point of the slab. Wonderful stuff.

CURSET *** 4+ (MVS 4b) 20m
Start just to the right of the centre point of the slab and trend slightly right until it is possible to step back left over a bulge into a shallow groove. Climb this to steeper rock which is crossed on good holds to reach the same lower-off as the previous climb. Oddly named, considering how pleasant it is!

To the right of the slab is a rather scruffy-looking, left-trending groove to the left of a gorse bush and with a prominent peg runner low down.

BABA ** 5 (HVS 5a) 24m
A worthwhile climb that is better than it looks. Climb the initial groove past a bolt to the peg then continue up the sustained right-hand branch until it curves over to the right. Make a dainty traverse below the overlap then pull back leftwards over the bulges to a padlocked belay/lowering point below the crest of the wall.

To the right is a clean triangular slab, 15m high, with twin white perched flakes on its summit. The next four routes start up this. The first route climbs the left side of the lower slab and the shallow groove above, and is pleasant if somewhat unbalanced.

Willie Jeffrey near the top of the superbly sustained RECORDS DE BUNYOLA, 6a+ (E2 5b) at Creveta

1	Coordina Coordinador ***	4+ (VS 4)	7	Hyperion Derecho **	5+ (E2 6a)	13	Ta Ma Pagaras **	6b+ (E4 6a)
2	Curset ***	4+ (MVS 4b)	8	Els Corderos Atacon		14	150 Spits **	5+ (E1 5c)
3	Baba **	5 (HVS 5a)		de Nuevo **	6a (E2 5c)	15	Records de Bunyola ***	6a+ (E2 5b)
4	Camisasaque *	5 (HVS 5a)	9	Jerita ***	6b (E3 6a)	16	El Sant Crist ***	6a (E2 5c)
5	Krilin *	6a (E1 5c)	10	Hussain ***	6c (E4 6b)	17	Som-hi ***	5+ (E1 5c)
6	Hyperion **	5+ (HVS 5b)	11	Terapia de Grupo ***	6a+ (E3 6a)	18	Ball O'en Banyeta Verda ***	6a (E3 5c)
			12	Ca, Magre Puses *	5+ (E2 5c)	19	Somni Bucòhlic ***	5+ (E1 6a)

CREVETA

CAMISASAQUE * 5 (HVS 5a) 24m
Climb the left side of the slab to its apex (quite tough but very short) and continue passing the perched flakes to enter the pale shallow groove above. Up this pleasantly to join and finish as for the previous climb.

KRILIN * 6a (E1 5c) 15m
The centre of the triangular slab gives a pleasant 'quick-tick' protected by four bolts. Absolutely no deviations are allowed at the grade!

The next two climbs share a common start up the right side of the triangular slab and then find their different ways up the rock above to a shared belay below the bulges that cap the wall.

HYPERION ** 5+ (HVS 5a) 24m
Climb the tricky right side of the triangular slab (maybe just 5b) then follow the easy ramp line to its tip. From the flakes here step right then continue straight up the wall until it is possible to move right to reach the belay.

HYPERION DERECHO ** 5+ (E2 6a) 24m
The initial section is the same at the regular route to the ramp. From here (bolt above on the left) step out to the right just above the overlap and make a difficult couple of pulls to get established just to the right of a bubbly grey streak. Continue first right then back left to the same lower-offs as the regular route.

The next four climbs all start from a domed ledge system 5m from the ground. This is most easily reached from the left. A direct approach involves crossing some highly abrasive vegetation, and if your second does not fancy an involuntary trip through this it might be worth considering taking a belay on the ledge system. The left-hand route above the ledge is:

ELS CORDEROS ATACON DE NUEVO ** 6a (E2 5c) 24m
From the left edge on the ledge climb the awkward slab to a thin ledge occupied by some shrubs then make baffling moves up and left, using small pockets, to enter the diagonal scoop. An entry from further left is a bit of a cop-out and risks a prickly landing in the event of a miscalculation. Once established in the scoop climb to its top before stepping left onto the wall and following good holds to the lower-off.

The next three routes are amongst the most difficult on the cliff offering fine sustained and fingery climbing. Exactly how hard you find them is a direct reflection of
 a) your resistance to pain;
 b) how rapidly you find the best holds;

c)   how stiff your boots are.

JERITA *** 6b (E3 6a) 25m
The left-hand line starts just to left of the centre of the curving ledge and climbs direct past a small but prominent semi-circular scar. Above this sustained moves and plenty of protection combine to guarantee a classic outing. From the lower-off it is possible to check out the rather harder route to the right, and even place the quick-draws (if that's allowed).

HUSSAIN *** 6c (E4 6b) 25m
The central line climbs directly up the steepening slab into a shallow scoop and makes thin steep moves out of this (try a left-facing 'rock over') to thankfully reach an easier crack line and the lower-off some distance above. The climb is rather easier if you stray too far to the right of the 'true path'.

TERAPIA DE GRUPO *** 6a+ (E3 6a) 25m
The right-hand line is thought by some to be the best of the bunch, though the grade is just a touch tight-fisted! More thin sustained climbing following the thin white streak on razor-sharp flakes and pockets. If you are really keen to do this one it is probably best not to leave it to the last route of the day!

The right side of the steep slab is bounded by an open black scoop. This is most easily reached from the right and is climbed by:

CA, MAGRE PUSES * 5+ (E2 5c) 27m
A pleasant route with short-lived difficulties. Climb to ledges then continue easily up the white slab into the scoop. Make technical moves up the steepening groove, and continue past broken flakes and up the scoop on crozzly holds to a flaky section where it is possible to step out left to reach the belays.

To the right of the black scoop is a steep barrel-shaped buttress climb by the oh so painful:

TA MA PAGARAS ** 6b+ (E4 6a) 20m
Climb to a ledge then up a blunt rib to more ledges and the start of the difficulties. Head up the steep buttress with a short jig out to the right at the third bolt on some of the sharpest holds in the world. Single bolt belay. A route for real masochists or those with skin like chain-mail.

Ten metres right is a clean lower slab with a palm tree growing at its bottom left corner, close to the rock. Four metres to the right of a 3m high, white, perched flake is the optimistically named:

150 SPITS ** 5+ (E1 5c) 24m
Climb the straightforward lower slab to the prominent horizontal break, then continue more steeply to a move using an insubstantial 'razor' to reach better holds. Continue up the right side of a corner then step right to the belays.

RECORDS DE BUNYOLA *** 6a+ (E2 5b) 28m
Three metres right climb past a detached-looking flake at 3m to the base of this superb 'blank' face. Gain the base of the wall using an undercut two finger pocket and continue by sustained moves to the left edge of a large curving hole/pocket. Make a long reach then continue up the centre of the upper wall (still sustained but on surprising holds) to a lower-off just to the left of a bush in the centre of the upper slab. If you are using a 50m rope take note of the length of this pitch!

EL SANT CRIST *** 6a (E2 5c) 28m
Great climbing with a sudden transition from 'jugs to razors'. Climb the lower slab above two large blocks, past the horizontal break to a position below the left side of the horizontal cave half way up the face. Pull steeply rightwards out of this to gain the upper wall then trend right to the lower-offs.

SOM-HI *** 5+ (E1 5b) 28m
Start just to the right of the blocks at the foot of the face and climb the sustained slab past an obvious horizontal orange-stained overlap. Smoother rock leads to the bulging wall above which is best climbed quickly before the whole affair becomes too painful.

BALL O'EN BANYETA VERDA *** 6a (E3 5c)
An excellent route marked by alternating black and white bolts. The technical lower slab gives fine sustained climbing past a constriction in the horizontal break. Continue (crux) to the bulges that are best crossed by a tricky move left followed by a romp back to the right past a huge 'ringing' flake. Easier rock remains.

SOMNI BUCOHLIC *** 5+ (E1 6a) 28m
The last route on the face has a tough crux and plenty of good climbing as well. Climb the slab just to the right of a thin crack to reach the bulges that cross the face. Step left and make a couple of unlikely thin moves (especially so for the short) to reach better pockets which give sustained but easier moves until it is possible to step left to reach the huge 'ringing' flake of the previous route. Finish rightwards up easier rock.

*Classical face climbing on BALL O'EN BANYETA VERDA,
6a (E3 5c) at Creveta*

To the right is a vegetated corner and beyond this an attractive zone of rock. In April 1994 there were three chains installed above this section and the locations of the bolts had already been marked on the cliff, though they had yet to be placed. The routes under preparation here looked as if they should be of similar quality to those on the main face.

FRAGUEL ROCK

Character

A glowing golden bowl of truly 'tufatastic' routes and a genuine Mecca for those in search of high standard, high quality climbing. For a while Fraguel was the best kept secret of the Majorcan climbing scene. Only a short distance from the town of Bunyola and the well known cliff of Gubia, the locals found a valley stuffed with rock and set about developing one of the more impressive cliffs in it, producing some stunning and very tough climbs in the process. Originally the intention was to keep the place hush-hush from visiting climbers but inevitably (considering the quality of the climbing) the crag has gradually become known to a wider audience and now it is firmly on the island's regular climbing circuit. I have deliberated long and hard as to whether to include this cliff in the guide but the number of unofficial topos in circulation means that the place really is no longer a secret. Whilst one can feel sympathy with the locals having had their private playground usurped, I have no doubt they have numerous other 'Fraguels' tucked away in the Majorcan mountains that they can retreat to when the invaders from the frozen north arrive on their annual winter migration.

At present there are almost 50 routes here and most of them are hard to very hard. There are also a few more moderate offerings scattered around the edges of the cliff and so the place is worth at least one visit by most parties. People training for the harder routes on British limestone could spend all week here and still come back for more.

Almost all the routes are steep and involve either pocket-pulling or doing powerful battle with impressive hanging tufa systems. The cliff faces south-east and goes out of the sun shortly after midday. Sun worshippers will need to arrive early and of course the place makes an excellent after lunch venue when it is too hot to climb full in the sun.

I have only recently come up with names for the climbs and even the grade of many of the routes is open to question. The information recorded here is a distillation of a whole series of sources; blame me for any inaccuracies. Any updated feedback would be very welcome.

All the routes are fully equipped with 10mm bolt runners and almost all can be done to the lower-off and back to the ground on a 50m rope. The lengths included here are approximate and are intended for rough guidance only.

Access

The cliff is quite difficult to locate on first acquaintance. On the south-eastern side of Bunyola (on the road running towards Santa Maria), immediately before the town sign is a rough road running towards the hills. This is followed past houses and around a small valley and it then begins to climb rapidly. The road it not metalled, is quite rough in places, and is followed for a bum-numbing 5 kilometres. An unexpected 900m section of tarmac arrives and just past the end of this, and the 5 kilometre marker, is parking space on the right by a 'respect the mountains' sign on a tree. A good track leads down into the woods here and is followed for 100m (passing camp fire rings) to a charcoal-burning circle hidden in the trees 5m to the left of the track. (The circle is unmistakeable, being about 4m across and covered in bright green moss.) At this point the cliff top is dead ahead and can be approached by a long abseil if you are carrying a spare rope. The base of the wall is reached by a long loop to the left. Pass round the left side of the circle to locate a narrow track running off into the trees. This is followed gently downhill past one zigzag to a large block (and occasional cairn) by the track, where a slabby rock band and then an awkward 10m groove can be descended to reach the base of the cliff. (If this proves too steep for non-climbing members of the party it is possible to continue along the main track to an easy scramble down and then double back along the cliff base.) From the foot of the rock band turn right (facing out) and follow various indistinct trails to where the cliff becomes more impressive; 15 minutes from the car. The final section of the approach passes some rock that could be developed to produce less intimidating climbing than on most of the rest of the cliff. *Note:* If all else fails try heading downhill always making sure not to walk over the cliff top, into the bottom of the valley where there is a good track. From here the cliff can be located and reached by 5 minutes of re-ascent.

The first climbs start off a narrow ledge where the approach path to the cliff climbs up a short rise.

F1 CRIS LINE ** 4 (VS 5a) 15m

Closely spaced red bolts up the rib starting from the ledge system at the end of the approach path. A pleasant but very untypical pitch which is obviously on the wrong cliff.

F2 CHURRU PINO * 5+ (E1 5b) 20m

The steep groove with *in situ* tree and gold-coloured bolts. A tricky start over the bulge gains the right wall of the groove which is followed with interest.

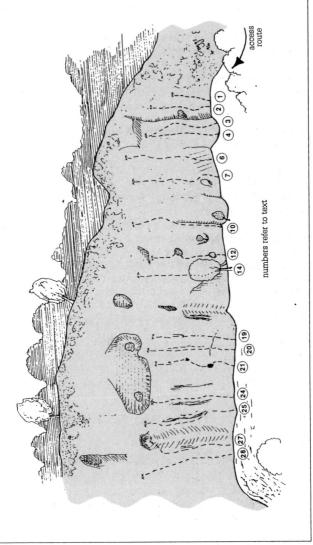

FRAGUEL ROCK

access route

numbers refer to text

To the left is a steep orange tower capped by a tilted prow, home to three lines.

F3 ? *** 6b+ (E3 5c) 22m
The right-hand line has a sharp start and an upper section that is climbed on a continually surprising set of holds.

F4 MARMADE ** 7a+ (E5 6b) 22m
The central line on small sharp holds leads to a belay in common with the previous climb.

F5 PEEP SHOW'S GARRIGA 7b+ 22m
The left-hand line looks tough.

To the left is a slabbier section of cliff and towards its left side a 4m high club-shaped flake leans against the rock.
To the right of the flake is an easy angled slab.

F6 ? ** 6b+ (E4 6a) 20m
The easy slab is climbed to pockets, then steeper orange rock leads with difficulty into an open finishing groove.

F7 LA CADENA DEL WATER ** 6a (E2 5b) 20m
Climb over the flake with care and head up the sustained and interesting pocketed wall above.

To the left is a rounded rib before the cliff becomes much more spectacular. Two routes start up this past a prominent peg runner.

F8 SEMEN TIR ** 6a (E3 5c) 20m
Pass the peg then move out right to the line of gold bolts. The midway bulge proves troublesome.

F9 COMANDO RASTA ** 6b+ (E4 6a) 20m
Up the rounded rib past the peg runner, then follow the line of oldish bolts up the gradually steepening wall.

Around to the left of the rib is a shallow groove running out into steeper rock.

F10 COUS COUS *** 6c (E4 6a) 22m
Up the groove then step right and climb the steep wall with the crux around bolts number 5 and 6 and a slightly run out finish.

To the left is a small tree in an orange hollow 7m up the cliff.

F11 COTORROT * 7c 20m
The bolt line rising from the right side of the hollow and forging on up the steep wall. I have also seen *(E6 6b)* as the grade for this route; one of them must be wrong!

F12 SETEBE EL PLUMERO *** 7b+ (E6 6b) 20m
Five metres left of the tree in the hollow is a hole 8m up the cliff. Enter this easily then step left and do battle with the next section until it is possible to pull right to gain a respite in another hole. Step out left and make a precarious couple of moves to easier ground.

F13 PASTANAGA PUNYERTA *** 8a (E7 6c) 20m
The steep orange rib immediately to the left and just right of a pine tree standing close to the rock. Sustained and on tiny holds.

Left of and behind the pine tree is a tufa-covered lower wall 7m high and capped by a leaning, ginger section of cliff. There are four tough-looking routes on this section of wall.

F14 ON ES L'AVI *** 7a+ (E6 6b) 22m
The right-hand line keeping to the edge of the ginger wall. Good climbing but hard for 'dwarves'.

F15 CUENCAMELO *** 7b+ (E6 6c) 22m
The next line left follows the edge of the tufa and then forges straight up the wall.

F16 ROC PUNK *** 7c+ (E7 6c) 22m
The next offering lies just left again.

F17 ? *** 7c+? (E7 6c) 22m
The final route here is located just to the right of the large groove system.

Left again is a major overhanging groove leading to an elongated cave half way up the cliff. Off-width and chimney freaks please note that this feature is unclimbed at the time of writing. Left of the groove is a prominent triple tufa and left of this is an innocuous looking open orange scoop running up the cliff to fade out into steeper rock.

F18 TETE DE PENE *** 7c (E7 6c) 24m
The open scoop system leads to the bulging rib where things turn tough. The first of a host of hard routes on the central section of the cliff.

Starting in the same place and initially trending left is a line up a leaning wall passing a prominent and permanently chalked up mono-doigt. This is the first of five routes that have lower-offs on the large ledge in the centre of the cliff.

F19 GLASNOST ** 7c+ (E6 7a) 20m
Gaining and passing the 'mono' both prove problematical, especially the former. A route that used to be a tough 7b is now harder after the removal of a crucial hold.

F20 ALOHA FROM HELL *** 7b (E6 6c) 20m
Just to the left a white wall leading to a line of unhelpful pockets marks the line of this butch piece of exercise. Improvise up these then exit leftwards with difficulty.

To the left the cliff becomes ever steeper.

F21 MIGUELIN AND THE TEST TUBE BABIES *** 7c+ (E7 6c) 20m
A lower leaning section leads to a large orifice above which the wall is climbed rightwards. The difficulties are continuous and a mite excessive.

To the left the wall is steeply tilted and it runs into another major (and steep) groove system. There are four lines on this section of wall, all of which utilise tufa formations.

F22 PANTANO BOAS *** 7c (E7 6c) 20m
Follows the large, thick, 'shark's fin' tufa. Could do with rebolting.

F23 NO NAME ? 8b+ 20m
The steepest part of the wall utilising sporadic tufa systems was a long-time project but has now been completed.

F24 HUMANOIDE *** 7c+ (E7 6c) 20/40m
The rather larger tufas just to the left again (two systems out from the deep groove). The extension above the lower-off looks harder.

F25 BODO DODO *** 7b/c (E6 6c) 20/40m
The set of tufas before the deep groove with a short jig left at half height. The climbing is 7b to the fifth bolt (maillion in place) and 7c to the seventh bolt. Again the extension above the lower-off looks even harder.

The big groove itself is:

F26 MISS PALMA *** 7b (E5 6b) 20m
Steep bridging is the order of the day, easier for long legged chimps and just a little run-out. The continuation is 8a+.

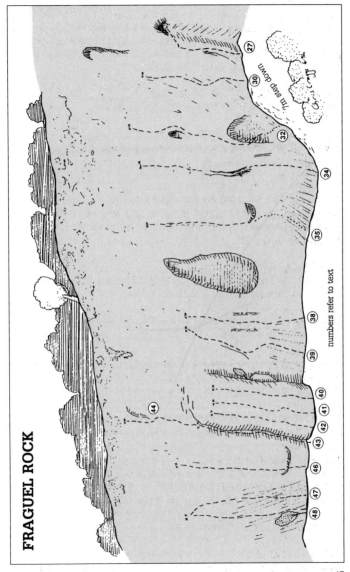

FRAGUEL ROCK

numbers refer to text

F27 FES LO QUE PUGUIS ** 7a+ (E5 6a) 20m

In the left wall of the groove is a set of twinned tufas which are followed (crux low down) until a traverse can be made to the right to the lower-off of the previous climb. One of the easiest climbs in the central section of the cliff and much used as a 'warm-up', hence the polish.

F28 TERRE D'ADVENTURE *** 8a 35m

The second line left of the big groove looks tough.

F29 FRENCH KISS *** 8b+ 30m

The smooth wall just left again is obviously over-desperate and is one of the longest pitches on the cliff.

F30 RAMADAN *** 8b+ (E7 6c) 25m

The steeply tilted wall just left again. As far as the fixed karabiner on the fifth bolt is the warm up for this area at * *6b (E3 5c)* and involves the use of a rather rickety tufa. Above this the angle increases and the difficulties escalate dramatically.

F31 SHABADA *** 8a+ 25m

Just above the step down in the base of the cliff is a line up prominent tufas. It is 7a+ to the maillon and much harder above.

To the left the foot of the cliff drops down a 7m step. Just above the foot of this is a route starting out of an orange cave.

F32 FUTBOL FAN *** 7c+ (E7 6b) 28m

One of Fraguel's finest. Climb leftwards out of the hollow following a line of jazzy purple bolts. From a rest in another hollow battle the leaning wall above with the crux just short of the lower-offs.

To the left a slabby section of rock leads to two separate tufa pillars. The belay for these routes is bolts linked by a long sling high above.

F33 AMNESIA ? 8b+ 25m

The right-hand and shorter tufa.

F34 LE GORILLE A UN BON MINE *** 7c (E6 6b) 25m

Another major classic. The left-hand tufa leads to an open groove high on the face and the route requires two dynos from most mortals, one at half height and one to grab the lower-offs.

F35 GOO-GOO MACK *** 8a (E7 6c) 28m

To the left of the slab at the foot of the face is a small hollow with a line of blue bolts rising from its left side and climbing through a zone of short tufas and small pockets. Looks good to me.

Left again is a 15m high alcove of unsavoury-looking orange rock. The right side of this is (not) climbed by two projects.

On the left side of the cave is

F36 SOLO SEX 8a 28m
...or is it a project?

Immediately left again is a line of pinky/purple bolts climbed by:

F37 JUNGLE HOP *** 7a+ 23m

F38 PSICHO-KILLER ** 6c 20m
The white slab and steepening wall passing between two grey streaks into and out off a niche looks excellent.

F39 FAKIR ** 6c 20m
The slab trending left to a broken flake and then on up easier angled rock above.

To the left is a grotty-looking open chimney with *in situ* bush and beyond this the cliff juts forwards as a steep grey pillar with three bolt lines on its front face.

F40 ROSA DE SANITARIO ** 7b+ 18m
The right-hand line over an overlap.

F41 CACA DE COLORES ** 6c+ 18m
Central line on very sharp and slightly overhanging rock.

F42 ? ** 7a? 18m
The left-hand line is a slightly more amenable angle but is still very spiky.

F43 PANTERA ROSA *** 5 (E1 5b) 20m
The left side of the pillar is bounded by a steep twisting bridging groove which offers a good pitch.

F44 EL GALLINERO ** 6b+ (E4 6a) 20m
From the lower-off above the last route step left and finish up the steep wall and hanging rib above. Sharp! A right-hand variant looks steeper but is on better holds (6a).

To the left of the pillar is a section of steep rock rising from a yellow bay with two bolt lines above it.

F45 HARISA * 7a 30m**
The right-hand and harder-looking line using pockets.

F46 TABASCO ** 7a 32m
The left-hand line into an open scoop, fine if you like slabs, but if that's the case what are you doing here?

Left again the crag becomes slabbier (or at least a little less vertical). Despite this the two routes here are no pushover.

F47 ? * 6b+ (E3 6a) 35m**
The right-hand line steepens as it rises and eventually bears away leftwards. There is also an upper pitch.

F48 OJO CLIMBICO ** 6b (E4 6a) 40m
The penultimate line on the cliff is marked by blue bolts that become purple higher up the cliff. Again there is an upper pitch.

The cliff continues leftwards for some distance but not on the grand scale already passed. At the present there is one climb LA CASA DE LA PRADERA * 6a (E1 5b) 20m. The rest of the cliff awaits a devotee. The spectacular cliffs on the opposite side of the valley are rumoured to be on private land; that's a great pity!

SA GUBIA

Character

'Gubia' is without a doubt the premier rock climbing location on Majorca. It is the best-developed crag, has the widest range of routes and remains the most popular climbing destination on the island. The name Sa Gubia means 'his trowel' and at certain times of the day the shadowy hollow in the centre of the cliff bears a passing resemblance to a huge gardening implement. The extensive cliffs here consist of ten separate 'sectors' spread around the entrance to an open ravine that cuts deep into the Sierra de Alfabia. This is located close to the small pleasant town of Bunyola, 15 kilometres to the north of Palma. Each sector has its own atmosphere and as they face almost all points of the compass it is usually possible to choose whether to climb in the sun or the shade. Routes range from 4 bolt 'quickies' to 8 pitch expeditions, and in grade from 4 (VS) to Majorcan 7b+ (E7). There really is something here for everyone, including the person who just wants to get away from it all. The rock ranges from perfect fluted grey sheets, through pocketed walls to incredible tufa pillars, and is impeccable almost without exception. Bolt protection is the norm and is usually frequent and substantial, as are the belays and lower-offs. The whole ambience of the area is quite magical with vultures high overhead, the blossoms on the almond and olive trees in the fields below the gorge and in the far distance the blue waters of the Mediterranean. If you think the crag is worked out just take a 5 minute walk past the base of the *Gubia Normal* and get a look at the cliff high on the right. Impressive or what?

The sectors are described in anti-clockwise fashion (right to left as the cliff is approached); the short pen-portrait of each one given below should give you a good idea where to head for first depending on how you like your sport.

The first seven sectors are all situated on the eastern side (right looking up the gorge) of the dried-up stream bed and are reached from the narrow path that cuts right through the gorge.

The sectors are:

1. The *SECTOR SILICONA* is up to 22m high, faces due south and is generally slabby in nature. It contains ten routes from 4 *(VS)* to 6b *(E4)* half of which are in the *E1/2* category.

2. The *SECTOR EXCALIBUR* runs up the side of a steep gully and is a south-facing wall up to 40m high. It contains ten routes from 5+ *(E1)* to 7b+ *(E6)* with a spread across the grades and climbing that is mostly steep.

3. The *SECTOR WHY* is the steep, red, west-facing tower directly above the path at the first narrowing in the gorge. It is up to 60m high and contains nine routes from 5+ *(E2)* to 7b+ *(E7)* with a spread of grades. Most of the climbs are strenuous, following strong natural lines.

4. The *SECTOR FINA Y SEGURA* is a north-facing area based around a deep water worn groove. There are thirteen routes from 6a *(E2)* to 7a+ *(E5)*. The routes here are generally short except for the longer classic of *SEXO DEBIL*.

5. The *SECTOR PRINCESSA* is the 160m high west-facing wall that towers above the bay in the centre of the cliffs. Only one fully equipped route is described here, but what a route. Another half a dozen routes are covered briefly.

6. The *SECTOR POLLA BOBA* is the attractive south-facing wall of excellent rock situated below the ridge climbed by *GUBIA NORMAL*. It is 45m high and is home to five good routes in the 5 *(HVS)* to 6a+ *(E3)* category.

7. The *SECTOR ESPOLON* is the massive ridge that stabs skywards at the narrowing of the ravine. It faces south and west and is home to 13 short

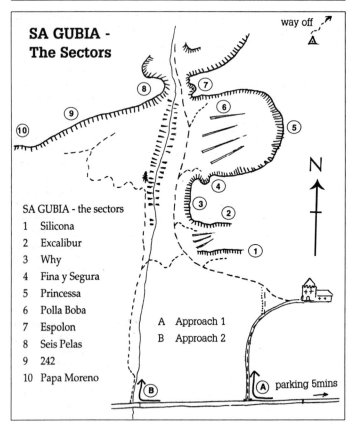

**SA GUBIA -
The Sectors**

way off

SA GUBIA - the sectors

1 Silicona
2 Excalibur
3 Why
4 Fina y Segura
5 Princessa
6 Polla Boba
7 Espolon
8 Seis Pelas
9 242
10 Papa Moreno

A Approach 1
B Approach 2

parking 5mins

routes, most of which are quite tough, the great 8 pitch classic of *GUBIA NORMAL*, and the recently bolted gem of *SUPER NOVA*.

The final three sectors are located on the western side of the dry steam bed and are known collectively as the *PARET DELS COLOMS* (the Wall of Pillars). The cliff generally faces south-east.

8. The *SECTOR SEIS PELAS* is the right side of the wall, to the left and right of where a strange black hole disappears up into the cliff. There are 14 routes on this 60m high face and their grades vary from *5+ (E1)* to *7b (E6)* with many of these climbs being major classics.

9. The *SECTOR 242* is the impressive central section of the *PARET DELS*

COLOMS. There are 13 routes here graded from *6a+ (E3)* to *7b (E6)*. The routes are steep to very steep, and some are even steeper than that! Many involve climbing strange tufa features and formations.

10. The *SECTOR PAPA MORENO* is situated around to the left side of the *PARET DELS COLOMS*. It is largely undeveloped and at the moment contains only four routes, *5+ (E1)* to *6b (E3)*. A leaning orange wall some distance up the hillside might repay a visit from a suitably armed team.

Access
Note: Please follow the directions closely, park sensibly, and avoid crossing cultivated land wherever possible.

From Palma follow the main road (the C711) northwards towards Bunyola and Soller for 15 kilometres. The crag becomes visible on the left after about 12 kilometres with the striking arête of Gubia Normal being particularly conspicuous. Immediately before the complex junction that provides a right turn into Bunyola is a small track on the left that doubles back towards the cliff. The third track on the right leads to a farm and is wide enough to allow parking for about ten cars on its right side on rough ground. Please park sensibly. There are two approaches, the first of which is the normal one at present. If the gate leading to the big white house has been fortified then use the second approach described below.

Approach 1
From the car park continue down the track for 5 minutes to the first rickety gate. A short distance beyond this is a gate on the right that bars access to the track leading to the large conspicuous white house which is also known as Sa Gubia. Climb carefully over the left side of this, or use the 'sheep hole' and follow the track until it bends right towards the house. Walk straight up the slope (ignoring the track branching off to the left), past the local rubbish dump, and join a well made path that bears away to left towards the cliff. The *SECTOR SILICONA* is reached in 20 minutes from the car.

Approach 2
Continue through the first rickety gate to another similar one about 10 minutes from the car. Pass through this to immediately reach a dry stream bed. Scramble 'upstream' for 50m then clamber up into the field on the left. Follow the side of the stream up towards the cliffs through fields of Biblical stoniness, taking care with a couple of wire fences, until the path redescends gradually into the stream bed. For the Sectors to the right of the stream scramble out of the stream to reach the path that comes from the big white house that is prominent to the right of the cliff. This runs right through the gorge.

51

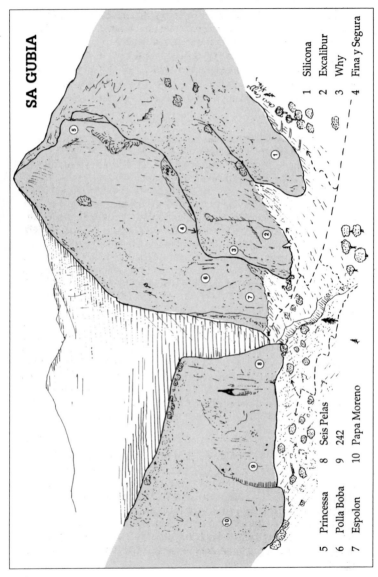

SA GUBIA

1 Silicona
2 Excalibur
3 Why
4 Fina y Segura

5 Princessa
6 Polla Boba
7 Espolon

8 Seis Pelas
9 242
10 Papa Moreno

For the Sectors on the left side stay in the stream bed for another 50m until directly below the last large solitary pine on the left. Scramble up here, keeping left of any outcrops, until a good path leads up to the base of the cliff. A direct link between the opposite side of the gorge is best avoided because of the incised nature of the stream bed and the dense and thorny vegetation.

SECTOR SILICONA

A great place to start your Gubia apprenticeship, with a fine collection of pitches that are full in the sun for most of the day and are on superb rock. They are described from left to right up the bank.

HAWAY ** 4 (VS 4b) 16m
The left edge of the wall is formed by a clean rib that starts from a bent-over tree. The rib is followed on great rock past six bolt runners to a final juggy steepening and a substantial lowering chain.

SILICONA * 6b (E3 6a) 15m
The smooth wall 6m right of the arête has been rebolted, though the climbing is as thin and fingery as it ever was. It is possible to continue up the wall from the initial lowering point following a line of older bolts to reach the belay of the next climb (* 25m).

LULU ** 5+ (E2 5c) 24m
Start just right of bushes where a red groove leads to a flat roof at 7m with a conspicuous bolt above its lip. Climb the groove and trend left over the roof to reach the base of a thin crack. Climb this with difficulty then continue up the steeper wall on a pleasantly surprising set of holds.

PROTEINA VEGETAL ** 5+ (E1 5b) 20m
Start left of the large tree and climb up the tricky slab to steeper rock. Step left (or do it direct 5c) and follow pockets to a belay in a hollow.

Directly above the large tree is a prominent white scar at 15m. The next climb reaches this from immediately behind the tree. It is:

TOTOM FA EL QUE VOL ** 5+ (E2 5c) 20m
A sustained and interesting lower wall (very thin if you are totally puritanical about it) reaches the base of the scar. Clip a high bolt then step right and climb the centre of the scar on holds that keep appearing all the way to the belays.

To the right is a section of walling/terracing and above where this meets the rock is an open groove taken by:

RESACA * 5 (E2 5c) 20m
The lower groove is straightforward but just when you thought the route was in the bag at a pleasant *HVS* it turns nasty. A very thin sequence (*6a* until you find the right holds?) leads to pockets and then the belay. The Spanish grade is just a bit ungenerous.

Three metres right of the walling is a broad clean rib leading to steeper rock.

GRAN PIS ** 6a (E2 5c) 22m
Climb straight up the broad rib then either pull straight over the overhangs and swing right or trend right through the bulges to reach the belays. Failure to clip the bolt in the centre of the crux moves may result in a grand pisser.

RUSTIC POGO * 6a+ (E4 6a) 22m
A route with a short fierce crux section: try bouncing. Climb the scoop to the right of the previous climb then step right to the foot of a steep wall. A layaway is used to get established on this and then a series of powerful moves lead right and then back left to better holds and an easing in the angle. Good value at *6a+*!!

Just to the right is an attractive slabby apron leading to steeper rock. This is climbed by possibly the best route on this section of cliff:

ROCA BUENO *** 5+ (E2 5c) 25m
Up the pleasant slab as directly as you fancy to a large hold at a flowstone pillar. A thin section leads up the steeper wall, with a pull leftwards on razor blades gaining easier rock. Quite excellent and not too high in the grade.

To the right of the crux section of the last route is another line of rather older looking bolts.

ROCA SOSO 6a (E3 6a) 22m
Either start as for the previous climb or approach the bolt ladder from directly below via an easy but unprotected and somewhat shrubby slab. The steep wall gives thin and rather unsatisfying climbing until it is possible to swing left to the belays of the previous route.

SECTOR EXCALIBUR

The steep side wall of the gully behind the *SECTOR SILICONA* provides a good collection of pitches on excellent rock. The area is rarely crowded and gets the sun all day. The routes are described from left to right and the first offering starts at the left edge of the wall where a 3m high 'tombstone'-like finger of rock gesticulates arrogantly skywards.

NA GUARRA * 5+ (E1 5b) 18m
From behind the 'tombstone' (not an auspicious start) step left and climb the smooth-looking rib on well hidden holds until a steeper pull gains easy ledges. As the bolts change from attractive silver to sombre black move right and climb the sharp crack in the right wall of the groove (no bridging out left at the grade) to a lower-off above. If this is the last route of your holiday it might be worth considering not clipping the frequent bolts by the finger crack and placing wires instead; after all, you are going to have to get used to the idea again!

HORRIBLE BELLEZA ** 6c+ (E4 6b) 16m
The flat orange wall directly above the lower-off of the previous climb gives a fingery test piece. Trend right up the lower section then head back left using a poor series of shallow pockets to reach a lower-off above the final difficulties.

Immediately to the right of the 'tombstone' is an attractive slabby ramp that cuts diagonally rightwards across the face to eventually fizzle out below a deep groove. This is the line of the original route of this section of cliff, the excellent:

EXCALIBUR *** 5+ (HVS) 55m
1. 26m   5+   (5a)   Follow the ramp rightwards into an increasingly dramatic position sandwiched between overhangs until below an orange groove. Climb the right wall of this (crux) to a restricted stance and three bolt belay by a tree.
2. 28m   5   (5a)   Climb the sustained groove behind the stance until it bends to the left and then fizzles out. Cross the bulge directly above to gain entry to an exposed crack line which is followed in a dramatic situation to the cliff top where a lower-off (or tree belay) will be found. Descend by one long (45m) or two short abseils.

Starting in the same place as *EXCALIBUR* is another worthwhile route at a reasonable grade, and if you fancy something just a little tougher, then that is catered for too.

OCHO * 5+/6a (HVS 5a/E2 6a) 15/20m
Climb onto the slab as for *EXCALIBUR* and continue straight up the wall and rib past an orange flake to a swing right onto steeper rock. This is all quite tough if climbed direct so use a bit of lateral thinking! Just above the steep section is a lower-off; thus far the route is a pleasant * 5+ *(HVS 5a)*. If you have had enough, lower off; if you fancy a challenge use pockets to swing right on to the steep wall and make a quick pull on a razor blade (ouch, that smarts) to reach easier rock and another lower-off, *6a (E2 6a)*.

The next three routes climb through the bulges that run above the ramp line of EXCALIBUR. All are worth doing though the oldest is the best because it offers rather more balanced climbing than the other two.

NO HACES MAS GRADO PORQUE ERES ENANO ** 6b+ (E4 6a) 20m
Pull easily over the bulges to the right of the start of *EXCALIBUR* then climb the easy slab to where things start to steepen. Follow the left-hand line of bolts up the thin technical wall which is climbed using three tiny layaway flakes to a final difficult (crux) stretch for the break. The steeper rock above has good though spaced holds; just keep cranking. The name suggests that the originator of the climb found it tough because he is a dwarf, though maybe it is tough anyway!

CUARTO * 6a+ (E3 5c) 20m
Start as for the previous climb and cross the bulge on the left easily. Follow the big new bolts up the slab then make tricky moves up the steep wall to a baffling pull over on to the slab above (*6a* if you fail to locate the best holds rapidly). A lower-off is found just above.

IL PANZEROTTO * 6a (E2 5b) 20m
Start as for the previous two climbs but trend right up the pleasant slab to enter and climb the steep shallow groove to the left of the scoop of *EXCALIBUR*. Pull left onto the rib then climb the final steepening by a couple of beefy pulls on good but spaced holds. Lower-offs are available both on the left and the right.

The final three routes in this area are harder offerings located further up the gully; pass round the back of a tree and climb a slippery scoop to a hollow beneath some impressive bulges, where there is an ancient three bolt belay.

BOFETADAS DE PLACER * 7b+ (E6 6c) 20m
Step left on to the leaning grey rib and climb past paired bolts (clip the newer ones!) using fiddly tufas and sharp pockets to a shake out on a large flake/ jug. When recovered press on to the lower-offs. Tough!

CARISMATICS ** 6b+ (E4 6a) 20m
Fine strenuous climbing up the scoops and hollows directly above the flat area. Bridge up and out right crossing a series of roofs to a well chalked (and well glued) flake. From this pull onto the wall above, crux, and continue up the leaning wall on a series of juggy tufas to easier angled and sharper rock. The lower-off is just above. Steep almost to the point of being silly.

To the right is an orange pillar and beyond this is:

HOT CONSUELA * 6c (E4 6b) 20m
The last route on the wall climbs an open scoop in grey rock to a large hole. Head up and right past a large *in situ* (and well irradiated) thread and continue up the tilted wall to the lower-offs. Good technical climbing rather spoilt by the difficulty of clipping some of the bolt runners.

SECTOR WHY

The steep red barrel-shaped tower that overlooks the open flat section of the path (good picnic or base campsite) has a fine collection of steep powerful lines. The area generally faces west and so is in the sun from midday onwards. The most conspicuous feature of this area is the bulging central crack line which does not quite reach the ground. This is climbed by *ZARAGUAY*. The climbs are described from right to left and the first route is located to the right of the easy angle skirt of rock that runs around the lower section of this wall, and just around to the left of the tombstone-shaped flake at the left edge of the *SECTOR EXCALIBUR*.

KGB ** 6b+ (E4 6b) 20m
Start just to the right of an easy right-facing corner below a smooth grey face leading to steeper rock. The lower wall is climbed on sharp holds until it steepens and a traverse to the left is required. This involves highly technical laybacking until some large pockets are reached. At this point a rest on the ledges down to the left is to be avoided to get the full effect. Follow the holes steeply to where they end, leaving a final sprint to the belay.

ZARAGUAY ** 5+ (E2 5c) 22m
The central crack system is approached up easier rock. Actually reaching the base of the crack constitutes the crux of the climb and is best done quickly using thin finger jams or some small polished flakes. Once gained the crack gives a good old-fashioned thrash, combining mainly jamming and bridging moves until it is possible to step left to gain a multiple bolt (all eight of them!) belay and good stance. Skinny-fingered gritstone virtuosos

might argue that the grade of the route is a bit generous, though sausage-fingered gritstone veterans won't.

To the left of the crack of *ZARAGUAY* is an impressive bubbly arête tackled by the dramatically exposed pitch of:

CORTO CIRCUITO *** 6a (E3 5c) 22m

Approach the arête direct or from the base of the crack on *ZARAGUAY* and head up it with an increasing sense of apprehension using good but well spaced holds. The prominent hole through the arête is best passed on the left lest you get inextricably stuck out in space. Easier climbing leads to the ledges above.

WHY *** 6a+ (E3 6a) 22m

The steep open corner to the left of the flying arête gives an excellent and unusual piece of climbing. Amble up the straightforward rock to the base of the corner then make awkward moves to gain a projecting 'boss'. Swing right onto the wall then step back into the corner where a tricky rock-over leads to the final obstacle in the form of a smooth section of corner containing a solitary hold. Use this to levitate to easier terrain then step right to the belays. People of less than average stature might feel the route to be *E4*, and those even shorter than that might find it impossible!

Above and left of the belay/lowering point used by the previous three routes is a stunning leaning prow:

AGARRATE MALDITO *** 7b+ (E7 6c) 22m

The magnificent flowstone festooned prow that hangs in space above the corner of the previous climb is a well bolted beckoning piece of rock architecture. Approach by any of the lower pitches (solo!) and throw yourself at the prow, which gives a superb route requiring muscular thumbs for all that tufa pinch-gripping. It is just a pity that the climb is so damn tough!

GIGOLO ** 7a (E5 6b) 22m

The slanting crack that forks leftwards out of *WHY* gives a sustained and admirably protected tussle, well bolted but with the awkwardly spaced holds dictating a technical approach.

To the left of the open corner of *WHY* and before the cliff swings round to face north is a zone of red bulges approached by a short bushwhack through shrubbery and blocks. There are four climbs that pierce these bulges.

BONGO BONGO ** 6c (E5 6b) 20m
The right-hand line is steep (aren't they all?) and is followed using a series of pockets that vary in size from generous to tight-fisted (or at least tight-fingered). Once round the lip a crimpy crux sequence leads to the belay. Just about worth *E* (for effort) 5.

PHANTASMAGORIA ** 7a (E5 6b) 20m
The line through the centre of the bulges is harder, steeper, more sustained and on poorer holds. Most definitely worth *E* (for effort) 5.

The next line leftwards on the bulging red wall is the start of the extended and classical:

ISLA BONITA I *** 5+ (E2 5c) 90m
Start at a gap in the vegetation where easy angled rock leads to steeper terrain about 6m right of the point at which the cliff swings round to face north. The start of the route is marked by a bolt on the lip of a small overhang 3m off the ground.
1. 20m   5+   (5b)   Climb the easy rib to a steepening and make a short series of powerful moves to a narrow ledge and possible stance, or continue.
2. 22m   5+   (5b)   Starting just left of the belays a couple of tricky moves gain good holds then continue steeply up a bulging crack until forced to swing left to easy ground. Belay 6m higher.
Note: The route can be done this far as a strenuous ** 5+ *(E1 5b)* followed by an abseil descent either down the line of the route or by moving left for 6m and making a 22m abseil to the ground.
3. 20m   5   (5a)   Climb the slab directly above the belay to its apex then saunter up easy rock (beware of occasional loose blocks) to a stance in a shrubby niche below a superbly fluted grey wall. All very Chinese.
4. 28m   5+   (5c)   Trend left past a thread to gain the left-hand bolt line and follow this up the fluted razors by bridging, jamming and anything else that helps until it is possible to move right to a belay. A most unusual pitch. Descend by two or three abseils.

PLACA NUEVO ** 6a+ (E3) 42m
A well bolted new route with a pleasant first pitch at *(E1 5b)* and a finely positioned second one that is much harder.
1. 20m   5+   (5b)   From clearing a short distance to the right of the arête of the cliff slant slightly leftwards up awkward slabby rock to steeper moves up a rib on the left side of a recess. After a tricky start, jug-pulling leads to a good ledge and belays. This far the route is a worthwhile ** *(E1 5b)*.

2. 22m   6b   (6a)   Climb the steep sustained and fingery wall that hangs over the stance to easier rock and, some distance higher, a belay station. Descend either back down the line of the route or by moving left for 6m and making a 22m abseil to the ground.

SECTOR FINA Y SEGURA

Immediately after the path passes under the steep red tower of the *SECTOR WHY* the cliff opens out into an immense bowl. On the right here is a curious water-worn groove whose back wall sprouts an unsightly growth. This is the base for a small number of climbs of very varying worth. The climbs here tend to face north and so the area makes for a suitable venue in high summer, always assuming you can cope with the walk in. In keeping with the approach the routes are described from right to left.

Starting on the right side of the scoop is the first pitch of the long and very worthwhile *ISLA BONITA II*. Unfortunately the top pitch is much harder than the lower two though it is a classic piece of climbing in its own right if you are up to it.

ISLA BONITA II *** 6b (E4 6b) 66m
1. 22m   6a   (6a)   Climb the right-hand line in the scoop with a painful start on 'razor edges' then follow better holds directly up the wall until it is possible to move right to a stance below a well bolted, easy angled slab. This pitch can be done on its own at *6a (E3 6a)* **.
2. 20m   4   (4c)   Climb the over-protected slab then easy rock to a belay in a floral niche shared with Isla Bonita I, at the foot of the grey fluted wall.
3. 24m   6b   (6b)   Follow the right-hand bolt line with increasing interest until the rock becomes 'blank' and a short desperate sequence is made up a blunt rib and then out left to better holds. Falling off the lower part of this pitch would be akin to sliding down a bread knife; don't even consider it!
    Lower back to the previous stance then make one or two abseils back to the base of the cliff.

Just to the right of the growth at the back of the scoop is a short new route leading to a large, single, ring bolt just over the bulge.

PRINGA EN EL METIDECO 6c (E4 6b) 10m
Short, sharp and well 'ard, could this be Malham 7a+?

On the left side of the scoop and just to the right of an easy groove is the rebolted line of the route that gave its name to the whole sector:

FINA Y SEGURA 6b (E3 6a) ** 22m

The new bolts are nice and close together in the lower wall, which is straightforward until a couple of thin moves are required to reach a rest out on the right. The upper wall is just as hard as the lower section, and the bolts are rather further apart. Step back left, take a big breath and go for it. The route might be worth E4 to the timid.

The left edge of the scoop has a short and fingery three bolt exercise that is;

INDIGNO 6c (E3 6b) 12m

A short pitch with some nice moves but spoilt by the fact that the hardest thing about the route is trying to follow the line of bolts. Avoiding the difficulties on the left or the right is strictly taboo.

Up the slope to the left of the scoop, and before the cliff swings round to face west again, is a magnificent wall that only gets the sun late in the day. There are several routes here: some fairly trivial affairs and one major classic which is well worth seeking out, the superb and alluring SEXO DEBIL. A hundred or so metres up the slope from the water-worn scoop is a steep wall with three new climbs. The right-hand line is 6b, the central one (starting in the same place) is 6a and the left-hand one is CAPERUCITA ROJA Y DESPLOME FEROZ 6a+. Further up the slope is a slabby stepped section of wall which has three recently-equipped low grade offerings, useful for escaping the midday heat or for using as a pleasant introduction to the sport.

CANNABIS IN VITRIO * 4 (VS 4b) 20m

The right-hand line on this section of cliff.

EL JARDIN DE LA ABUELA * 4+ (VS 4c) 20m

The central line heads straight up the slab apart from a slight jig to the right to get past the tricky overlap just above half height.

POTAJE ESPANOL * 5 (HVS 5a) 20m

The left-hand line follows a ramp initially then heads straight up the wall to lower-offs on the lip of a bulge.

The classic route of this part of the cliff is located a little further up the bank from the flat area at the foot of the previous offerings, where a low profile 'bent' pillar leans against the slabby lower section of the face about 20m off the ground. Start directly below this.

SEXO DEBIL ***** 6a (E4 6a) 127m

A titillating brute that leads you on to the point of no return, then drops you right in it! The latest topo to the island grades the four main pitches F6b which is a bit nearer the mark!

1. 35m   5   (5a)   The gentle introduction. Climb the easy slab to steeper rock and continue on good holds to belays at the foot of the steep wall. This pitch is well worthwhile on its own as a ****** *5 (HVS 5a)*, followed by an abseil descent.

2. 22m   6a   (5c)   The come on. Trend right up the wall following the bolts and make one hard move to gain access to a hanging corner. Above this, easier but incredibly rough rock leads to belays in a bay with *in situ* chimp!

3. 24m   6a   (6a)   Walk along the scoop to a line of tufas supplemented with bolt-on holds - honest! These are so far apart that the integrity of the pitch has not been spoilt too much. Power up the wall (just to add a touch of spice one of the 'bolt-ons' is loose) then traverse left with more delicacy to a cramped stance in a dramatic position.

4. 24m   6a+   (6a)   The trap is sprung. Make a thin traverse left then follow better holds up and left to the foot of a scoop. Swing left and climb the steep rib to belays but no stance. It is probably better to continue.

5. 22m   6a   (5b)   Trend right to regain the scoop by an exciting swing (stay low) to reach the easy groove that leads to the cliff top and the end of an admirable route.

DESCENT: Either drop off the back of the ridge and keep bearing left (facing out) until it is possible to head down right to the foot of the first wall on the cliff, or, much faster, and much more scary, abseil 40m to a tufa foot hold and triple bolt belay, then make another 45m abseil, free hanging, back to the ground.

According to the local topo there are also two short routes located on the steeply tilted wall to the right of the third pitch of *SEXO DEBIL*. These are *MI PICHICA 7a+* and *MIJU 7b+* and they are probably worth seeking out if you really want to get away from the crowds. I can guarantee you will be alone up there.

Colin Binks on the crucial ramp on the 4th pitch of SEXO DEBIL, 6a+ (E4 6a),
Sector Fina y Segura, Sa Gubia

SECTOR PRINCESSA

As the path through the gorge passes the red tower of the *SECTOR WHY*, the cliff falls back into a huge bay with a soaring south-facing back wall riddled with caves and festooned with tufa pillars and other geological oddities. There are just two routes that tackle the full height of this impressive wall and only one of these is fully equipped at the time of writing, the magnificent *PRINCESSA*.

The other route is something of an unknown quantity, this being the excellent-looking *EL ANGEL*. This expedition of six pitches utilises the huge right to left diagonal system of hollows that cut across the right side of the face. Through binoculars it is apparent that the route does not contain a lot of fixed gear, though some of the belay stations are in place. It climbs into the base of the hollow in two pitches by following a grey ramp that runs across the lowest section of the face rightwards to a belay and then trending back left on red rock to enter the caves. It then climbs to the apex of these before tackling a steep wall (crux 5+) then gaining a crack system and following this to the cliff top. The UK grade should be about *E1 5b* and the route looks well worth doing. A descent is possible by abseiling back down *PRINCESSA* providing you can find the belays (see below), going over the top of the mountain as for *GUBIA NORMAL*, or dropping off the back of the ridge and trending to the left (looking downhill) to get back to the approach route to the cliff. A machete may be required on this third alternative.

Starting 30m left of the grey ramp at the foot of *EL ANGEL* is the outstanding:

PRINCESSA *** 6b (E4 6a) 157m

A right regal outing up the highest part of the face offering one of the finest climbs on the island. Protection is perfect. The difficulties are limited to a few thin and well protected moves three-quarters of the way up the first pitch and it is possible to abseil off after this, though with the crux cracked the rest of the climb is well worth enjoying.

Start at the highest point of the bay where scratched arrows point the way up slabby rock to a small bush and the discreet belay bolts.

1. 48m   6b   (6a)   Climb up and left to reach the line of bolts and follow them, on good holds, straight up the steep impressive wall until things turn nasty (at an ominous trio of bolts). A thin sequence, perhaps slightly easier on the left, leads to good holds and just a little higher a

---

Jim Rubery on the ramp of EXCALIBUR, 5+ (HVS 5a),
Sector Excalibur, Sa Gubia

small stance.

2. 36m   5   (5b)   Trend left past a solitary bolt and then climb directly up easier rock until it is possible to move right to a good ledge, complete with shady trees, below a steep wall.

3. 33m   5+   (5b or 5c if you don't find the best holds)   Climb straight up behind the stance to the line of bulges that are crossed (rapidly?) on large holds to gain the fine sustained wall above. Up this trending gradually to the right to reach an exposed 'foothold stance' below a left-trending groove.

4. 40m   5   (5b)   Swing round the right-bounding corner of the groove and traverse easily to the right for 8m before climbing straight up the sustained and sharp wall to reach the cliff top and the end of a great outing.

DESCENT: After a trip round the rugged and headily scented rock garden of the cliff top there is the minor problem of getting back to the gear to be addressed. There are three alternatives (always excluding staying on top of the cliff). Firstly, the stances on the route are equipped to allow an abseil descent back to the base of the wall (providing you brought double ropes). This is speedy but a bit of a gripper, especially locating the stance at the foot of the final pitch as it lurks below an overhang. A second alternative is to go to the top of the mountain and descend as for *GUBIA NORMAL*, trainers recommended. A third possibility is dropping off the back of the ridge and trending to the right (looking downhill) to get back to the approach route to the cliff.

The area of rock to the right of *PRINCESSA* and *EL ANGEL* has recently been developed, the lower slabs have some pleasant routes and the steep walls above contain some real challenges! The first route on the lower wall is *6a+* and the one to the right of this is also *6a+*. Right again is *MOCO DE PAVO 7b+* and above the lower-off on this is *FARACORDA* which may be *8b*. Right again is *IDEM 7b+* and above the lower-off on this is *DE GORRONES HASTA LOS COJONES 8a*. The final route before the leaning pillar of *SEXO DEBIL* is an unnamed project.

Willie Jeffrey following the crucial middle pitch of STRICHINA 5+ (E1 5b), Sector Seis Pelas, Sa Gubia. The impressive chain is the belay at the top of the first pitch of TIA MELIS 5+ (E2 5c)

SECTOR POLLA BOBA

Below and to the right of the soaring ridge of *GUBIA NORMAL* is an attractive face of rock, 50m high and split horizontally by a narrow ledge system. (This should not be confused with the much smaller bolt spattered face near the toe of the buttress which is part of the *SECTOR ESPOLON*, see below.) The *SECTOR POLLA BOBA* has a small collection of worthwhile routes that are not too tough, are well protected, are on great rock and which face south: altogether not a bad combination. The lower wall contains two pitches which are interchangeable with the five pitches that continue from the midway ledge. There are no real stances above the top of the routes so lowering back to the stance in the centre of the wall is the easiest option. With a bit of organisation it is possible to tick the whole sector in a couple of very pleasant (or hectic) hours' climbing.

The routes are described from left to right.

Note: The two initial pitches make worthwhile objectives in their own right, and at a lower grade than most of the climbs above, if you do not feel the need to extend yourself high off the ground by venturing on to the upper walls.

At the base of the face is a well beaten area directly underneath the centre of the lower wall.

LA LEY DEL DESEO *** 5 (HVS 5a) 100m
An excellent and long climb offering a perfect introduction to continental (or island!) ethics. Newcomers to the game might feel that the crucial second pitch merits *(E1 5b)*, though old hands will probably be happy to stick with the *(HVS 5a)* tag.

1. 22m   5   (5a)   From the flat area at the foot of the wall step left on to the wall then follow the line marked by nice new 10mm bolts, with a tricky move over a bulge to reach a stance at the left edge of the ledge system.

2. 23m   5   (5a)   Climb directly above the stance on excellent rock following the bolt line with sustained interest to reach large holds by the final bolt. From here continue with a touch of faith; good holds continue to arrive and lead to the substantial belays not too far away!

3. 20m   4   (4c)   Continue up the line marked by the silver dots; pleasantly sustained climbing leads up the open rib to a stance where the cliff rears up again and things look a touch more serious.

4. 30m   5   (5a)   Climb the steeper rock via a tricky sequence then more sustained climbing in ever more dramatic situations leads to paired bolts at a cleaned ledge. There is also another pair of bolts 5m

higher. From here either continue up *GUBIA NORMAL* (you are just below the stance at the foot of pitch five) or abseil back to the ground. At this point it may occur to you that double ropes might be a good idea.

SOURISA VERTICAL ** 5+ (E1 5b) 46m
1. 22m   5   (5a)   Follow either line of bolts up the lower wall, the right-hand one being marginally easier, then move right or left to a stance.
2. 24m   5+   (5b)   Climb up to pass to the left of the prominent bush right of the arête. From here continue directly up the wall before bearing away left with plenty of protection and a goodly set of holds to eventually pass a peg runner and reach a stance on the arête of the cliff.

MASTER *** 5+ (E2 5c) 47m
The central line on the wall is one of the best hereabouts with the upper pitch being steep, sustained, direct and interesting.
1. 23m   5   (5a)   From the flat area follow the right-hand bolt line up scoopy rock immediately to the left of a low profile yellow tufa. A bulging section is taken on good holds then easier climbing leads to a move right to a cramped stance on a flake with a wire cable belay. The remains of the battered bush that just manages to survive behind the flake are guaranteed to snag your ropes and fray your nerves.
2. 24m   6a   (5c)   Climb directly up the wall to the bulging section and press on straight through it to easier terrain just beyond. Continue in the same line to another tricky and rather run-out section to arrive thankfully at a large pocket then cross the final bulges on a series of excellent holds to a hearty lower-off point.

POLLA BOBA *** 5+ (E2 5c) 45m
The original route of the wall remains well worth doing.
1. 23m   5   (5a)   As for the first pitch of *MASTER* to the wire cable belay.
2. 22m   5+   (5c)   Climb up the wall trending slightly rightwards (though not as rightwards as the next route) to a bulge which cuts across the wall and contains some odd calcareous growths sprouting from the rock. Cross the bulge with difficulty then continue on good though spaced holds to the lowering station of the previous climb.

MEJICO LINDO ** 6a (E3 5c) 45m
A worthwhile if somewhat unbalanced route with the second pitch offering the hardest climbing on this section of the cliff.

1. 23m   5   (5a)   As for the first pitch of *MASTER* to the wire cable belay.
2. 22m   6a   (5c)   Follow a line just to the right of the right-hand bolt ladder (or fourth from the left if any new lines have appeared further right) until it is possible to swing right under a bulge. Cross this by fingery moves and continue up the ensuing scoop until it blanks out. Lurch up and left with difficulty to reach the lowering point just a little higher.

Up the bank to the right of the *SECTOR POLLA BOBA* are three other bolt lines.

OASIS ** 6a+ (E2 5c) 30m
The first one starts to the left of a well trampled area and gives one long pitch, steepening as it rises.

A DE LOS BOMBEROS *** 6a+ (E3 5c) 110m
Starting at the well trampled area (suggesting it is popular) is this route protected by gold-coloured bolts that run a long way up the cliff. There are four pitches, 5+, 6a, 6a+, 6a+ and descent is most easily achieved by abseiling back down the line of the routes.

HAMBE ETERNA ** 6a+ (E3 5c) 25m
Further right is a line of silver bolts up a gradually steepening wall to a lower-off by grass.

SECTOR ESPOLON

On the right side of the narrowest point of the gorge at Gubia a striking ridge shoots skywards. This is in fact the protruding end of the extension of the sheet of rock that forms the *PARET DELS COLOMS* on the other side of the ravine. Located here is a small collection of short routes on the grey and yellow wall just to the right of the toe of the buttress and the much longer (and much more worthwhile?) classics of *GUBIA NORMAL* and *SUPER NOVA*. The short routes are described first, from right to left. The first of these starts just up the bank below the right arête of the wall.

TRANKY COMPI ** 5 (HVS 5a) 16m
The right edge of the wall (just left of the easy vegetated groove that separates this area from *SECTOR POLLA BOBA*) gives a pleasant sustained pitch on sharp rock past half a dozen bolt runners. Any mathematicians should be able to work out that 16m divided by six bolts = well protected fun.

The next four routes all start at a flat area, in the bushes below the centre of the slab that runs up to the middle of the wall.

PUTA PERRO * 6a+ (E2 6a) 16m
Climb the slab easily rightwards to the first bolt then use a couple of unusual 'stuck on' holds to get established on the steep wall above. A difficult couple of moves (marginally easier on the right?) on sharp holds leads to better pockets, and a quick sprint over the final bulge reaches the belay on the previous climb.

The next route is the easiest and arguably the best on this section of rock.

FI DE RIC ** 5+ (E2 5b) 15m
Climb up the centre of the slab then link a line of good but well spaced pockets and flakes up the centre of the widest orange streak by a series of long reaches to gain easier rock. The lower-off is just above.

JODETE ET BAILA 6b (E4 6a) 15m
Hard climbing with rather antiquated protection. Climb the centre of the slab and from the patch of yellow rock below its right edge pull into the prominent 'blank' scoop. Up this to a lonesome bolt lower-off.

CHARLY DANONE * 7a (E5 6b) 15m
For the final time today climb the easy slab then continue up the thin grey wall to gain the foot of an unusual crozzly tufa. Sharp climbing up this leads to the singular bolt lower-off shared with the previous route.

CHITAS MARCHITAS * 6b (E4 6a?) 17m
The final route here starts just to the left of a prickly bush and close to the left edge of the wall. Climb the easier lower rib then continue past two small white tufas and up the final grey pillar on tiny sharp holds to reach the prominent red lower-off.

The next two routes share a common and undistinguished first pitch which starts at the narrowest point of the ravine. Above this the first, *GUBIA NORMAL*, follows the classical ridge towards its right edge whilst the other, *SUPER NOVA*, takes the left bounding arête of the ridge.

GUBIA NORMAL (a.k.a. ALBAHIDA) *** 4 (VS 4c) 240m
The most striking feature at Gubia offers a magnificent outing at an amenable grade. The route follows the eye-catching ridge which is clearly visible from the island's airport, if you know where to look. It then follows easier rock to the top of the mountain. A descent back to the base of the

route is not an easy option as the climb is not equipped for an abseil descent and so the simplest arrangement is to carry trainers or a light sack and then descend the back of the mountain (see below). The route contains quite a bit of fixed gear but much of it is old; carry a light rack, and double ropes if you have any doubt about your ability.

The detailed description here is from my ascent of the route. Many other variations are obviously possible at much the same grade, some of which may have more fixed gear. If in doubt keep heading upwards! Many of the stances are numbered in rather faded red paint and there are occasional red arrows, usually at the stances, to indicate the general direction of the subsequent pitch.

START at the foot of the left-hand spur of the ridge at some red painted writing and a red cross. There is also a start up the right-hand spur that is supposed to be rather harder and may contain rather more fixed gear. It may be worth *HVS* though I have not done it.

1. 40m   3   V Diff   Follow the easy ridge up to the right and then back to the left to below a vegetated groove (no fixed gear). The arête on the left of the groove gives the safest option and leads to a recess with a bolt ladder (*SUPER NOVA 5*, see below) rising out of its left side.

2. 28m   4+   (4c)   Step out past bushes to reach the right rib of the recess and climb rough rock to an insubstantial *in situ* thread (a much bigger thread is available just above, not *in situ*). Continue up the steep sharp wall (first crux) until the climbing begins to ease and it is possible to trend up and left to a belay in another recess. There may be an easier variation to this pitch further to the right.

3. 28m   3+   (4b)   Move out right onto the exposed rib and climb ⇗ into a shallow corner passing a discreet peg that is well past its 'sell by date'. Follow the ridge above on great rock until a comfortable stance (and hiding place) in yet another recess is reached.

4. 34m   3+   (4b)   Head up and right to reach the obvious flake crack (prominent orange peg) and climb it, taking care with one or two large blocks, to gain access to the face above. Continue up this to reach ledges on the right with two brand new bolts and then climb an easy open groove to a belay 8m higher in a recess containing a large tree.

5. 40m   4   (4c)   Behind the tree is a steep wall which is best approached from the right. Climb up to an old peg then trend left across the wall (second crux) to better holds before climbing straight up again to regain the open crest of the buttress. Continue undeviatingly up this past a selection of *in situ* threads (and possible stances) to a foothold stance at two of the larger threads.

6. 35m   3   (Severe)   Continue straight up the rib on great rock (easier but inferior floral variations are available to either side) to a stance

below the bulge that blocks the ridge.

7.   35m   3   (4a)   Move awkwardly right into a crack behind a
bush and climb round the arête to a deep corner. Climb this, taking care
when passing the huge jammed block, then either climb the groove or
the rib to its right to arrive at a projecting shoulder and just a little higher
is the sudden end to the climbing. Thread and tree belays. If you have
timed things right you should have at least an hour's daylight left. If not
it is time to get a move on!

DESCENT: From the top of the climbing the easiest way off the cliff is to
continue up the ridge. This is exposed in places and care is needed with
occasional loose blocks, though a rope should not be needed. Most tricky
sections can be passed on the right (especially as there is a huge drop to the
left) and gradually the ridge opens out to where slabby scrambling leads to
the top of the mountain; about 20 minutes from the top of the climbing.

From the ruined buildings on the summit an indistinct path leads
northwards through bushes to reach a well made gravel road in 5 minutes.
Turn right along it. This weaves its way downhill (45 minutes) to arrive at
a farm complete with a big dog on a long chain (try barking back at it!) Just
beyond here is the main road; turn right and walk for $1\frac{1}{2}$ kilometres (passing
the inviting taverna after 1 kilometre if you can) to arrive back at the car.
(About $1\frac{1}{2}$ hours from the end of the climbing.)

Running parallel to the left of the *GUBIA NORMAL*'s pitches 2 to 5 is
a clean rib of rock with a three pitch bolt ladder up it. This only requires ten
quick-draws and double ropes and is the excellent:

SUPER NOVA (a.k.a. QUAN ES FA FOSC) *** 5 (HVS 5a) 133m
A great climb, steep direct and exposed on marvellous rock and with the
added bonus that it is well bolted.

1.   40m   3   V Diff   As for *GUBIA NORMAL* to the bolt belay in the
recess.

2.   30m   5   (5a)   Eight clips. Step left and climb the rounded rib
on very sharp rock until the angle drops back and a small uncomfortable
stance in a hollow is reached.

3.   30m   5   (5a)   Nine clips. Traverse out left from the recess
then follow the bolt ladder, generally trending slightly rightwards until
again things ease off and a stance in a yellow bay is reached.

4.   33m   5   (5a)   Eight clips. This pitch might be considered the
crux, mainly because it is steeper and more exposed than those below
rather than its being any more technical. Step left out of the recess and
enjoy the situations! Now follow the rib with sustained interest to arrive
eventually at two large bolts equipped with maillions.

Either continue slight rightwards up the easy upper section of the *NORMAL*, approximately 70m to the top of the ridge (see above for the way off) or descend the line of the route by abseil.

Just beyond the foot of *GUBIA NORMAL* the gorge starts to open out again. High on the right is a huge and very impressive west-facing wall that will doubtless keep a couple of generations going with 'super-projects'. Immediately ahead at this point and just above and to the right of the path is a dark slab climbed by the rather tatty-looking *FAKIR 6a*, whilst on the other side of the stream bed is another dark slab tackled by the marginally better looking *VITAMINA 6a+*.

PARET DELS COLOMS

The magnificent west wall of Gubia is home to over 30 routes, a good number of which are great classics. They vary in length from 20m to three pitches and in grade from *5 (HVS 5a)* to tough *7b+ (Hard E6)*. The whole area is known as the *PARET DELS COLOMS* and is rather arbitrarily divided into three sectors, from right to left, *SEIS PELAS, 242* and *PAPA MORENO*. Although the face generally varies in angle from steep to very steep there are some more reasonable pitches scattered amongst the 'E big numbers', especially on the slabbier skirt of rock that runs along much of the base of the cliff. The whole cliff looks rather intimidating when seen from the opposite side of the gorge but it turns out to be more friendly on close acquaintance, especially in the morning when it is full in the sun. Many of the harder climbs follow bizarre tufa pillars and chandeliers and some of these weep after prolonged rain. Other climbs, most notably those on the clean barrel-shaped buttress at the right side of the face, dry very rapidly after rain.

The foot of the cliff is most easily approached by walking up the dry stream bed to a point immediately below the last large solitary pine tree on the left side of the valley. A steep path, difficult to pick out at the start, weaves up the hillside to arrive right below the centre of the cliff, which is in the sun until a couple of hours after midday.

Note: It is best to avoid attempting to cut directly across the ravine because of its incised nature and some very exotic (ie. prickly) scrub.

In keeping with the rest of the cliff the routes are described from right to left.

PARET DELS COLOMS

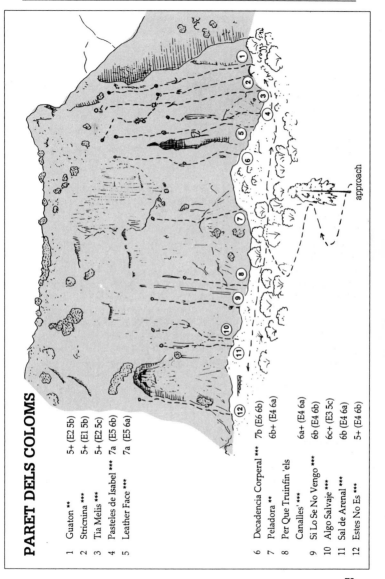

1	Guaton **	5+ (E2 5b)
2	Stricnina ***	5+ (E1 5b)
3	Tia Melis ***	5+ (E2 5c)
4	Pasteles de Isabel ***	7a (E5 6b)
5	Leather Face ***	7a (E5 6a)

6	Decadencia Corperal ***	7b (E6 6b)
7	Peladora **	6b+ (E4 6a)
8	Per Que Truinfin 'els Canalles' ***	6a+ (E4 6a)
9	Si Lo Se No Vengo ***	6b (E4 6b)
10	Algo Salvaje ***	6c+ (E3 5c)
11	Sal de Arenal ***	6b (E4 6a)
12	Estes No Es ***	5+ (E4 6b)

approach

SECTOR SEIS PELAS

This section of cliff stretches from the right-hand boundary of the face, as far left as an area of slabby, scrappy rock about 10m to the left of the big black hole that disappears into the heart of the cliff.

The first routes described start from a small hollow at the very right toe of the buttress. This is reached by a short diagonal scramble up a brushy slab and is recognised by having a trio of old bolts set in its left side.

Note: There also appears to be a route which starts up the scruffy slab to the right of the first climb described (*GUATON*). The bolted second pitch up the convoluted red rock up and to the right looks well worthwhile but no grades are available.

To the right of the trio of old bolts is a line of large and brand new bolts heading straight up the face. These are the protection on the common first pitch of two excellent face climbs.

GUATON ** 5+ (E2 5b) 44m

A fine climb with two good pitches, the lower one of which makes a worthwhile objective at *5 (HVS 5a)* **.

1. 22m 5 (5a) Follow the new bolts by climbing rough rock directly above the stance then continue up smoother rock, keeping to the left of a recently cleaned flake to pull over a bulge to reach the base of a projecting tufa pillar. Climb the left side of this by laybacking and fat pinch-gripping to a small, comfortable stance with substantial belays.

2. 22m 5+ (5b) Step out right and climb up to gain the line of golden-coloured bolts running up the wall. Follow these directly or slightly more easily by climbing the red hollows just to the right. At the level of a very large (unoccupied?) bird's nest head straight over the bulge, finishing with a long reach for the chains.

DANZOMANIA *** 6a (E3 5c) 90m

An excellent sustained route, the longest on this side of the ravine.

1. 22m 5 (5a) As for the first pitch of *GUATON*, to the small stance; see above.

2. 30m 6a (5c) Climb straight up the wall past a couple of old bolts and a peg then trend left following new dark speckled bolts by very sustained moves on sharp holds until a tricky sequence leads to a bulge. Once through this easier climbing protected by rather spaced and more elderly bolts lead to a stance below an open grassy groove.

3. 28m 6a (5c) The left wall of the open groove is approached easily and then gives more sustained and sharp climbing until things

ease and your tattered fingers can be given a rest. Abseil descent.

CHUNGUI CHUNGUEZ *** 6b (E4 6a) 52m
The second pitch offers superb, sustained and fingery face dancing. The first is a worthwhile outing at ** 5 *(HVS 5a)*. Start at the trio of old bolts on the left side of the hollow directly below a white tufa at 20m that has a vague resemblance to a pale pair of buttocks when seen from this position (honest).

1. 22m   5   (5a)   From the trio of old bolts climb straight up the wall to reach the white pillar. Awkwardly gain a standing position on this then continue more easily to a stance in a small hollow with multifarious belays.
2. 30m   6b   (6a)   Directly above the stance is a line of closely spaced and occasionally paired bolts. This is followed with escalating difficulty to a 'thread' handhold from where harder moves lead up and left to steeper rock and better holds. From this point things ease, though the interest is maintained to an odd set of belays and a cramped stance. Lower back to the previous stance or belay here and then descend by abseil.

Using the same first pitch as the previous route is a fine excursion that follows a sneaky line up this impressive buttress. Good protection, perfect rock and exciting positions combine to make a classic outing:

STRICNINA *** 5+ (E1 5b) 67m
A great climb with only a couple of tricky moves which are very well protected. Start as for *CHUNGUI CHUNGUEZ*.

1. 22m   5   (5a)   From the trio of old bolts climb straight up the wall following a line of rather coy bolts, to reach the 'buttock shaped' pillar. Gain a standing position on this with difficulty then continue more easily to an isolated stance in a small hollow with an interesting selection of belays.
2. 20m   5+   (5b)   Crossing the wall to the left of the stance is a vague line of weakness which is followed into the middle of nowhere. The belay chains above the first pitch of *TIA MELIS* (see below) offer a substantial running belay to protect the crux moves up and left to a discreet peg before it is possible to swing left into a shallow cave. After clipping the chain and bolt belays, regain your composure, then you can begin to enjoy the positions.
3. 25m   5   (5a)   A serious feeling pitch with rather spaced fixed gear. Bridge carefully out of the roof of the cave (spooky) then continue straight up the wall above until it is possible to trend right into an open shallow groove. Pull onto the wall above this then trend slightly right for 8m, at which point a choice presents itself. Either traverse horizontally

left past a peg runner to a substantial tree in a hollow with threaded chain belays, or trend up and right to reach fixed belays close to the second stance of the previous climb (no stance). From either belay a 45m abseil leads to the ground.

On the left side of the buttress tackled by *STRICNINA* is the magnificent 'drop of water' line followed by:

TIA MELIS *** 5+ (E2 5c) 47m
1. 25m   5+   (5c)   Start left of the shallow hollow at the foot of *STRICNINA* by a stunted tree and climb to a bolt (difficult to spot from below) by a patch of orange rock immediately beneath a small hole in the cliff. Once this is located continue directly up the face by sustained climbing then make thinner moves up smoother rock to reach a prominent diagonal flake crack with orange staining below it and just a little higher the chunky chain belay (no stance).
2. 22m   5+   (5c)   Make a couple of thin moves up and out right to a hole then climb directly up the cliff by more superb sustained climbing (no sneaking off left) to the belays which allow a 150ft abseil back to the foot of the cliff.

To the left of the direct line of *TIA MELIS* a line of grassy hollows trends slightly leftward up the cliff face. The odd piece of ancient fixed gear points to this having been climbed in antiquity though it is not marked on the present edition of the local topo. Re-equipped it would offer a great low grade way up the cliff. Any philanthropic takers?

To the left of the easy break is an impressive smooth wall, the most eye-catching feature of which is the red 'drainpipe tufa' climbed by the classic *LAS PASTELES DE ISABEL*. Below this section of wall is a grey apron of rather shrubby rock, bounded on its left (directly below the 'drainpipe') by a cleaner slabby section with bolt runners. The next three routes start up this.

VOL DE NUIT ** 6a+ (E3 5c) 30m
Fine steep wall-climbing spoilt only by the possibility of escape to the right part way up the pitch.

Climb easily to the apex of the slab (10m) and clip the first bolt on the steeper section of *GAY POWER*. Step right and climb the wall, right then left, to reach a rather fragile fretted pocket. From here continue directly up the wall by steep climbing on good holds to eventually climb a short bulging section and reach the cave stance above the second pitch of *STRICNINA*. Continue this 5 *(HVS 5a)* and/or make an abseil descent.

GAY POWER 7a+ (E5 6b) ** 30m
Very thin face climbing that is especially difficult if the largest of the many
micro-holds are not chalked up. Climb to the top of the slabby grey apron
(10m) then head up the wall on an increasingly sketchy series of holds. The
crux arrives just before things ease and a lower-off is reached a little higher.
A second pitch *6c (6a)* ** is available by moving left on to the next climb,
as the obvious direct continuation does not appear to behave been re-bolted
at the time of writing.

The 'drainpipe' is climbed by the major classic of:

PASTELES DE ISABEL *** 7a (E5 6b) 35/60m
1. 30m   7a   (6b)   Start up the slabby grey apron as for the two
    previous climbs then step out left onto the wall and make thin moves
    on small holds to reach the base of the tufa (*6a* with an extended reach?).
    Shin up the left side of this by sustained climbing to gain a squatted rest
    on its top with difficulty, then loop out left and back right to reach and
    follow better holds over a bulge to a small stance and lower-off.
2. 25m   6c   (6a)   Head up the easier angled wall above the
    lower-off until things begin to rear up and more fingery face climbing
    is required to reach another set of chains and the end of a great route.

To the left is the great black cave that disappears into the cliff, and below
and to the right of this is the left-hand edge of the slabby apron that runs
across the base of this section of the cliff. The last route on the smooth wall
to the right of the hole starts here and provides brilliant pocket pulling.

LEATHER FACE *** 7a (E5 6a) 35/60m
1. 35m   7a   (6a)   Either start as for the previous routes and then
    trend left to a spiky tree at the base of the steepest part of the wall, or,
    perhaps better, reach the same place from directly below by climbing
    the lower section of the next route. From the flattened area behind the
    spiky tree step out right (no climbing up left and stepping in!) onto the
    wall. This gives very sustained and gradually steepening pocket pulling,
    with thin moves up left to a juggy tufa. Above this the angle increases
    and fortunately the holds get bigger and better; keep on cranking. Just
    above the bulges a small stance and/or lower-off is reached.
2. 25m   6c   (6a)   The fine face above the stance has been rebolted
    and now gives more superb and gradually steepening face climbing to
    double the pleasure and the pain.

The rock around the great black cave that disappears up into the bowels
of the cliff has been developed to give a selection of pitches across a range

of grades. There are three short pitches into the cave and from the mutual stance in the base of the black hole there are two harder ways on. There is obvious scope here for mixing and matching.

A prominent scoop runs up into the base of the cave and to its right is a steep rib rising above a hollow and leading onto a slab.

LAMPARA ROCA ** 6a (E3) 42m
A good climb with a bizarre second pitch which provides an appropriate introduction to the tufa climbing at Gubia.

1. 20m   5   (HVS 5a)Climb the edge of the hollow, then steeper rock (jugs galore) to reach the slab. From here trend left passing below the tree on *LEATHER FACE* until it is possible to drift up and left to a belay in the base of the chimney. A worthwhile pitch in its own right, * with one short hard section.

2. 22m   6a   (5c)   Cross to the right side of the chimney and climb the groove until it is possible to tackle the bizarre chandeliers by some monkey business (taking care not to pull the whole affair down) to a bulge which is crossed by a quick powerful sequence. A lowering point is located just above.

CENTRO * 5 (E1 5b) 20m
The central line just right of a prominent scoop is steep to start, quite sustained and is on very sharp rock. From the belay in the base of the chimney go exploring the beckoning hole above or lower off rapidly back to sanity.

COMECHOCHOS ** 6a (E3 5c) 42m
A bizarre climb following the prominent scoop and then the inside left wall of the chimney. The first pitch makes for a worthwhile climb at *5 (HVS 5a)* ** and the grade of the second pitch depends on how soon you can (or are able to) make use of the opposite wall of the chimney with the grade being somewhere between *E2 5b* and *E4 6a*!

1. 20m   5   (5a)   Climb the scoop by pleasant bridging to a belay below the orifice, an excellent pitch at mild *HVS*.

2. 22m   6a   (5c)   Climb the left wall above (using holds on the right when required) until things steepen and the roof is crossed with difficulty until it is possible to bridge across to the opposite wall. The belays are just above the lip of the overhang, and if required there is a resting ledge a little higher on the other side of the chimney. Don't you have an urge to see where that hole goes to?

The fine grey pillar immediately to the left of the black hole is climbed by the first-rate though arduous:

DECADENCIA CORPERAL *** 7b (E6 6b) 60m
1. 30m   6b   (6a)   Start just around to the left of the groove that
    runs up into the hole and climb rightwards before swinging back left at
    a well hidden peg runner. From here sustained climbing using poor
    pockets and thin edges leads to a final steep sprint to a set of chains in
    a hollow. An excellent pitch at *E4 6a ****.
2. 30m   7b   (6b)   The bolts continue up the steep wall and so do
    the holds, but only just! A fantastically sustained piece of climbing on
    which it is difficult to identify a crux move, though it is probably the one
    that you fell off.

Immediately to the left of the first pitch of *DECADENCIA CORPERAL*
is another and recent bolt line running straight up the fine face:

PELLOJO DE TIBURON ** 28m 6c (E4 6b) 28m
More thin climbing, never too steep, but quite taxing enough due to its sharp
and sustained nature.

To the left of the grey pillar climbed by the previous two routes is an easy
looking left-slanting break that was the line chosen by the original route on
this section of face: *SEIS PELAS*. The first pitch trends left up this break and
passes a steeper section to a set of shoddy belays in the base of the large
orange hollow high on the face. The second and crucial pitch trends right
following the top edge of the grey pillar to a belay at the top of *DECADENCIA
CORPERAL*. The lower pitch does not appear to have been re-equipped at
the time of writing though I have heard rumours of the route being *** *6b
(E4 5c,6a)*. Are there any Doctor Livingstones out there?

The last piece of rock to be described on this sector is the clean wall
below and to the left of the initial pitch of *SEIS PELAS*. There are two short
but excellent and amenable face climbs here. These are directly below the
right edge of a prominent huge orange bowl high on the cliff. The right-hand
line is:

MES RAPIT SUC EL VENT ** 5+ (E2 5b) 25m
A fine sustained pitch, well protected and generally on good but sharp
holds. Keep clipping and keep pulling all the way to the chains.

HUMI ** 5+ (E2 5c) 28m
The left-hand line is the harder twin and has steep sustained lower section
and a tricky bulge thrown in for the crux.

To the left is another section of tree-ridden grey rock that is initially
slabby and runs up into steeper orange terrain above. This is the right-hand
end of the central part of the cliff, *THE SECTOR 242*.

SECTOR 242

The central section of the *PARET DEL COLOMS* is the most impressive developed wall at Gubia (look at the amazing tilted sheet of rock to the left of *SEXO DEBIL* for the most impressive undeveloped wall). This section of cliff is bounded on the right by a slabby apron of grey rock directly below the huge orange bay high in the centre of the cliff and on the left by the smoother slabby face left of the deepest caves directly above the old stone-built platform. Between these two features are a dozen or so routes offering some of the hardest pitches in the area. Many of the climbs follow most unusual tufa features and the climbing is generally steep and powerful rather than overly technical. Chipped and drilled holds are quite a common feature on the harder climbs!

On the right edge of this area is a brown wall bounded by grey streaks to left and right. There is a recently bolted route up the centre of this which looks good and hard though I have not been able to find a grade for it.

Starting up the grey slabby apron at the right side of this section of the wall is the well worthwhile:

PELADORA ** 6b+ (E4 6a) 24m
Climb the easy slabby rock to where the colour and angle change. Steeper sustained and quality climbing on pockets leads to lowering chains just as the angle falls back. May be worth *** if you like the style of climbing.

Climbing the left side of the same section of rock is the marginally less worthwhile outing:

PESADILLA FINAL * 6a (E2 5c) 28m
Climb the grey slab then trend left up steeper orange rock using a fine selection of pockets until a final tricky move over the bulges leads to a belay just above the change of angle. There is a second easier pitch 5 (5a?) up the walls above but the skull and crossbones plus the description 'roca molta decomposta' on the Spanish topo suggests where the route name *'FINAL NIGHTMARE'* came from, and, after all, you are on holiday.

Left again and just before the most imposing section of the wall is an indeterminate area of rock with several bushes and some large orange patches of rock 10m off the ground. The two pitch route *MORGUE 5,6b* climbs this though it does not look like an especially edifying exercise, being a bit too reminiscent of some of Cheedale's better offerings.

Left again the rock becomes ever more impressive. The lower section of the wall is marked by three grotesque phalluses sprouting from the rock. To the right of these is a large, pale grey active tufa and right again is a cleaner grey wall. The wall is climbed by the excellent:

PER QUE TRUINFIN 'ELS CANALLES' *** 6a+ (E4 6a) 22m
A fine sustained pitch of face climbing on sharp holds and with the crux sequence involving a short leftwards traverse at half height. The lower-offs are situated at the point where the rock becomes dirty; now there's a novel idea.

To the left is the long impressive tufa system described earlier. This is one of the last to dry out after seepage begins. To the left of this are the unmistakable large growths mentioned above. These have been described as 'elephant's legs' and other less repeatable comparisons; the mind boggles. Two hard and excellent routes start here:

SI LO SE NO VENGO *** 6b (E4 6b) 28m
Climb between the growths then press on up the sustained pocketed wall to technical and fingery moves past the fourth bolt to gain a slender ramp on the right. Easier climbing reaches a good rest on a 'sheep's head' at 25m then a final tricky sequence reaches a belay just a little higher. A second pitch continues up and left before heading up the crest of the wall, 22m 6a (6a?), though it does not appear to have been rebolted.

Also starting by the protrusions is a route regarded as one of the best routes on the wall by those in the know. It is certainly one of the hardest.

PINON FIJO *** 7b (E6 6b) 28m
From the growths climb the wall trending slightly leftwards following the pale grey streak past a hollow and a difficult clip (reinforced extension sling in place) to an optional breather in the cave of ALGO SALVAJE. Step back right and continue to the chains by some large, and some not-so-large holds.

To the left is the only white streak on this section of the cliff. This is tackled by the easiest route in the area, though it is no pushover. This is the great classic of:

ALGO SALVAJE *** 6a+ (E3 5c) 26m
Climb up rightwards to the white streak via an overhanging scoop which leads to some large holes. Exit right from the scoop and battle up to and past a large hanging lump to reach an overhang. At this point the translation of the name ('something wild') becomes ever more apt. Cross the overhang to reach an overdue resting ledge before stepping left and climbing the juggy wall to the lower-offs. Superb.

242 *** 7b (E6 6b) 23m
A tough climb which offers some brilliant moves despite (or because of) the drilled pockets. This route has been incorrectly called ZUZ on some topos

81

(I blame the originator's handwriting!). Start as for the previous route but trend left up the smooth wall before making moves right then left past a disappointing pocket to a mono-doigt from where the crux span up and rightwards can be made. A short sprint to the belays remains. Steep.

To the left is a section of orange scoops. Climbing through these is:

TRES MENOS CUARTO ** 7a+ (E5 6c) 22m
Bridge up through the scoops and tufas to a 'curly' overlap and thread where the rock turns grey. Continue up the grey streak using an undercut mono-doigt to reach better holds from where an immense reach gains a distant edge. Thankfully easier climbing leads to a lower-off below a large clumpy bush.

SAL DE ARENAL *** 6b (E4 6a) 22m
A shortlived but excellent piece of exercise climbing the right edge of the large area of red rock, to the right of a tall white tufa with a bush on top. Trend left up slabby rock then climb the wall past a small tree via a ragged crack. From the last resting place storm the twin tufas by frantic upside down laybacking to reach a thread and two bolt belay to right of a prominent bush. The route might be considered 5c by the criminally muscular.

To the left is an impressive though undeveloped area of face right above the old stone platform. The cliff here consists of a large inverted funnel with a variety of holes disappearing up into the rock. There is obviously scope here for some exciting trips into upside down land though the rather scrappy approach up slabs has delayed development.

ESTES NO ES 5+ *** 6b (E4 6b) 28m
A good route with some wild positions and a fierce and spectacular crux. The name (You may be 5+, this is not) is very true. Start to the left of the old platform and climb a slab past bushes to reach a prominent pocket with an orange streak below it. Climb over bulges on prickly rock then continue to ledges below steeper country. Layback up the tufas until all appears lost, from where a massive reach leftwards off a poor layaway gains brief respite at jugs. Pull back right with difficulty from where better holds lead to a lower-off on the slab above.

To the left, roughly following the arête of the wall, is a route called *ES POAL* which is given the odd grade (considering the chipped holds on other parts of the cliff) of *6a & A0*; no other details are known, though the topo in the climber's bar does not give it any stars.

Around to the left is a much more open and slabby section of cliff that only contains one route at present. The slab is climbed by the thin:

PEOR IMPOSIBLE ** 7a (E4) 39m

1. 15m   4   (4c)   Climb the lower slab trending right to a stance on ledges below the smoother rock.
2. 24m   7a   (6b)   Trend up and left to bypass the first bulge before heading back right towards the centre of the face. This gives thin sustained climbing on razor edges until another bulge is passed and easier moves lead to the lower-off.

SECTOR PAPA MORENO

The final sector at Gubia is the band of rock that runs leftwards up the hillside to the left of the caves and tufas of *SECTOR 242*. At present there are only four climbs here though there is obvious scope for more, especially further up the hillside.

The first route is the three pitch *PUEUTE AEREO 5,5,5+ (E1 5b?)* which climbs the lower walls to reach a groove high on the cliff. Further up the slope is a pedestal and starting on top of this is *PAPA MORENO ** 6a+ (E3 5c)*. Still further up the hill past some impressive tufas are the final two climbs, both of which are two pitches long. On the right is *AMOR BRUJO 6a,6a* and on the left is *PECHO LATA 6b,6b*.

CALA MAGRANER

The climbing shop in Palma (see appendix) sells a collection of rather rudimentary topos for 400 pesetas. Generally speaking these consist of a series of rather rough hand-drawn maps of the better known areas. Amongst these is a climbing location on the south-east coast known as Cala Magraner, though unfortunately I have been unable to locate its exact whereabouts on my last visit to the island. The notes below have been supplied by Roger Briggs and friends, (to whom I am indebted) they must have better exploration skills than me!

Character
A line of south-facing walls in a secluded setting on the south-east coast of the island. The 30 minute or so walk to the cove ensures that it is always quiet and some who have visited the place describe it as perhaps the most idyllic climbing setting on the whole island. There is a good spread of grades

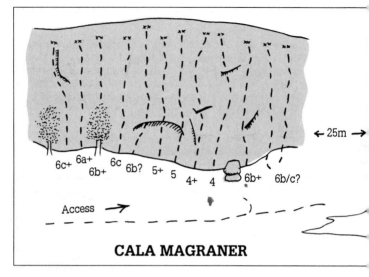

← 25m →

6c+ 6a+   6c 6b? 5+ 5   4+ 4   6b+ 6b/c?
        6b+

Access →

CALA MAGRANER

with several very well bolted easier climbs, away from the madding crowd, and then there is always the sea!

Access

The cliff is situated on the south-east coast of the island between Porto Cristo and Calas de Majorca. Eight kilometres south of Porto Cristo is the impressive castle/fortified house of Son Forteza Vey. Driving south from here the road descends some sweeping bends for a kilometre until a parking place at the entrance of an unsurfaced road on the right (with an assortment of post boxes on its right side) is reached. Cross the road and follow the dried-up river bed gently downhill all the way to the sea. The first 10 minutes are easy going then as the streambed narrows a path on the left can be followed for another 10 minutes. A couple of gates on the right are traversed and just beyond these the track leads into a mini-gorge with a lake separated from the sea by a pebble bar. To the right of the centre of the climbing area is a ruined building, the location of which aids finding specific routes.

As mentioned above the cliffs are in a south-facing valley that contains a small lake, and which runs out into the sea. The latest topo information I have shows almost 30 climbs (and development continues), all of them are unnamed. The given grades are presumably 'Majorcan French', though they may be 'French French'.

On the far left just before the crag peters out is a *6a* and right of this a

84

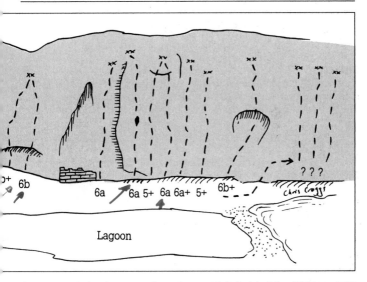

6c+ starting behind a tree and running up a left-facing flake. Right again is a 6a+, a 6b+ and a 6c, the middle one of which starts behind another tree. Right again is a 6b? and a 5+ through a curving overlap, with a 5 up its right edge and beyond this two good low grade routes, a 4+ and a 4. Starting behind (or on) a block is a 6b+ and just to the right are two steep 6b/c? routes. A 25m gap separates this area from the one behind the ruined building.

On its left are a 6b+ and 6b that pull over an overhang and go their separate ways to a common lower-off. Behind the building is a cave and on the right edge of this a 6a, whilst to the right of this (and running through a narrow hole/cave?) is a 6a. Right again are two climbs that go up a slab and over bulges to a common lower-off in a bay at the top of the cliff. These are 5+ and 6a. Right again is a wall with a 6a+ and a 5+, and just above the shingle bar there is a 6b+ running diagonally rightwards through a cave. To the right the cliff extends out over the sea, and ledges are reached by a short scramble and easy traverse. There are at least half a dozen lower grade climbs here to enjoy.

LAS PERCHAS

Character
An amazing little cliff with a small number of exceedingly steep climbs; the place is like a larger (and steeper) version of Yorkshire's Hollywood Bowl. The crag faces due north but this hardly matters; it is so steep that even if the cliff faced due south it wouldn't see much sun, such is the angle of the rock! Not surprisingly the climbing is very powerful, relying on pockets and sporadic tufas to climb walls that vary in angle from very steep to indecently steep. This is definitely a suitable destination for the criminally muscular. Slab climbers had better look elsewhere for their sport, unless they can find a way into the interior of the cliff and climb the 'other sides' of the leaning walls. Along with Ses Tret this cliff is a 'DIY' crag, as I only have complete details for some of the routes. The rest are described briefly for completeness. Feel free to do them all, and fill in the grades yourself.

Access
From Inca follow the road north to Selva and onto the small village of Caimari tucked in close under the hills. Drive north out of Caimari for a short distance to the 'Luch 10 km' sign. Just past this are several narrow entrances on the left; take the one with the small red arrow on a gate post. If you reach the first sharp bend as the road begins to climb into the hills then you have gone too far. Drive down the track, over the river and past a settlement for 300m to limited parking below the cliff; you are unlikely to miss the crag.
Note: Parking on the narrow track below the cliff is difficult and very limited. Turning round is also difficult. The best place to turn is 400m further up the track as long as the gate is open. If not it may be necessary to reverse back to the settlement and turn or park there.

   The climbs are described from right to left and as I have been unable to come up with names for the climbs I have simply numbered them. At the right edge of the cliff the crag runs out into ivy-coated hillside. The first short route starts 7m left of the ivy.

P1 * 7c 10m
Climb the white scoop to reach grey rock above and the solitary lower-off bolt. A short route offering hard, well chipped face climbing. Three clips.

P2 ** 7b (E6 6b) 15m
Starting 2m to the left and just to the right of a prominent blackened cave. Climb the leaning lower wall on pockets to prominent tufas. Battle powerfully up these to the lower-offs. Five clips.

P3 ** 7c 15m
Start from a pair of 'elephant's legs' in the back of the cave (paired bolts at start). More butch climbing up overhanging tufas, blobs and flanges. Six clips.

P4 ** 7c 20m
Five metres left the overhanging orange wall is climbed on well chalked pockets, passing a 'black hole' to eventually reach a tufa and then the lower-offs. Five clips. Climbers over 6ft can only claim a 7b+.

P5 *** 7c+ 22m
Three metres left the next offering starts at low relief tufa with a pocket in its top left corner, and climbs a line past an old wooden wedge at 5m. Once past this climb through a hollow then trend gradually leftwards up the face passing a hole. Seven clips.

P6 ** 7c 20m
Three metres left climb up to black holes at 5m using a series of 'chips', then continue into and up the steeply leaning ramp/groove above. Six clips.

Left again is a large hour-glass-shaped pillar below a large cave. There are no routes on this section of cliff at present, though some lines are obvious.

P7 ? 24m
To the left of the hour-glass-shaped pillar is a cave/recess with a small fire ring in it. The route climbs the groove just left of this and then continues on up a leaning rib above until forced out right into a groove. A route that looks both tough and sparingly bolted.

To the left is a prominent small tree 10m up the cliff growing under a large overhang.

P8 *** 7a+ (E5 6a) 22m
Just left of fall line from tree. A tricky leaning lower wall to a good rest (you will need it) on ledges on the right. Step back left then tackle the tufa-encrusted roof to reach a leaning wall above. The crux moves lurk here and involve getting up and right to the lower-offs. Seven clips.

Left again and under the right edge of the major cave is a tall thin cave entrance. The next route starts directly above this and is reached most easily by scrambling round to the left, though the belayer may want to stay on the ground rather then risk being pulled off the ledge by an airborne leader.

P9 *** 8b+ 25m
Swing out right then trend left across the never ending roof to belays around the lip. As far as the fixed karabiner on the fifth bolt this may be a juggy *6a (E3 5c)*. At least ten clips.

P10 ***? 8c? 25m
Start in the back left corner of the main cave. Climb across the overhang to a hole in the centre of the roof, and then continue in the same vein to the twin bolt lower-offs around the lip. I am not sure what grade this is, but it certainly isn't *5+*. Astounding. I counted seven clips, though there may be more.

The final three routes are to be found around the left arête of the cave.

P11 ** 7c+ 22m
Another steep number. The overhanging wall right of the arête is followed rightwards to a belay in the right wall of the large groove around the lip. Seven clips.

P12 * 7a+ 20m
A slight rib to the right of the hole is climbed steeply to easier angled rock to the lower-offs. Six clips.

P13 * 6b (E3 6a) 12m
The easy looking groove in the left arête of the cliff is the warm-up for the rest of the cliff. Steep climbing up the juggy groove leads to a more technical exit. Four clips.

A short distance up the road beyond the turn-off to 'biceps city' the road starts to climb into the hills. Just beyond the third bend is *HAIRPIN CRAG*, recently developed with six inconsequential climbs. The safest parking is on the first bend from where a track and short scramble leads to the cliff, otherwise park on the third bend right by the cliff. Quite why the locals choose to develop this with so much rock on the island escapes me!

From right to left the routes are:

HP1 6b+ 10m
The first bolt is a 'gripper-clipper'.

HP2 * 5+ (E1 5b) 12m
A shoddy start but gets (a bit) better climbing the right side of the slab.

HP3 * 6a+ (E2 5c) 15m
Start as for the last route but keep left. Possibly the best on the crag.

Pete (POD) O'Donovan on one of the 'easiest' routes at Las Perchas, P8, 7a+ (E5 6a)

HP4 5 (HVS 5b) 10m
Just around to the left, poor!

HP5 6b+ 10m
Fingery climbing trending to the right to reach the lower-off of the previous climb.

HP6 6c 10m
Start as for the last climb and trend left up the rib.

PUERTO PI

Character
A slightly scruffy bouldering area whose main asset is its great accessibility, being situated on the southern side of the bay only a short drive from Palma in one direction and from the resorts of Palma Nova and Magaluf in the other. I have no doubt that there are many other areas of greater worth scattered around the island, but if you are looking for somewhere for a quick work-out, only minutes from the road, Peurto Pi fits the bill admirably. The rock consists of a long 5m high outcrop that overhangs considerably for much of its length. The rock is pocketed and is generally exceptionally rough. Fortunately the sea is very close if it all proves a bit much.

Access
Follow the road around the harbour at Palma in a southerly direction to the first turnoff, located at a major junction, with traffic lights, just a short way past the military harbour. Take a left turn here. If coming from the resorts to the south, a right turn is made at the foot of the long hill that runs down to the harbour. Follow the road up the hill, then as it bends round to the left, roadside parking is available where there is a break in the chain on the right.
Leave no valuables in the car
The rocks are reached by a short scramble down the bank. Enjoy the setting and get pumping.

SANTA PONCA

Character
A small cliff of good rock which is worth a visit if you are in the area, and can climb to a suitable standard. The cliff faces north east and so can be a

shady retreat on hot days.

Access
The cliff is the conspicuous smooth white lump that overlooks the golf course at Santa Ponca. Take the coastal road past Palma Nova and Magaluf and on towards Andraixt. At a roundabout with a newly restored windmill turn left towards Santa Ponca and follow signs for 'Golf'. At the entrance to the golf course turn right and take the road that winds up the hill towards the cliff sticking out of the trees. Park on the roadside at a long right-hand bend then follow any one of a series of tracks that wend up through the trees to reach the base of the cliff less than 5 minutes away.

Leave no valuables in the car

The routes are described from left to right.

SP1 ** 5 (HVS 5a) 14m
Climb a short easy crack then step onto the wall and follow a continuously surprising set of pockets. Steep and satisfying.

SP2 * 6a+ (E3 6a) 15m
Start as for the previous climb but swing awkwardly right onto the face and make a couple of moves on razors to reach better holds, leaving a short steep sprint to the belays.

Just to the right the cliff swings round to face north; the arête that divides the two faces is climbed by:

SP3 *** 6c+ (E5 6b) 15m
The overhanging arête is steep, sharp and technical. Climb diagonally leftwards on poor pockets then head straight up the sustained pocketed rib above.

SP4 ** 7a (E5 6b) 15m
Start to the right of the arête. Pull through the roofs with difficulty then continue up the smooth white wall with more of the same.

SP5 ? 15m
The line just to the left of the scruffy gully that divides this section of the cliff looks worthwhile though I do not have a grade for it.

SP6 ** 7a (E5 6b) 16m
To the right of the gully is a discontinuous crack line that runs out into steeper rock just below the cliff top. The crack is much harder than it looks, being largely holdless and precarious to boot. Eventually good holds are reached and more thuggish climbing leads to the lower-offs.

SP7 ** 7a+ (E6 6b) 16m
The last route on the cliff is an open white scoop that gives a technical,
precarious and sustained pitch. Most definitely not one for strong arms.

SES TRET

Character

Note: The cliff is also known as Roca Blanca on some topos. A most unusual
crag for Spain in that part of it has been quarried in the past. Before you turn
the page in search of something better, be assured: this is no Horseshoe
Quarry. Indeed the rock is generally very solid. Unfortunately the angle of
the cliff means that all the climbs are of a high standard of difficulty, with
virtually nothing to interest climbers operating in the 'fours','fives' and
'sixes'. The crag faces due north and so is sheltered from the sun and much
of it is steep enough to stay dry even in heavy rain. Rather conveniently, due
to the quarrymen's activity, the base of the crag has a continuous 'dotted
line' painted along it with the dots being a standard 1m apart. This does
away with the need to find names for the climbs though it does make for
rather boring climbing talk, adding ever more numbers to the melting pot.
   "I though *23.2* was more like *7a+* than *E5 6b*, and a Yank I met said it
was 5.12b!!!"
   This is one of the two sections of this guidebook that are pretty much
'DIY'. I have included all the information that I have been able to come up
with, though sadly this is far from complete. For routes that have no grades
and no star rating please feel free to add your own!

Access

The crag is hidden just off the main road from Palma to Valdemossa. Fifteen
kilometres to the north of Palma the road cuts through a short rocky ravine
with a prominent slabby cliff above the road on the right. Immediately upon
exiting from this there is an extensive (and scruffy) parking area on the left.
This is easily overshot on the first visit; a couple of kilometres further up the
road is a right turn that allows you to turn around and have a second go!
Leave nothing in the car, then follow the left-hand track, past a locked gate,
as it rises gradually until the cliff appears on the left 400m down the track.
A short steep scramble leads up to it. Several other buttresses are passed
on the way to the main cliff though they are largely undeveloped at present
and are all rather uninspiring.

   The routes are describe briefly from left to right and the painted numbers
are used to locate them.

Number 35 8c? 12m
Head straight up the wall which leans at an angle close to 45 degrees. Not all of the holds are entirely natural!

Number 34 * 8a+ 12m**
Up the wall following gold then red bolts trending slightly leftwards to a lower-off in the groove above.

To the right is an even steeper prow of rock with no routes at present.

Number 27 * 7c (E6 6c) 18m**
A fearsomely steep line up the crag tackling the leaning lower wall to a 'rest' on the ramp of the next climb, and then attacking the severely tilted rock above 'with gusto'.

Number 25.1 ** 6b+ (E4 6a) 15m
A diagonal pocketed ramp line is followed steeply leftwards to ledges and a lower-off at the world's largest karabiner. A good warming 'pump up' for this section of the cliff, though stripping the gear can be problematical.

Number 25.2 ? 20m
Start at the foot of the ramp and initially climb straight up the crag. At the third bolt trend left up the steep sustained ragged crack line.

Number 25.3 ? 20m
As for *25.2* to the third bolt then straight on up the overhanging orange rock above and over a prow to the lower-offs. Undeniably steep.

Number 24.1 ? 24m
Start at a right-trending seam. At the fifth bolt (with fixed karabiner) move left into an orange scoop and then press on over the roof above. The lower-off is located just below the top of the cliff.

Number 24.2 * 8b 24m**
Start up the right-trending seam and press on to reach a rest in an orange niche. From here do battle with the square roof and the black prow that hangs over it.

Number 19 ** 8a 22m
Straight up the 'easier angled' wall to the right to enter an orange rounded scoop. Climb out of this to reach a ragged crack line and then a tufa which is followed to the lower-offs. As far as the fixed karabiner on the second bolt is a rather trivial *5 (HVS 5a)*.

Number 17 ** 6b (E4 6a) 15m
Head up right to reach ledges below a ragged crack line then press on up this, before trending leftwards to reach a lower-off where the wall becomes smooth.

Number 13 *** 7a+ (E5 6a) 22m
Despite its allotted number this is one of the best routes on the crag, with a technical lower section and exciting finale plundering the centre of the head-wall.
    Climb the smooth lower wall then press on up a tufa, passing an overlap with difficulty. Climb into a bay for a breather then push on up the leaning wall using a discontinuous crack system until it is possible to step left and then lean back right to reach the lower-offs. Stunning.

Number 12 7b 20m
Climb the ragged crack to an optional lower-off in bay, or if you feel up to it, continue up the tilted prow via a thin crack.

Number 11 ? 22m
A very fingery-looking pitch up the centre of the wall just left of the prominent groove line, protected by white bolts and finishing over the big prow.

Number 8 ** 6a+ (E3 5c) 20m
The twisting bridging-groove that defines the right side of the central section of the cliff is protected by bright red bolts. The warm-up for the cliff. Despite being the only climb on the cliff suitable for normal mortals it is considerably steeper than it looks, and thus requires some powerful climbing.

Number 5 ** 7b+ 18m
The short leaning buttress is obviously no pushover.

    Around to the right are three more steep lines on a planet-sized boulder. Unlike the main cliff this section of rock does not bear any numbers but to continue the theme of the main sector of cliff they are:

Number -1 ** 7a+ (E5 6a) 15m
The leftmost line up an overhanging rib has a tricky start and is climbed mostly, and surprisingly, on its steeper left side.

Number -2 * 7a+ (E5 6b)
The central line follows the previous route to the third bolt and then swings

right to climb a steep orange scoop and formidable roof on pocketed rock.

Number -3 ** 7a+ (E5 6b)
From boulders reach a chiselled hold which is used to pull into a series of scoops. Step left and climb the overhanging groove precariously on sloping holds and then the final easier leaning wall direct.

SOLLER (S'ATALAIA)

Character
A cliff of contrasts, in a pleasant if slightly scruffy setting, and easy of access from the town of Puerto Soller; which is itself difficult to get to from almost anywhere on the island! The cliff is divided into a short set of rather scruffy walls with a selection of lower grade routes and an impressive tufa cave with some more memorable offerings. Development of the left side of the cliff is continuing at the present and judging by the extent of the rock will go on for some time. It is worth mentioning that the cliffs are in the sun from about mid-afternoon until it sets. Once the sun bathes the rocks in golden light any imperfections in the setting are soon forgotten.

Access
Soller is reached most easily via the C711 that runs north from Palma passing the cliff of Gubia and the town of Bunyola. Unfortunately the crossing of a high pass shortly after Bunyola makes the journey a bit of a nightmare. (You try and count how many bends there are!) A tunnel is being driven through the hill and this will cut out most of the bends and make the journey a lot easier. Unfortunately at the time of writing the tunnel has been under construction for five years! A pleasant alternative to the drive is to take the train to Soller and then catch the tram to the terminus at Puerto Soller, a steep 5 minute walk from the cliffs. See appendix for train times.

With your own transport cross the infamous pass then drive past the town of Soller and along the sea front at Puerto Soller. Follow the railway track to its end and take the last available right turn (by a leather boutique) which winds steeply uphill until there is an opening on the left by the Bar Nautilus. Turn down here and park anywhere away from the big drop into the sea. The routes are described from right to left as this is the usual approach. I have been unable to come up with names for most of the routes and so have simply numbered them with the prefix 'S'. The first selection of 14 climbs have little to recommend them apart from involving themselves in bolt clipping in the sunshine. Then again, perhaps that is commendation enough.

The initial routes lie below the projecting hotel wall that juts out high above, and the first offering is up a tall grey tower at the right end of cliff directly below the corner of the wall.

S1 * 5 (E1 5b) 20m
Climb the rib up the right side of the face and continue up the upper arête. A lower-off is available thus avoiding the need to enter the palatial grounds above.

S2 * 5+ (E2 5c) 20m
Start up the tricky bulging face to the left of the arête and pass these obstacles to gain the easier and well positioned upper section.

S3 5 (HVS 5b) 14m
To left are flat ledges at 3m. From these climb to more ledges then scale the wall directly above via a slippery bulge (chipped holds) to reach the chains in the base of the easy groove above.

S4 4+ (HVS 5a) 10m
Two metres to the left is a short bulging wall with diagonal right to left cracks crossing it. Climb directly up the centre of this to a lower-off on the ledges above.

The white wall to the left is prominently spattered with old and new bolts. On the right side of this is a groove.

S5 3+ (VS 4c) 10m
Climb the open groove to the right of the white wall. The start is steep and the rest is much easier.

S6 5 (HVS 5b) 10m
The centre of the well bolted white wall has tricky moves past the third bolt to reach a quick sprint to a lower-off above.

The next two routes start from a couple of flat rocks on the ground.

S7 4+ (HVS 5a) 10m
Take a line up ruddy rock via a prominent and recently excavated niche.

S8 4 (VS 4c)
To the left is a left-trending bolt line passing more recent red rock scars; indeed some of the rock still feels rather temporary so climb it with care.

Jim Rubery in spectacular setting on SHORTY 5+ (E1 5b),
the upper crag, Valldemossa

A typical winter's day at Buda, Ibiza
The East Face of La Catedral, Tenerife, with the lava fields beyond.

Five metres left is a bizarre line of seven huge homemade brackets. These provide the very encouraging protection on:

S9 6a (E1 6a) 10m
A very sharp lower wall is climbed starting off a small ramp, and with the climbing easing rapidly as height is gained.

S10 * 5+ (E1 5b) 13m
Just left of the 'mega-brackets' is a bulging wall and shallow corner leading to a small robust tree. A short distance above is a solitary bolt and Krab lower-off. One of the better routes on this section of cliff.

Several hundred metres further along the track a small scrambly path leads to a prominent pale rock-scar with four short and hard-looking routes, the three right-hand ones sharing a common lower-off. They do not look especially worthwhile but who knows? For completeness these are:

S11 7b? 12m
The right-hand line.

S12 * 7a 12m
Straight up the wall.

S13 * 6b 12m
The left of the trio.

S14 6b+ 12m
Left again.

SECTOR SA COVA

A short distance left again the cliff becomes more worthwhile starting with an impressive tufa cave which is home to seven routes. This is the *SECTOR SA COVA*. Generally each climb is a grade or so harder than the one to its right, so start at the right edge of the cave and see how far you get! Almost all of the routes here climb some amazing tufa features; please treat them gently. The cave is a superbly sheltered sun-trap late in the day when the sun hammers straight into it. Just the spot for boosting up the tan. The first two climbs here share a common start up the right rib of the cave.

S15 * 6a+ (E2 5c) 22m**
A good climb with a tough finale. Swing onto the initial rib then trend right past a hole, towards a hanging 'dong'. Just short of this move left then make steep pulls (lowering off from the fixed karabiner here is worth ** 5 (E1 5b)) to where a swing right along a diagonal crack gives access to a final difficult sequence to the chains.

S16 *** JA SOM FIVE 6b+ (E4 6a)
Start as for the previous climb then climb the edge of the cave until the wall starts to lean. A demanding sequence past a series of 'stuck-on' tufas reaches sloping ledges and (possibly) a hidden jug, then a baffling final set of moves allows a rightward exit onto a slab to reach the belay. It is also possible (and a cheat!) to step left to join the finish of the next route.

Inside the the right edge of cave are the next three contributions to the area's climbing. The first one parallels the previous pair of routes with the other two crossing the impressive roofs further left.

S17 *** CLUB SUPER TRES 6c+ (E5 6b) 22m
Great climbing, powerful and sustained. Pull onto the wall over a tricky overhang and continue up 'tufatastic' rock to where it starts to lean severely. A hard move on disappointing pockets gains a hanging proboscis then easier but still steep moves up the wall conclude a great pitch.

The next two climbs share a common start and find separate ways around the lip of the cave, with one finishing direct through the roofs and the other trending left below lip to pull round onto the leaning head wall.

S18 *** CHICALITO 7c (E6 6c) 20m
Step right out of the back of the cave (gluttons can start as for the previous climb) then pull over a roof to tufas and a good deep hole. From this power straight through the overhangs above with great difficulty to eventually reach better holds.

S19 *** PHANTONMAS 7b (E6 6b) 22m
A great test of stamina. Follow the previous climb to the 'good deep hole' then trend left below the lip to a bigger hole and a semi-rest. Tackle the bulge directly above using a series of good but spaced pockets to reach black tufas and the lower-off. Butch work.

The compelling line out from the back of the cave is unclimbed at the time of writing though it looks an obvious challenge. At the left side of the cave is a route that traverses the whole of the underside of the lip from left to right:

S20 *** VIRGIN 8b (E8 6c?) 25m
An obviously over strenuous outing despite the size of many of the holds, and a suitable challenge for those who thought the last route 'duff'.

Overheard: Climber 1. "That route is never *8b!*"
              Climber 2. "Oh, have you done it then?"
              Climber 1. "No"!!!!

*Pete (POD) O'Donovan silhouetted in spectacular setting at Soller on
S16, JA SOM FIVE 6b+ (E4 6a)*

Follow the underside of the left edge of the cave to eventually (after two more years in the gym?) join and finish as for the previous route. Use of the midway lower-off makes for a softer option, *(VS 4b?) 8a+* actually!

S21 ** DIT I FET 7a+ (E4 6b) 12m
Starting at the left edge of the cave is a ragged seam running straight up the wall and into a brown bay. A short but action-packed pitch which is rather 'sequential'.

To the left of the cave is an area of more amenable rock consisting of an open scoop and then a rounded buttress. This area appears to have been largely ignored up to the present day. With a little effort there could be some fine lower grade climbs here. A solitary bolt 10m up and just above a small bush (to the left of the main scoop) is the only sign of activity. Beyond the rounded buttress is a tree growing just to the left of an alcove. Climbing out of this (the alcove, not the tree) is:

S22 ** 6a+ (E3 5c) 20m
Exit from the scoop via the prominent undercut and tootle up the white tufa-streaked wall to a steeper section of grey/brown sharp rock. Finish up this with gusto!

To the left of the last route described above are another five more bolted lines (at the time of writing), and although they all look worthwhile I have not done any of these. Brief details are included here for reference.

Immediately left of the previous route is an inviting, open, brown groove, unclimbed at present.

S23 ** 6a+ 18m
To the left of a tree standing close to the rock are some spiky bushes on the wall and then a bright white buttress climbed on its right side by a line protected by silver bolts. The route heads left of a grey streak past large holes, then up the tilted brown wall, to chains on its rim.

S24 ** 5+ 15m
Left again is a line marked by dark red/brown brackets running straight up steep white wall to a short leaning section and on to a lower-off in a cave. It does not look too hard.

Left again the cliff gets considerably higher, and it is slabby in its lower section.

S25 *** 6c 30m
A line of large gold ring-bolts runs left across the lower slab to a hollow

(stance?) below much steeper rock. Then it trends back right across a weakness in the steep head wall to a large, silver, solitary lower-off bolt in a cave. The route looks excellent.

S26 *** 7c 35m
To the left again and behind a big tree is an easy groove most easily reached from the right and leading to a short wall running into the hollow of the previous climb. The continuation forges straight up the steep wall above and is much tougher.

The final offering at present is a short distance left in the back right-hand corner of a flat-floored bay (which doubles as a sun-trap and toilet).

S27 * 7b 12m
This last route climbs a steep wall and large formidable looking roof to chains on its left arête.

The rock continues leftward and a small cave contains three bolt lines, from right to left *8a?*, *7a?* and *6c?*.

PLAYA DE TIJUANA

Character
A fine set of generally tough climbs in a superb setting. The climbing is generally fingery and is on very sharp rock that is not as soft as first appearances might suggest. The cliffs have the atmosphere of Pembroke's Trevallen, with the added attraction of continental-style protection and the blue Mediterranean as a backdrop instead of the Bristol Channel. Mention should also be made of the superb beaches, bars and cafes nearby; why fly half way round the World to the Seychelles when paradise is a lot nearer than that? All the routes here have fixed protection though some of the bolts had suffered serious corrosion due to the proximity of the sea. Through the winter of 1993/4 a replacement programme was going on with almost all the old bolts being replaced by substantial glued stainless steel affairs. It is to be hoped that this trend will continue.

Access
The cliffs are located below the headland to the east of the superb beach and inlet of Cala Santany. On first acquaintance the easiest way to get to the cliffs is thus. Take the main road across the island to the town of Santany (Santanyi on some maps) where signs lead, in 3 kilometres, to a right turn to Cala Santany. The road winds down into a narrow valley where there is parking for the beach. Drive past this (if you can) and up a winding road past

several hotels. Take a right turn at a triangular roundabout containing a tree, then take another right turn signed Hostal Villa Sireno & Apartments at a tear-drop shaped roundabout with plants. Continue for 300m to yet another right turn (signed Inmobiliaria Brossa, Palmeria and opposite a plaque in the wall: Carrer de S'Atalaia Vella). A short distance further on parking is available at an open area by a derelict lighthouse.

Leave nothing valuable in the car

Facing the sea, walk right through scrub for 200m, past a collapsed stone wall, and descend easy slopes to the extensive wave cut platform that runs below all the cliffs. On hot days the sea is very inviting though the undercut nature of the rock makes getting in and out of the water tricky, especially if there is a swell running. Perhaps a visit to the beach at Cala Santany is a better idea.

The Climbing

Walking back towards the car along the wave-cut platform you can see a rather indeterminate horizontally striated wall just before some huge boulders perched on the edge are passed. A large cactus hangs over the top of the wall and its right side is bound by a deep red corner. There are three routes on this wall and although they are not especially spectacular their setting makes them worth the effort if you climb in the lower grades. The routes start from a long narrow conglomerate ledge reached by a short unsavoury scramble.

EBAAGUM 4 (VS 4b) 15m
Start from the left end of the ledge, 3m right of a tree, and climb directly up the lower wall and bubbly black slab above. It is worth noting that the final bolt runner can be removed by hand! A lower-off is available just to the left of the cactus below the crest of the wall.

EBAM 4 (VS 4b) 15m
The central line. Climb an orange bulging wall leftwards to slabbier rock and then follow a crack line rightwards up easier rock to a lowering point to the right of the cactus bush.

EBAMSA 4+ (VS 4c) 15m
Start 2m left of the main corner and climb straight up the gradually easing black slab. Passing the first bolt is the crux of the climb and a belay is available just to the left of the overhang near the top of the cliff.

The large red corner offers an obvious challenge to any traditionalists who have brought a rucksack full of big nuts on holiday and who are suffering withdrawal symptoms from 'real climbing'. The pale striated wall

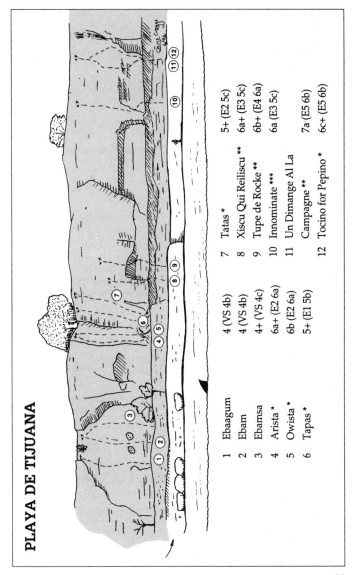

PLAYA DE TIJUANA

1 Ebaagum   4 (VS 4b)
2 Ebam   4 (VS 4b)
3 Ebamsa   4+ (VS 4c)
4 Arista *   6a+ (E2 6a)
5 Owista *   6b (E2 6a)
6 Tapas *   5+ (E1 5b)

7 Tatas *   5+ (E2 5c)
8 Xiscu Qui Reiliscu **   6a+ (E3 5c)
9 Tupe de Rocke **   6b+ (E4 6a)
10 Innominate ***   6a (E3 5c)
11 Un Dimange Al La
   Campagne **   7a (E5 6b)
12 Tocino for Pepino *   6c+ (E5 6b)

and massive roof to the right offer a more modern challenge; out with that bolt gun.

Around to the right is a scruffy corner and starting from the ledge at its foot, and reached by a short scramble, are four short but interesting climbs.

ARISTA * 6a+ (E2 6a) 15m
The left arête of the bay is climbed on its right side with one short taxing section which can be climbed by 'barn-door laybacking', or a quick jump. Easier rock remains.

OWISTA * 6b (E2 6a) 15m
The centre of the left wall of the corner has a short 'blank' central section that is passed by precarious use of a couple of razor edges; it may be thought *(6b)* by technical duffers.

TAPAS * 5+ (E1 5b) 14m
Just to the right of the corner the steepening wall is rather harder than it looks, offering steep fingery moves past thin diagonal cracks.

TATAS * 5+ (E2 5c) 15m
The centre of the right wall of the corner is a bit longer and a bit harder. It sports a mixture of old and new bolts. The route starts off with a slabby section and then steepens to a long reach through bulges using an unhelpful set of 'stuck-on' flowstone holds. Twin lowering bolts are found 1m below the cliff top.

A solitary bolt below the right side of the wall suggests that this may be the next line to be done here. Around to the right the buttress is severely undercut with a sharp arête in its centre. The left side of this is climbed by:

XISCU QUE REILISCU ** 6a+ (E3 5c) 18m
A short but action-packed pitch. Power over the initial overhang from the right, then glorious jug pulling leads up the leaning grey wall above to lower-offs where the angle eases.

TUPE DE ROCKE ** 6b+ (E4 6a) 18m
Start just to the right under the centre of the wide white roof at 7m, and climb up to it. Step right and pull back leftwards across the edge of the roof with difficulty before heading straight up to the chains.

Running to the right from the previous climbs the cliff is undercut by a series of flat white overhangs 3m off the ledge. Despite some obvious lines this section is undeveloped at present. Twenty-five metres along the ledge and just right of a hanging corner is a red arête. On its right side is the

UN DIMANGE AL LA CAMPAGNE, 7a (E5 6b), Tijuana.
Pete (POD) O'Donovan with the cliff to himself

recently rebolted:

INNOMINATE *** 6a (E3 5c) 20m
A great pitch of contrasting styles. After a tricky start over a roof, juggy
climbing leads leftwards up the lower wall. This is best completed quickly
to gain easier angled rock above. A couple of technical moves up the wall
give access to easier rock and the belays.

A short distance to the right is a hanging left-facing corner rising above
the flat roof. The wall to the left of the corner is climbed by:

UN DIMANGE AL LA CAMPAGNE ** 7a (E5 6b) 20m
Gain the bolt ladder from the corner then step left and sprint up the leaning
wall to reach (marginally) easier angled rock above by a tricky move. This
is still tricky and climbed trending rightwards to an artificial-feeling last
couple of moves to reach the belays.

The hanging corner still contains old bolts at the time of writing. It is
climbed in part by:

TOCINO FOR PEPINO * 6c+ (E5 6b) 20m
Climb directly into the base of the corner using a long reach to pass the roof
then follow it until forced out onto the left wall. Step left again and join the
final tricky section of the previous route.

To the right the roof gets ever larger and the rock below it leaves something to be desired. There are several routes in this section though quite how they get across this formidable obstacle is somewhat open to question. Either the local climbers are *very* tall or some form of combined tactics has been used to reach the initial holds on many of the routes. Bringing a short step ladder might not be bad idea.

Eight metres to the right of the corner of *TOCINO FOR PEPINO* and just past an open scoop is a steep crack line with new bolts (and old rust marks) running alongside it.

FLESH FOR DANI *** 7b (E6 6c) 20m
The roof is 3m across and 3m off the ground! Improvise a way around this using drilled holds then follow the steep sustained and technical crack line up the gently leaning wall to the lower-offs.

COMPIEDRAS ** 7a+ (E5 6b) 20m
Eight metres right again is a shallow crack in a groove above the lip of the overhang. Again the roof proves formidable! Once through it step left and follow small holds by sustained climbing up the brown-streaked arête which eventually eases.

Just to the right is a route with odd-looking rather rusty bolts set in much fresher looking glue.

DARSA PRISA ** 7a+ (E5 6c) 25m
Climb the initial overhang then trend left into the shallow open groove. Up this then continue (if you can) up the more open wall above. The route offers good climbing, rather spoilt by a final hideous move.

MIGUIELS *** 7a (E5 6b) 25m
Start as for the previous route to get through the initial overhang then follow the line directly up the leaning wall at the junction of the yellow and brown rock. Magnificent technical climbing throughout with a baffling sequence up the final blind groove.

LA CALLE DEL RITMO ** 7b (E6 6b) 23m
Starting above a huge white block on a vegetated section of the ledge is an open groove in the left side of a bay. Start right of the groove and climb the centre of the smooth white face before trending slightly left to enter and climb the red groove by fierce sustained moves.

PSICCOMAMBO *** 6b+ (E4 6a) 23m
At the right side of the open bay is a line of bolts above the lip of the overhang. Pass the roof by using a prominent red pocket. Once over the roof

PLAYA DE TIJUANA

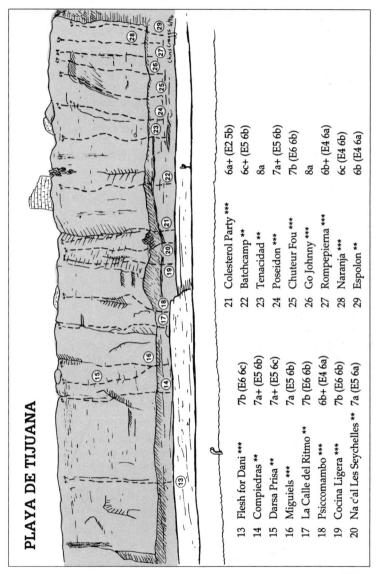

Chris Craggs 6/94

13	Flesh for Dani ***	7b (E6 6c)
14	Compiedras **	7a+ (E5 6b)
15	Darsa Prisa **	7a+ (E5 6c)
16	Miguiels ***	7a (E5 6b)
17	La Calle del Ritmo **	7b (E6 6b)
18	Psiccomambo ***	6b+ (E4 6a)
19	Cocina Ligera ***	7b (E6 6b)
20	Na c'al Les Seychelles **	7a (E5 6a)

21	Colesterol Party ***	6a+ (E2 5b)
22	Batchcamp **	6c+ (E5 6b)
23	Tenacidad **	8a
24	Poseidon **	7a+ (E5 6b)
25	Chuteur Fou ***	7b (E6 6b)
26	Go Johnny ***	8a
27	Rompepierna ***	6b+ (E4 6a)
28	Naranja ***	6c (E4 6b)
29	Espolon **	6b (E4 6a)

swing awkwardly out right then step back left to follow the pleasantly technical open groove. The sting in the tail is a final tricky (and fingery) sequence to the lower-offs.

To the right the ledge that has run below the whole face fizzles out and the base of the cliff steps down 3m. Around the arête to the right is an impressive red corner severely undercut at its base and rising above a cave that tunnels up into the cliff. This corner is the classical *COLESTEROL PARTY*. To the left of the corner there are three much steeper routes. Climbing the impressively steep left arête of the cliff is a new route, no details known.

Climbing the centre of the severely overhanging face and marked by new bolts is:

COCINA LIGERA *** 7b (E6 6b) 25m
Climb through the initial overhanging wall by zig-zagging left then right before pulling out left onto the impressive left arête of the corner. Up this in a dramatic position to the lower-offs.

NA C'AL LES SEYCHELLES ** 7a (E5 6b) 20m
Start just left of the big corner and head up the short awkward wall into the base of the cave. Step left and climb steeply through the bulges trending leftwards until it is possible to pull over onto the wall. Up this to a crucial blind reach (try up and right) to easier climbing that leads to lower-offs in the centre of the wall above.

COLESTEROL PARTY *** 6a+ (E2 5b) 25m
A superb pitch, and the best lower grade route on the cliff by far. Climb a short soft wall to ledges below the cave that disappears up into the cliff. Pull through the roof left then right on a collection of massive holds then follow the main corner by sustained bridging past plenty of bolts to a lower-off in the left wall just below the cliff top.

To the right of the big red corner a huge prickly pear cactus hangs threatening over the cliff top. Sunbathing directly below it is probably not a brilliant idea as it drops spiky fruit at irregular intervals!

BATCHCAMP ** 6c+ (E5 6b) 22m
The blunt arête to the left of the fall line from the cactus is well bolted and well 'ard, offering thin sustained climbing with a difficult clip thrown in for good measure.

TENACIDAD ** 8a 24m
Five metres right of the fall line from the cactus is a bolt line up the centre

of a leaning red wall. It is climbed direct apart from a slight jig to the right at about half-height. A tough pitch on tiny holds, obviously for the tenacious only.

Two metres further right and just to the right of a thin wriggling crack line a set of new bolts runs straight up the wall and protects one of the best pitches on the cliff:

POSEIDON *** 7a+ (E5 6b) 24m
An easy slab leads to gradually steepening rock and more technical moves to reach a baffling sequence through bulges using pockets. Above this more steep moves (just keep going!) lead to the lower-offs. A great pitch on which a three-pronged fork up the backside might just give you the impetus to succeed.

CHUTEUR FOU *** 7b (E6 6b) 24m
Just to the right is a bulging arête with a shallow white leaning groove up its right-hand side. Climb easily into the base of the groove and then follow it as it leans to the right with considerable and sustained difficulty.

GO JOHNNY *** 8a 22m
Start to the right of the leaning white groove and climb into the centre of a bay 7m up. From here take a deep breath and then head straight up the sustained leaning wall, always bearing the route's name in mind.

ROMPEPIERNA *** 6b+ (E4 6a) 22m
To the right again and 10m before the arête of the cliff is a prominent brown stripe with bolts up it. Streak (not literally) up this to good holds amongst tufas high up and then finish more easily. The name means 'break a leg', but you don't have to.

NARANJA *** 6c (E4 6b) 20m
Just before the arête of the cliff is a bright orange wall. This gives excellent climbing on good though often hidden holds and with two hard moves thrown in just to keep you on your toes.

ESPOLON ** 6b (E4 6a) 20m
The right arête of the main section of the cliff gives a good introduction to the harder climbs the place has to offer. Start on the left and make difficult moves up and right on improving holds until a rest in a hollow can be had. Step back left and pull over the bulges to the (toilet) chain belay.

Around to the right the cliff is undeveloped apart from one route up the blankest section of wall, no grade known. There are obviously some strong natural lines available across a spread of grades on this section of the cliff, and as it faces the morning sun it is only a matter of time. Across the next inlet the cliffs continue to Cala Figuera and beyond. There has been a little development here on some of the larger boulders and there is scope for lots more.

TORRELLA

Character
A recently developed cliff that gives an indication of what still waits to be 'sorted' on this island. The cliff is located in the mountains between Soller and Pollenca, overlooking the former. It offers good climbing on great rock and with expansive views. As the crag faces north-west winter can be cool up here but conversely the crag makes a good summer venue. Development is in its infancy.

Access
The cliff is rather awkward to get at from the resorts on the south coast being situated 'in the middle of nowhere'. From Soller (a trek in itself) follow the road up into the hills in the direction of Pollenca. After 10 kilometres is a large tunnel (the first) where there is a viewpoint on the right. Park on the left here (good views!) and follow a clearly marked track up to the left through the trees, passing over a large wire cable and a stone wall. The walls here have been stripped of ivy, they await complete development. Most of the present climbing is on the left end of the cliff, though the first bolt lines are nearer the car.

The first three lines passed all look like very hard pitches.

T1 ? ? 25m
The first bolt ladder, close to the road.

T2 ? ? 25m
Just up the slope from the cable. Climb the central streaks left of the orange wall.

T3 ? ? 25m
Up the slope beyond the stone wall follow a shallow groove.

Further up the slope past an impressive undeveloped wall, some boulders and ivy is:

T4 ? ? 40m
A long hard pitch.

T5 ? ? 40m
Left again and below the streaks climb the wall trending-right then straight up.

Up the slope is the best developed area at present and two climbs that are the reason for most visits.

T6 ** 6b 30m
A line to the right of the prominent streaks passing some holes near the top.

T7 *** 6b+ 28m
The pocket wall is climbed on good holds becoming more sustained towards the top, just keep pulling, superb.

T8 *** 6a+ 25m
Step off a flake and climb steeply to bulges at 15m which are passed on good finger slots. The wall above leads to another bulge where a 'sprag' allows access to the chains, stupendous.

T9 ? 7a? 22m
Just to the left, trend leftwards passing a bulge.

T10 ? 7a? 20m
The wall to the left again.

T11 * 6c 18m
The groove on the left edge of the wall.

T12 * 4 15m
The rib on the left edge of the cliff.

Forty metres further left is a smart-looking and tough prow.

VALLDEMOSSA

Character
A pleasant set of very accessible climbs in a magnificent setting. The cliffs are in the sun from shortly after midday until it slips majestically into the Mediterranean. As might be expected with such an accessible piece of rock there has been quite a bit of development here since the 1990 guide. Despite this there is still an awful lot of undeveloped rock in this valley. The name of the place appears to have many and varied spellings.

Access

From Palma follow the road that runs due north for 15 kilometres (not the almost parallel 711 to Soller) to the small pleasant town of Valldemossa. Drive through here following the coastal road westwards towards Andraitx for a short distance until a signed right turn points to Port de Valldemossa. This twists round a small valley and then begins to descend past a quarried wall rising directly from the tarmac. Just past an impressive overhang that juts out over the road there is limited parking on the right in a layby. If this is full there is further parking, either before the road starts to descend or further on down the hill.

Note: Despite its constricted width, the road sees quite a lot of traffic, including occasional large lorries. Please park with common sense and keep an ear alerted for traffic.

The routes are described from right to left. The first routes are located 50m back up the road where a clean grey pillar of rock rising straight from the road is liberally spattered with bolts. The five routes here offer pleasant enough sport on quality rock. Be prepared to skedaddle if you hear approaching traffic.

RIGHT RIB * 6a+ (E3 6a) 18m
The rightmost line is a clean grey rib which is gained via a tricky lower wall and is followed by sustained and fingery climbing on small sharp holds.

The next four routes to the left share a common belay. With that being the case it won't have escaped your notice that if you get up the easiest line the other routes can be top roped for a bit of safe exercise or as a stress-free way of upping the route tally for the holiday.

RIGHT ROUTE * 5 (E1 5b) 18m
Start just left of a recess and use big holds to attain easier angled rock which is followed leftwards onto the face. Up this by pleasant climbing until a final couple of tricky moves gain the belay.

The next three climbs are very crowded; the creator of these would have done a better job just putting up two lines here and giving them a bit more independence.

RIGHT TRIPLET 6a (E3 6a) 18m
Gain a ledge at 3m and then swing right to the foot of the bolt ladder; this leads steeply at first to a couple of taxing moves past a 'long gone' flake hold and then on more easily to the lower-off.

VALLDEMOSSA

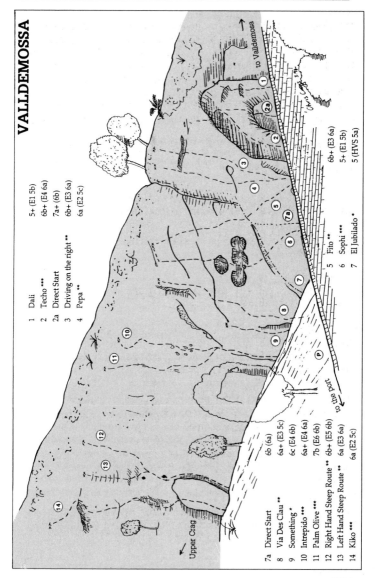

1	Dali	5+ (E1 5b)
2	Techo ***	6b+ (E4 6a)
2a	Direct Start	7a+ (6b)
3	Driving on the right **	6b+ (E3 6a)
4	Pepa *	6a (E2 5c)
5	Fito **	6b+ (E3 6a)
6	Sophi ***	5+ (E1 5b)
7	El Jubilado *	5 (HVS 5a)

7a	Direct Start	6b (6a)
8	Via Des Clau **	6a+ (E3 5c)
9	Something *	6c (E4 6b)
10	Intrepido ***	6a+ (E4 6a)
11	Palm Olive ***	7b (E6 6b)
12	Right Hand Steep Route **	6b+ (E5 6b)
13	Left Hand Steep Route **	6a (E3 6a)
14	Kiko ***	6a (E2 5c)

PERFIDO ENCANTO * 6a (E2 5c) 18m
The nicest of the trio. From the ledge of the previous climb head straight up the rib by sustained moves on good rock. An action-packed little pitch.

ROMPEDEDOS 6a (E2 5c) 18m
The left-hand line is sustained and tough, with the exit onto the upper slab offering a brief heart-flutterer. Move delicately up and right to the lower-offs.

A short distance down the road is an unspectacular route up a short rib.

LEFTMOST ROUTE 6a (E1 5b) 15m
A route that is rather better than it appears; that's not difficult as it looks very uninspiring. Start up an awkward groove then a steep couple of moves over a bulge lead to a short 'slap' to gain the upper wall.

Further down the road is a large roof that hangs right over the road. To the right of this feature is a nondescript route up a short tilted wall this is:

DALI 5+ (E1 5b) 15m
Climb the steep rib and ensuing bulge to twin bolts hidden on the ledge above.

TECHO *** 6b+ (E4 6a) 18m
Climb the right-slanting groove with difficulty (or do the first bulge direct with even more difficulty 7a+), then yard leftwards across the roof on buckets to a couple of powerful moves to the chains. When lowering off keeping an eye out for traffic, especially big lorries and double decker buses!

The wide slabby wall that backs the parking place now has a pleasing collection of worthwhile climbs across a range of grades. The first two of these both start up the steep arête immediately left of the cave of *TECHO*. Both routes climb the initial rib and then go their separate ways.

DRIVING ON THE RIGHT ** 6b+ (E3 6a) 20m
Up the rib then move out right onto the steep and generally holdless wall. Climb this and the overlap to a lower-off just below the tree covered ledges.

PEPA ** 6a (E2 5c) 20m
Start as for the previous route then trend slightly left up the steep and sustained slab and cross the overlap to reach easy ground, and the same belay as the previous.

Also starting from the edge of the tarmac is the original route of this section of rock.

*Colin Binks yarding across the roof of TECHO 6b+ (E4 6a), Valldemossa,
a sight to stop the traffic*

FITO ** 6b+ (E3 6a) 22m
Climb the easy-looking (it isn't) slab leftwards then continue up the centre of the steep wall connecting good holds by tricky moves until a final precarious and strenuous stretch gains the chains.

Just to the left is another bolted line that can be used as a more direct start to the above route with no change in grade. It can also be used as an illogically difficult direct start to the much easier upper groove of *EL JUBILADO* (see below).

Climbing through the strange collection of cavities in the centre of the wall is the elegant line of:

SOPHI *** 5+ (E1 5b) 22m
Start just right of a deep drain and climb a thin break leftwards (*5c* for technical dunces) then head up into the first hollow where a sit-down rest can be had. Pull awkwardly over the bulges then continue straight up the wall by sustained and interesting climbing on great rock until level with the belays on the right. Traverse right and lower-off.

An interesting route can be had by following the diagonal crack that runs rightwards across the lower part of the slab. Done originally as a traditional climb by a homesick OAP this has now been bolted up.

EL JUBILADO * 5 (HVS 5a) 22m
Start below the left edge of the large hollow at 10m and follow the rising crack line rightwards until the obvious upper groove can be reached. It can also be reached direct and leads to the trees; abseil off. The name means 'the retired one' after its first ascensionist.

To the left is another line climbing through a diagonal bulge just to the right of the point where the bank starts to rise:

VIA DES CLAU ** 6a+ (E3 5c) 22m
Start below the bulge and climb the sustained wall on continually surprising holds. Slant right to the left edge of the hollow in the centre of the wall then swing back left and scale the next bulge. The right edge of a shallow groove is followed until almost at the level of a ledge, then swing right to reach the belays via a classical high step.

Just left is a short innocuous-looking thin crack.

SOMETHING * 6c (E4 6b) 10m
A tough nut to crack (and it would be a tough crack to nut) being both very short and very sharp.

To the left is a short steep crack that leads to a grassy diagonal break at 12m, above the left edge of which rises an impressively steep wall with two bolt lines.

INTREPIDO *** 6a+ (E4 6a) 28m
Climb the stubborn crack to the vegetated break then step left and storm the well pocketed wall until a thin leftwards traverse (crux) gains a hidden flake. Swing right and make a final tough pull up to reach the chains, making sure that you clip them before you pump out. Almost too exciting to be a holiday route!

PALM OLIVE *** 7b (E6 6b) 28m
Start as for the last climb to the break then step left and follow the left-hand line by steep sustained and technical climbing with a particularly thin cross-hands move on razor edges forming the technical crux.

Left again the path rises up the bank and a short distance up here a tall fallen flake stands close to the rock. There are three routes here, two of which share a common start before going on to find their different ways up the head wall.

THE RIGHT-HAND STEEP ROUTE ** 6b+ (E5 6b) 22m
Climb the right side of the flake then take a deep breath, roll up your sleeves and when ready step out right onto the wall, and get battling.

THE LEFT-HAND STEEP ROUTE ** 6a (E3 6a) 20m
Climb the flake then step out onto the wall (easier higher up) before tackling the holes and bulges above in a generally leftwards direction. Pull over the final bulge to reach easier rock and the chain some distance above.

KIKO *** 6a (E2 5c) 22m
A fine strenuous pitch starting at the bottom left corner of the flake. Step right onto the flake and climb easily to its top. Cross ledges then follow the steep groove to another ledge and then storm the pocketed wall above. Keep slightly left to a frowning bulge then trend strenuously right under this to a resting ledge. Swing steeply back left to reach the lower-offs.

The rest of the routes at Valldemossa are situated a steep 5 minutes' scramble up the bank from the parking place, to reach the base of a large, open and rather unsavoury corner. This area can also be reached by parking before the road starts to descend below the main section, then following any one of a series of vague paths along the cliff top to a pleasant picnic-type area above the climbs. The base of the wall is most readily reached from here by abseil, and this is also the easiest way back down after completing any of the climbs. For continuity the routes here are described from right to left as they are approached up the bank.

The right wall of the corner has two routes that are well worth doing as long as you do not feel too 'altitudinally challenged' by their names.

SHORTY *** 5+ (E1 5b) 42m
1. 22m   5+   (5b)   At the right edge of the right bounding face of the grotty corner is a bulge 3m up. The name is painted just to the left. Pull through the bulge and climb straight up the face until a ticklish couple of moves can be made onto the slab on the left. Continue to bulges then either step right and take a hanging stance, or more sensibly step down and right to a small ledge and belay there.
2. 20m   5   (5a)   Move out right onto the 'smooth' rib and climb this on a continually surprising set of holds to a bulge which is neatly sidestepped on its left to reach the cliff top.

LANKY ** 5+ (E1 5b) 42m
Seven metres right of the large corner is an area of highly sculpted and well fluted rock.
1. 20m   5+   (5b)   Climb the flutings then step out left onto the steep slab. Shoot up this to a belay below an overlap on threads and bolts. The last move to the belays might be considered 5c by 'shorties' and as there is no real stance here it might be best to forego the unethical 'rest' on the belay and press on instead.
2. 22m   5+   (5b)   Gain the undercuts by the threads (this is probably the crux, and whether it is the last move of the first pitch or the first move of the last pitch is open to conjecture). Move right into a corner and climb up and out to a position just above the lip of an overhang. From here step right onto an open rib to reach an easier climb which leads to a spike (possible anchor) and just beyond, the cliff top.

The final few climbs are located on the left wall of the corner. I have to admit that I made the names of these climbs up (tut tut) in the 1990 version of the guide and four years later I have not yet managed to find any alternatives. I was quite amused to see that the second edition of the German guide *Sun Rock* had also borrowed these names. Until their true identities turn up I think it is safest to stick with these.

CRANK IT ** 6c+ (E5 6a) 43m
A fine steep climb up the leaning crack system to the left of the corner.
1. 23m   6c+   (6a)   The crack is climbed with escalating difficulties, passing a 'gnarly bolt' until things steepen up dramatically and rapid moves need to be made to reach the foot of a fine slab. Lower-off or saunter on to the cliff top.

The upper slab offers a fine pitch at ** *20m 5 (HVS 5a)* in a grand position. It is approached from the cliff top by a short abseil, and if it proves too much, another abseil will take you to the foot of the cliff.

LAYBACK * 6a (E3 5c) 30m
Left again is a wide crack that steepens and narrows as it rises. Grovel up the initial offwidth section (*5.8?*) then layback the imposing flake, at full tilt, until it is possible to swing left and extemporize onto a ledge; possible stance. Lower-off from here or step out left then back right to climb a rib and a spiky tree to reach a belay/abseil point just below the cliff edge.

THINK OF ENGLAND * 7b 22m
A left-hand variation to the layback section of the previous climb is much harder. Unfortunately it is impossible to avoid the initial offwidth section; get rooting!

LAST DITCH EFFORT ** 7b 22m
The final offering on the crag needs no description, just lots of stamina.

OTHER AREAS

This small section has been slotted in at the back of this section of the guide rather than in its logical alphabetical order purely for ease of reference, so look no further. Here are brief notes on a few localities that have at least some development and might be of interest if you are in the area or just want to get away from the crowds!

CALA SAN VINCENTE

This small but popular resort is situated at the end of the valley that runs parallel and to the north-west of the Boquer Valley. It is worth a visit to gaze across at the huge cliffs of the Caval Bernat across the bay and wonder just how good the rock really is. Between the resort's two beaches is a rocky headland sticking out into the bay. Acting on a 'hot tip' I visited here at Easter 1994. There are quite a number of old and very rusty bolts splattered around the wall that runs out over the sea, and the occasional name and grade are painted below some of the easier lines towards the right side of the face. Unfortunately much of the rock is not as good as you might have come to expect on the island. Further to the left there was a brand new bolt line complete with fresh drill dust, starting above the water. This looked far

and away the most worthwhile route here and appeared to be about grade
5 (E1 5b'ish). As the Mediterranean is effectively non-tidal, a calm day would
be needed to get at it. The cliff also has some obvious potential for girdling,
either with ropes and a full rack, or perhaps more appropriately with chalk
bag, swimming trunks and rock boots.

PUIG MAJOR ANTICIMA

On the southern slopes of the island's highest mountain is a superb tower
of clean white limestone, roughly 265m high and approached by what looks
like a 45 minute walk. Unfortunately there is a NATO listening station on top
of the Puig Major and there is a considerable military presence at the foot
of the road that leads to the peak. This is the spot where it would be
necessary to park to walk to the cliff, so there is little chance of sneaking on.
I have heard rumours of people climbing here in the past, and getting written
permission from the military in Palma, though enquiries have failed to
confirm this. The topo from Es Refuge suggests parking on a bend south of
the military base, and cutting through the woods before walking up the
valley to the foot of the face. If your Spanish is good enough it might be worth
asking at the base, if not and you find sport climbing a bit boring, a night
approach might get you onto the cliff (or a free view of the inside of a Spanish
gaol).

The topo shows four long routes, all partially equipped. From left to right
these are: *SOCU 5, 5, 5* (though shown as 8 pitches on the topo, four to a
ledge, an easy traverse right and then four to the top). *YEYE 6a+, 6a*, a direct
start to the above route. *PUIG 5+, 4, 6a, 6a, 3, 4* and finally *COSI 5+, 5+, 5+,
5, 5, 4, 4*, up the right edge of the cliff.

The descent is by walking off to the right or by abseiling back down
COSI (two 50m ropes recommended).

TORRENTE DE PAREIS

There are two areas of limited climbing development around the spectacular
gorge of the Torrente de Pareis. The descent of the gorge itself is a classic
half day through trip, passing some magnificent rock scenery. It is best
attempted after a dry spell and requires a pick up team to collect you at the
exit from the gorge. See June Parker's *Walking in Majorca* (Cicerone) for full
details.

The bottom end of the gorge, Sa Callobra, is reached by a tortuous road
usually occupied by many huge coaches shunting the tourists in and out.

There is a wealth of rock hereabouts but the inaccessibility of the place has led to very limited development. There are also some impressive pieces of rock halfway down the road at the point, most notably, where it passes between a huge tower and the mountainside. From the car parks, bars and restaurants, a series of short tunnels leads through the cliffs to reach the beach at the lower end of the Torrente de Pareis. Above the first of these is an old bolt ladder that runs a long way up the face and looks like an old aid route. Around to the left of the second tunnel a concrete walk-way runs under the cliff and above the sea. There are two recent-looking routes that start off this; both look worthwhile and not too hard. On exiting from the final tunnel there is a bay on the right with a black slab that runs up into steeper rock. There are two more climbs here that share a common start up the slab and then follow different ways up the steep upper section. While you are there check out the number of cats! In the centre of the gravel beach at Sa Calobra there is a rock tower about 20m high and there are three steep and worthwhile looking pitches on the western side of this obelisk. On the far side of the gorge is a tall wall that rises above a seasonal pool and contains at least one route. I have also heard rumours of routes on a steep fluted wall about 30 minutes' walk up the ravine, and on a large sea cliff around the next headland from the beach. Fancy an adventure?

The other area of development at Calobra is at the top end of the gorge and this is most easily reached from Escorca, which is the parking place for the start of the aforementioned through trip. A footpath is followed through olive groves and then it starts a long descent on a well made path to the top end of the narrow section of the gorge. On the descent the impressive tower visible on the far side of the gorge is where the routes are located. Opposite the point where the narrow side branch of Sa Fosca joins the main gorge from the left is the towering cliff of the Entrefoc. There are (at least) two multi-pitch climbs on this magnificent 300m pillar, and it goes without saying that they are not sport climbs. A full rack and double ropes would appear eminently sensible for an attempt on either of these routes. According to the topo I have seen to the cliff, starting at the crack to the left of the foot of the main arête of the buttress is the *VIA ANTONIO G. PICAZO* which is eight pitches long. The pitch grades are *4+, 6b&A2, 5+&Ae, 5+, 4+, 5&A1, 5&A1, 6a&A1,* and *5+&A1.* It may well be free-climbable at a not too lofty grade. Up the bank to the left is the more amenable sounding *VIA RECTAL* (up the backside of the cliff??) which starts at a right slanting ramp and has six long pitches graded *4+, 6a/b, 5, 5+, 5+* and *6b.* For both climbs a descent is available by scrambling off the back of the cliff and descending back to the point where the path from Escorca arrives at the river. Although these routes are long and something of an unknown quantity, they are probably nothing when compared to the walk back up to the car!

APPENDIX:
PRACTICAL INFORMATION

The *Majorca Bulletin*

This is a useful daily newspaper written for expatriate Britons. It is available in newsagents for 100 pesetas and is free in most bars. It always makes a big deal about the weather back home and is worth buying for that alone. It also carries a lot of useful phone numbers: police, ambulance, consulates, etc. and has a list of all the 24 hour chemists open each day.

Tourist Information

Every resort has a Tourist Information Office that will help you with accommodation, car hire, etc. The staff invariably speak English and are very helpful, though remember that office hours are the norm, and that in Spain office hours include a siesta. If you cannot locate the local Tourist Information phone the main Palma office on 712216 and they will point you in the right direction.

Shopping

There are several truly huge hypermarkets that are worth stocking up at, in the interest of economy, as savings are in the order of 25 to 30% over the smaller supermarkets. They sell absolutely everything and accept Visa as well as sterling! The Continente on the right side of the motorway when travelling towards Palma is convenient, though there are others on a similar scale scattered around the island. Also look for Mercadona and Pryca - you cannot miss them! Alcoholic drinks are especially cheap from the hypermarkets, eg. 90 pesetas for a litre of beer, 500 pesetas for a 750cl bottle of whiskey, and wine upwards from 70 pesetas a litre. Have a good holiday and don't forget the climbing!

Eating Out

The island has literally tens of thousands of good eating places. For cheapness (around 400 pesetas for chicken and chips) look for the places with photographs of the meals outside. For something more up-market, and not necessarily a lot more expensive, go for the restaurants with Spanish names. As you might expect the sea food is often exceptional.

Climbing Shops

The only climbing shop in Majorca is in the centre of Palma, on the square called the Plaza Palou I Coll, which is just to the east of the larger Plaza Major. The shop is called Es Refugi and it carries stock at prices slightly cheaper than back home. Boots are a better bargain but they do not carry a very large range of sizes, especially if you have got big British feet. Visa is accepted. The easiest way to get to the shop is to park in one of the Pay and Display car parks on the sea front and then to walk past the cathedral in a north-easterly direction. It takes about 15 minutes if you don't get lost. Try using a map!

The British Consulate
If you need the consulate (and fingers crossed that you don't) it is situated outside the western edge of the Plaza Major (Tel. 712445 or 712085), conveniently 2 minutes' walk from the climbing shop.

24-Hour Petrol Stations
Many of the island's petrol stations are not open on Sundays, or over Bank Holidays (and those appear to be almost weekly). There are 24 hour petrol stations at the airport, Campos, Callade la Calma, Santanyi, Manacor, Inca, Andraitx, Puerto Alcudia and of course in Palma. Not all of them stock unleaded. If in doubt keep at least half a tank full.

Train Times
Trains leave from the Plaza Espana in Palma for Soller and Inca.
Palma to Soller
    8:00, 10:40, 13:00, 15:15, 19:45.
Soller to Palma
    6:45, 9:15, 11:50, 14:10, 18:30.

Trains run to and from Inca, in the middle of the island, roughly every hour from 6:00 in the morning to 22:00 at night.

Ferries
Ferries run from Palma to the other Balearics and to the Spanish mainland. An island-hopping holiday is a possibility.

Ferries from Palma (winter timetable) to Barcelona 23:30 every day and 13:00 Tuesdays and Saturdays.
Valencia: 12:00 every day except Sunday. 24:00 Sunday.
Ibiza: 10:00 Wednesday and Friday.
Mahon: 9:00 Sunday.

Other Activities
What is there to do if you fancy giving your fingers a rest day? Well, apart from the hill walking, bars & restaurants, the beaches, the discos and the nicknack shops, there are a few other things to pass the time away. For starters try one of the show caves. They are warm, dry and on a scale unimagined in the UK. Entry prices initially appear rather high, though you

Sunset on the undeveloped cliffs at the first mirador, Formentor

will get your money's worth. If you fancy something different go wind-surfing, snorkelling or for a ride in a glass-bottomed boat. For more excitement give the water park Agualandia a try. It is located between Benisalem and Inca on the C713. Also at Inca are leather factory shops that are renowned throughout Spain - just the place for that last minute present. For something more relaxing try bird watching. Take a trip to the vast reed beds at La Albufera between Alcudia and Ca'n Picaort, on the north coast. There is a network of footpaths and hides, and rarities are commonplace!!

Useful Publications are *Walking in Mallorca* by June Parker and *Bird Watching in Mallorca* by Ken Stoba. Both Cicerone guides.

If all that fails to entertain you, get up in 'them thar hills', locate your own crag X, and get it developed.

Ibiza

INTRODUCTION

The rock climbing on the large island of Majorca has become better known to a gradually increasing audience, as has the general pleasantness of the island as a winter destination, especially its superb wild mountains. In fact, British hill walkers have been escaping the cold rain of our own hills for this Mediterranean paradise for a number of years and rock climbers are just beginning to catch on. It turns out that all of the Balearic islands are composed of limestone and although Minorca is generally low lying, the smaller island if Ibiza is quite rugged, with hills rising to almost 1500ft and extensive sea cliffs ringing large parts of the coastline. Of course Ibiza does have a famous place in the 'Brits abroad, summer on the Costa' syndrome and an August week spent in San Antonio would put most climbers off all forms of mortal life for ever. On the other hand the winters here are exceptionally quiet, the place has some of the finest beaches in the Mediterranean and Ibiza is reported to have the most equitable climate of all the Mediterranean islands. At the moment there is enough climbing here to fill a week for most folk, though the island is perhaps best used as somewhere to get a winter break in the sun, and to mix climbing with other less energetic activities. The proximity of Majorca and the existence of frequent ferry crossings points to the possibility of a two-centre holiday, if you fancy a change of scene or doing a bit of 'island hopping'.

Flights to Ibiza are cheap and frequent throughout the summer; in the winter they are rather less frequent and even less expensive. There is ample accommodation, though a base on the south coast is probably the best bet as this is the most central, with the roads radiating from Evissa (as the locals call Ibiza town) offering easy access to the whole island. A car is pretty much essential. See the Majorca section for the details of Premier Car Hire who have a depot on the island. Camping is generally discouraged, a throwback to the rosy days of hippydom when the island was a venue for the 'flower power brigade', though with a bit of discretion it would probably be possible to bivouac near the chief cliff of Buda. Sleeping on one of the beaches is liable to get you moved on by the local police, unless you can find somewhere well out of the way. At present there are only 15 or so climbers on the island and they are kept busy developing new cliffs. A call into the climbing shop in Evissa, which is at no.12 (the northern end) Calle de Ramon Muntaner (named after a local historical hero and not a climber), should elicit the

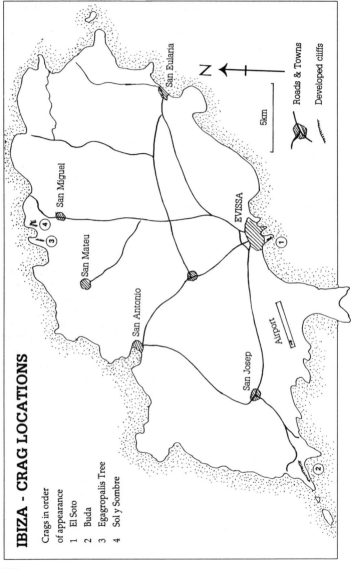

IBIZA - CRAG LOCATIONS

Crags in order
of appearance

1   El Soto
2   Buda
3   Egagropalis Tree
4   Sol y Sombre

Roads & Towns

Developed cliffs

5km

N

San Eularia

San Miguel

San Mateu

EVISSA

San Antonio

San Josep

Airport

whereabouts of the latest place to be and be seen. Buying any topos that are available will help with the cost of bolting new areas.

All of the routes described here are on limestone, much of which is very sharp. Good bolt protection is the norm, and as on Majorca the grades tend to be a touch on the tough side. There is one extensively developed cliff on the island and three other less important venues. These are described here in clockwise manner, starting actually in Evissa city. Enjoy your visit.

EL SOTO

Character
A fairly uninspiring set of climbs unless you especially enjoy short brutal overhangs. The cliff is close to Evissa town and the setting is pleasant, especially late in the day when the low sun shines across the bay onto the cliff. There is also the potential for some good traversing as long as you don't mind falling into the sea when you finally pump out.

Access
The cliffs are located in a west-facing position below the rocky heathland that is located on the promontory to the west of the fortified walls of the old city of Evissa. Tacking through the complex built-up area to this general vicinity should locate either one of a pair of rough roads that run out on to the heath. The higher one arrives on top of a small hill and the lower one ends close to the sea by a high wire fence. The cliffs are located under the highest part of the coast here, directly downhill from the higher parking point and a 2 minute uphill walk from the lower one (see map). A loose open gully located in the centre of the cliff is descended, keeping to the right until it is possible to turn left (looking out) at which point a short easy traverse should locate the first bolts in a prominent block overhang. The climbs are described from left to right as they are approached, and as they are all less than 10m high no lengths are given here.

Geography
The left and right extremities of the cliff both plunge straight into deep water and the developed section is located in the centre. This is split by an open corner that is wave-washed at its base and can be tricky to cross if any real size of sea is running. The present collections of climbs are centred around the two prominent overhangs that are the main features of the cliff.

After descending the gully and turning left (facing the sea) the first feature of note is a block overhang with two bolt lines through it. These are:

Y'ASTA 5+ (HVS 5b)
Gain the left-hand line from the left, pull powerfully over the roof and finish easily.

PATO 6a (E1 5c)
The right line tackles the roof at its widest point and gives a short, sharp struggle.

Around the arête to the right is a leaning wall starting from the water's edge or alternatively from an undercut ledge 5m up. This face is supposed to have been climbed by *MAS PIMIENTA MARIA* (grade unknown) though it did not appear to have been bolted on our visit.

To the right is a deep corner which can be tricky to cross if the sea is at all rough; traverse awkwardly round this or paddle across. On the other side of the inlet is a large block overhang above a slab, with the most worthwhile (though it's not that good!) route on the cliff crossing it:

TECHO MARGARITA * 7a (E4 6a)
Follow the bolt-protected crack line across the roof using good holds then at the lip swing right and make difficult moves to easier ground.

ARENOS NO SIGUES GOS 6b (E2 5c)
The right edge of the roof is followed past a thin green thread and bolts until it is possible to gain the slab above.

BOCATA DE LOMO 6a (E1 5b)
Around to the right is a right slanting white rib on the side wall, which is climbed to the lower-off used by the previous climb.

Around to the right is an easy ramp which slopes up to the right ending above a big drop into deep water. Above this ramp are three short climbs, only one of which is fully bolted at present.
Note: It is possible to escape back to the cliff top by climbing the short wall above the lower end on the ramp *(Diff)* to gain easy ground and thus avoid the paddling. The rock is a little suspect so don't fall off. Unfortunately this isn't a suitable way down, chiefly because of the difficulty of identifying the correct place from above.

The final three climbs end at a mutual lower-off and considering the poorly protected nature of two of these climbs they appear to make good candidates for top roping.

Mike Appleton on CHORRERA DE DIOS 6b+ (E4 6a),
Sector Colorado, Buda, Ibiza

PREPARADOS 5+ (E1 5b)
The left-hand line is climbed trending rightward to a lower-off just below the grass.

LISTOS 6a+ (E4 5c)
The central line is unbolted at present.

YA POR MISTOS! 6b (E2 5c)
The right-hand line has well spaced bolts: don't fall off until you have the first one clipped.

BUDA

Character

On the eastern side of the Cap d'Oliva close to the south-western tip of the island are the extensive and relatively well developed cliffs that go under the title of Buda. The rocks here look south-east over an idyllic bay and are in the sun until about 3 o'clock in the afternoon. The routes vary in height from a tiny 5m to a grand 120m, and they are almost without exception very well bolted. Much of the rock here is astoundingly sharp and a fall from most of the routes that are less than vertical is unthinkable, with severe lacerations to the ego being the least worrying consequence of such a tumble. On the harder routes the local climbers have taken to removing the sharpest edges from the holds; if you think this sounds like chipping, it is, but don't criticise it until you have tried a few of the routes and see what they are up against. It is perhaps worth noting that there is a large amount of undeveloped rock here including an especially spectacular wall on the far left side of the cliff; a walk down the track towards the sea will reveal all.

Access

From Evissa take the road that runs west across the island towards Sant Josep de sa Talaia. Three kilometres before the town is reached is a left turn to Es Cubells which cuts the corner and removes the need to go through Sant Josep. Rejoin the road to Es Cubells and then a kilometre before the village take a right turn and follow the recently upgraded road up the hill towards the tiny harbour of Cala d'Hort. Once over the crest of the hill the impressive towers of the island of Es Vedra come into view and a couple of hundred metres down the hill on the left is a rough rack with a plum-coloured sign to 'Torre des Savinar', almost directly opposite a concrete blockhouse with

---

*Unknown climber enjoying the sun on VIA DEL CESAR *** 6c+ (E4 6a),
Sector Psquiatrico, Las Canadas*

partially bricked-up windows. Turn down the rough track, initially passing a wider area then bearing left until a left turn leads steeply to a flat parking area on a col, close to the cliff. A rather unstable gully runs right under the base of the cliff, and a zigzag well out to the left offers a rather easier way down.

Note: It is worth taking the short drive down to the beach at Cala d'Hort for the impressive views of the rocky island of Es Vedra and perhaps a quick brew and a bite at one of the restaurants here (and maybe even a couple of hours on the beach!).

Mention should also be made here of the cliff's population of bright green and very tame lizards. When you get your 'buttie box' out prepare to be mobbed!

Geography
The cliff is loosely divided into five sectors though this division appears rather arbitrary due to the fairly continuous nature of the face. On the far right and just below the col by the parking is the *SECTOR RAMPANTE* running along the side of the steep descent gully, and home to many of the easier offerings on the cliff. Below this, towards the bottom of the slope and running leftwards almost to a prominent flat sandy area, is the *SECTOR COLORADO.* Beyond here is the rather nondescript *SECTOR ENTRESUELO* and left again the massive caves that mark the *SECTOR CUEVAS.* To the left the cliff reaches its highest extent in the *SECTOR VIDAS* and here lurks a small number of longer offerings amongst a lot of virgin rock. The impressive tilted wall even further to the left will doubtless offer some desperate sport in the fullness of time.

Each of the sectors and all of the routes are described from right to left as this is the usual direction of approach.

SECTOR RAMPANTE

The first section of cliff is the easier angled and rather shrubby walls that run along the side of the steep slope directly below the car park. Some of the Spanish grades are a touch on the mean side here and all the routes have their names painted on the rock, though some are rather faded.

At the top of the slope is:

CUERDAS Y CUCHILLOS 5 (HVS 5b) 10m
A short, steep and sharp wall starts behind a tree and leads to a ledge and cave. Continue up the wall above.

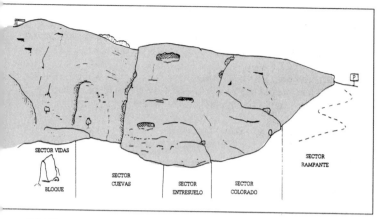

CAP DE FABA 5+ (E1 5c) 12m
Start from a small flat area and climb past a hanging block in the rim of a cave to where easier climbing leads to a lower-off close to the top of the wall.

Further down the slope is a 3m high flake.

E.G.B. * 5+ (HVS 5b) 20m
Start by the flake and trend leftwards up the lower wall then continue up a rib and the steeper rock above.

SI NO LO VES NO TE LO DES * 6a (E1 5b) 12m
Start below a conspicuous bright blue initial bolt just left of a bush. Climb the fine slabby rock to a possible belay on ledges. Lower-off from here or better continue up:

TARARI QUE TE VI 5 (HVS 5a) 10m
Follow the bolts up the wall above the lower-off of the previous route, trending slightly leftwards. Rather confusingly the name of this route is painted at the bottom of the cliff, next to the bolt line used by the next climb.

UNO MAS UNO (1 + 1) * 5 20m
Start behind a bush and climb past an odd rusty ring bolt into a hollow and on up the steeper rib above, before trending right to the lower-off used by the previous climb.

FAKSIMIL 4+ (HVS 5a) 15m
Left again, climb up past a yellow patch of rock onto rib and press on direct to ledges. Lower-off.

PARAGIRDLING * 5 (HVS 5b) 15m
A spelling mistake or a whole new sport?

A couple of metres left start up a rib of quality rock and press on over some yellow blocks to the lower-off of the previous climb.

VARIANTE DE LEVANTE 5 15m
A rather trivial rhyming variation start to the previous route, climbing a rib past bushes then moving right to join the parent route.

ESKUARTAKO 5+ (HVS 5b) 10m
The short leaning wall leading to a tree with *in situ* slings is unremarkable in the extreme.

SECTOR COLORADO

This sector starts at a rounded arête some distance up the slope from the lowest point of the cliff and behind some trees growing close to the rock. This is just to the left of and down the slope from the easy break/ramp that bounds the left side of the *SECTOR RAMPANTE*.

The first routes are on the smooth yellow wall immediately to the left of the rounded arête.

PLOU PLOC 6b (E1 6a) 10m
The short rounded arête is climbed on its left side and has a tough start and then eases rapidly. Wire cable lower-off.

STIRI 6b+ (E2 6a) 10m
Start just left up the right rib of a hollow then make fingery moves up the right-trending shelving ramp to join and finish as for the previous climb.

NUI FOR RENT 6a (E2 5c) 12m
The smooth-looking wall to the left is climbed starting from the left side of the hollow of *STIRI*. Up this on sharp holds (black bolts), gradually easing as height is gained. By the way, what is a nui anyway?

The next series of routes all climb up to and then cross the prominent narrow overhang that runs across the face 10m to 12m from the ground. The first two routes start in the same place just to the left of wiry bush growing close to the rock.

INKREDULO ** 7a (E5 6b) 12m
A fierce pitch. Start at a 1m wide hole at head height and climb the fingery and technical wall to a lower-off on the lip of the roof above.

BUDA - SECTOR COLORADO

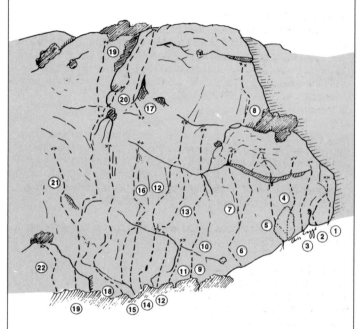

1	Plou Ploc	6b (E1 6a)
2	Stiri	6b+ (E2 6a)
3	Nui for Rent	6a (E2 5c)
4	Inkredulo **	7a (E5 6b)
5	Kolpez Kolpe **	6b+ (E3 6a)
6	Espasmos de Terror ***	6c+ (E5 6b)
7	Eduardo Aqui Tienes Argo **	7b (E6 6b)
8	Hand Made	??
9	Picapiedra	6b (E1 6a)
10	Toca Metodo **	7a (E5 6b)
11	Cantant Caramelles *	6a (HVS 5b)

12	Kemafisio **	5+, 6c+ (E4 6a)
13	Los Inocentes Indecentes **	7a+ (E5 6c)
14	Podenco Ibicenco	6a (E1 5b)
15	La Abeja No Me Deja *	6a (E2 5c)
16	En Palma la Abeja **	6c+ (E4 6a)
17	Red Hot	6c+ (E4 6a) *
18	Chorrera de Dios ***	6b+ (E4 6a)
19	Percu Jones ***	5+, 5+ (E1 5b)
20	Cave Man *	6a+ (E2 5b)
21	Gecco Blaster **	7a (E5 6a)
22	Madona Igual	6b (E3 6a)

KOLPEZ KOLPE ** 6b+ (E3 6a) 15m

Climb out left then up a small black tufa by technical moves. Cross the roof at a hanging 'dong', then trend left to a lower-off on the wall above.

ESPASMOS DE TERROR *** 6c+ (E5 6b) 20m

At present a large *in situ* thread marks the start of this climb. Start out left along a ramp then head back to the right to pass a potential (you wouldn't, would you?) hanging belay with difficulty until it is possible to pull through the roof just left of the dong of the previous climb and to share its lower-off. Using the optional stance is a highly unethical way of reducing the grade of the pitch.

EDUARDO AQUI TIENES ARGO ** 7b (E6 6b) 20m

Follow the previous climb until just short of its 'possible belay' then climb the tough wall trending left to reach and cross the roof at its widest point by the prominent wide crack.

Above the lower-off for the previous four climbs is a ledge and rising from this is the unknown quantity of *HAND MADE ??*.

To the left of the previous climbs and rising from the foot of the slope is a flat section of wall, 10m high and with shrubby ledges above.

PICAPIEDRA 6b (E1 6a) Almost 6m

The shortest route on the island climbs the wall on a series of chipped holds, protected by two white bolts. The crux move is reaching the good holds by the second bolt and can be problematical until you work out the correct approach. Single bolt lower-off.

TOCA METODO ** 7a (E5 6b) 20m

Above the previous climb is a newly installed lower-off and forging up the leaning orange wall just to the right of this is a tough cookie, easing gradually as height is gained.

CANTANT CARAMELLES * 6a (HVS 5b) 12m

A prominent right-facing flake crack is reached by a tricky *(5c?)* rock over and followed to a well bolted exit to easier ground. Lower-offs to left and right.

KEMAFISIO ** 5+, 6c+ (E4 6a) 33m

A good tough climb, the first pitch offering pleasant sport at a sensible grade, while the upper one is more challenging.

1. 13m   5+   (5b)   Climb the lower wall on sharp holds, passing a large thin flake and a mild run-out to the third bolt then move left to a cramped belay on a lower-off *(* HVS 5b)*.
2. 20m   6c+   (6a)   From the belay, two bolt lines continue upwards. Move left to the left-hand line then climb steeply rightwards on sharp holds to gain a scoop. Trend right out of this to join the easier angled upper section of *LOS INOCENTES INDECENTES*.

LOS INOCENTES INDECENTES ** 7a+ (E5 6c) 20m
Start at the cramped stance of the previous climb then move right and make hard moves on well spaced holds gradually easing in difficulty and angle.

PODENCO IBICENCO 6a (E1 5b) 10m
Two bolt lines to the left of the conspicuous right-facing flake is a line up a right-trending scoop starting at the lowest point of the cliff. This is followed on good pockets with the occasional long reach. Lower-off from below the steeper rock above.

LA ABEJA NO ME DEJA * 6a (E2 5c) 10m
Just left again is a white scar and this route climbing yellow rock past some conspicuous holes. The crux is reaching the largest of the pockets; from here sprint for the chains.

Directly above the previous climb is a line of bolts that heads leftwards up the wall. This is:

EN PALMA LA ABEJA ** 6c+ (E4 6a) 20m
Swing right then follow closely spaced bolts to the left across the tilted wall until a couple of blind moves gain easier angled rock. From the lower-off at the top of the slab either head down or bring up the second man and have a go at the spectacular:

RED HOT * 6c+ (E4 6a) 15m
Powerful climbing through the bevy of pocketed bulges above the lower-off of the previous climb.

Just to the left of the last route described at the base of the cliff *(LA ABEJA NO ME DEJA)* is a new route not listed on the present topo, offering steep thin face climbing. It starts from the foot of a ramp and trends slightly right to reach the lower-off above *LA ABEJA NO ME DEJA*. If looks are anything to go by the route appears to be at least *6c (E4 6a)*.

CHORRERA DE DIOS *** 6b+ (E4 6a) 28m
A tough pitch of high quality up the conspicuous flowstone pillar at the left

end of this section of the wall.

Follow the ramp up to the left then climb the undercut flake out to the right and make a vicious move on razors out right again to reach easier ground. Continue up the tufa system above on good but spaced holds then make more taxing moves to lower-offs in the steeper rock above.

Around to the left of the ramp and tufa of *CHORRERA DE DIOS* is a ledge at 3m with several short routes starting from it (technically this is really the right side of the *SECTOR ENTRESUELO*). Starting up the right-hand line of white bolts by two white paint spots is:

PERCU JONES *** 5+, 5+ (E1 5b) 40m
An entertaining route offering sustained and interesting climbing up a devious weakness.
1. 28m   5+   (5b)   Follow the bolts up the short wall to easier ground then continue until it is possible to move out to the right along a large flake and climb a tricky wall (crux) to less taxing terrain and then a stance below a slab.
2. 12m   5+   (5a)   Climb the very rough slab to a bulge and cross it into a groove. Follow this to a lower-off, or top out and scramble round to the right.

CAVE MAN * 6a+ (E2 5b) 12m
Really a right-hand finish to the previous climb. Start from the final stance of *PERCU JONES* then climb the slab rightwards to below the overhangs. Cross the bulges right then left on generous holds to finish close to (or on) the arête.

GECCO BLASTER ** 7a (E5 6a) 20m
Start as for the first pitch of *PERCU JONES* then move left to follow the bolts diagonally across the leaning wall to a lower-off where the situation eases. A strenuous and technical pitch.

SECTOR ENTRESUELO

A rather nondescript section of rock that nevertheless has some worthwhile climbs, the majority of which are rather on the short side. Perhaps the highlight of the area is the superb sandy 'beach' below the wall, just the spot to grab some rays! The first four routes start on the narrow ledge, 3m off the ground, that is also used as the launching pad for *PERCU JONES* (see above).

The first three climbs are short offerings that all end at the same lower-off.

MADONA IGUAL 6b (E3 6a) 10m
The right-hand route (the second bolt line left of the twinned paint spots) follows a thin ragged pocket line; short and not too sweet.

GROCK'N'ROLL 6c+ (E4 6b) 10m
Smooth-looking wall just to the left; short and savage.

FLUJO ROSA 6a (E1 5b) 10m
Start at the left end of the ledge and climb steeply on good pockets before trending rightwards past a tree with *in situ* thread to the lower-off.

The next route is of rather more substance than those to the right.

EXPLOITED CLIMBERS ** 6a+ (E3) 30m
1. 15m   5+   (5b)   Start as for *FLUJO ROSA* but when it bears right pull on to the slab on sharp holds then continue more easily to a belay in a bay below overhanging rock.
2. 15m   6a+   (5c)   Trend left up awkward rounded ledges to below an overhanging rib then battle up this on a generally unhelpful set of holds.

JOSELITO is the tough-looking line trending slightly to the right up the wall directly above the first stance of the previous climb. The pitch is 20m long and the grade is unknown.

A short distance to the left is another pair of short, hard climbs (the place is full of them) that share the same lower-off.

MI OSITO DE PELUCHE 7a+ (E4 6c) 12m
Running straight up the smooth brown wall is this vicious little number.

DELICATESSEN GROG 6b+ (E3 6a) 12m
An awkward start leads to a swing out right and a quick spring on spaced holds linked by high rock-overs gains the chains (you hope).

Left again are three more short climbs, all of which finish at a lower-off on top of a short tilted section of rock above the left side of the wall.

LA AVERICIA ROMPE EL FRENILLO 6c+ (E4 6b) 15m
Follow the line of white bolts past a prominent hole 7m up, then head up left along a ramp line to a finish up the right side of the tilted wall.

BUDA - SECTOR ENTRESUELO

1	Percu Jones ***	5+, 5+ (E1 5b)
2	Madona Igual	6b (E3 6a)
3	Grock'n'Roll	6c+ (E4 6b)
4	Flujo Rosa	6a (E1 5b)
5	Exploited Climbers **	6a+ (E3)
6	Joselito	??
7	Mi Osito de Peluche	7a+ (E4 6c)
8	Delicatessen Grog	6b+ (E3 6a)
9	La Avericia Rompe el Frenillo	6c+ (E4 6b)

10	Todo Por la Napia	6a+ (E3 6a)
11	Mis Primeros Spits	6a (E1 5b)
12	Con Faldas y a Lo Loco *	5 (HVS 5a)
13	Kristo Salva *	5+ (HVS 5a)
14	Menamorao **	6c+ (E5 6a)
15	Orake Iosi	??
16	Kotopaxi **	5+ (E2 5c)
17	En Technicolor **	6a, 5+, 4 (E1 5b)

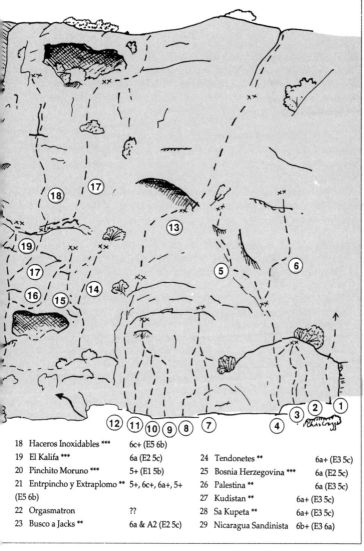

18	Haceros Inoxidables ***	6c+ (E5 6b)			
19	El Kalifa ***	6a (E2 5c)			
20	Pinchito Moruno ***	5+ (E1 5b)	24	Tendonetes **	6a+ (E3 5c)
21	Entrpincho y Extraplomo **	5+, 6c+, 6a+, 5+	25	Bosnia Herzegovina ***	6a (E2 5c)
	(E5 6b)		26	Palestina **	6a (E3 5c)
22	Orgasmatron	??	27	Kudistan **	6a+ (E3 5c)
23	Busco a Jacks **	6a & A2 (E2 5c)	28	Sa Kupeta **	6a+ (E3 5c)
			29	Nicaragua Sandinista	6b+ (E3 6a)

TODO POR LA NAPIA 6a+ (E3 6a) 12m
The central line on the wall is a tough cookie for the grade on a nasty collection of pockets. Finish up the leaning wall on a much better set of holds.

MIS PRIMEROS SPITS 6a (E1 5b) 12m
The easiest route of the three is still quite hard work. Start below the left side of the wall and climb past a diamond-shaped hole. Move out right then continue on up the tilted wall above on biffos, or cop out by climbing up and left and leaning across to reach the lower-off.

The next climb is a pleasant pitch at a more sensible grade than the routes to the right, and it also offers a lead in for some extensions up the shrubby-looking rock overhead.

CON FALDAS Y A LO LOCO * 5 (HVS 5a) 20m
Follow the bolts up blocky rock and short steep walls to a lower-off on a good ledge system above. Either head down from here or, better, follow one of the next two routes onwards.

KRISTO SALVA * 5+ (HVS) 50m
1. 20m   5+   (5a)   From the belay on the ledge system traverse easily rightwards for 8m then climb the steep wall to a stance in a large cave.
2. 20m   5   (5a)   Traverse horizontally right out of the cave for a short distance then climb the wall above the tree, firstly straight up then trending right to a stance.
3. 10m   4   (Severe) Easy rock with the odd moment of interest leads to scrambling and the cliff top.

Starting in the same place (at the top of *CON FALDAS Y A LO LOCO*) but taking a rather more direct line is:

GALVANA MENTAL * 5+ (E1) 40m
1. 15m   5+   (5b)   From the belay climb straight up the steep wall above to easier angled terrain, then trend right to a belay in the cave as for the previous climb.
2. 25m   5+   (5b)   Climb strenuously around the right edge of the cave roof to rapidly join and follow the rest of the previous route to the cliff top.

The final route in this sector starts from the cave stance of the previous two climbs and offers strenuous and exposed climbing in a rather out of the way setting.

SUPER HEROES DE BARRIO * 7a (E5 6a) 15m
Start under the right edge of the cave and climb across the roof leftwards until it is possible to claw a way round onto the head wall. Continue horizontally to the lower-off then once back in the cave try to talk your second into stripping the pitch.

SECTOR CUEVAS

To the left the cliff becomes gradually more impressive as it runs out towards the sea. The first feature of note is a large cave rising above the 30m high shrubby slabs at the foot of the cliff, and high above, barely visible from the ground, is a much larger cave. Despite the difficulty in getting at the upper cave the effort is well worth it to examine this amazing hole in the cliff face. To the left of the lower cave is an impressive slab bounded on the left by a shrubby gully and beyond this some impressively steep walls. Further to the left again is a fine pillar of grey rock which forms the left side of the *SECTOR CUEVAS* and is home to some of the finest pitches on the cliff.

The first four climbs described are based around the lower cave which is reached by a diagonal scramble from the right. Starting under the right edge of the cave is:

MENAMORAO ** 6c+ (E5 6a) 22m
Climb up then leftwards towards a cramped rest in a hollow on the rim of the cave, before heading straight up the bulging wall past a deep undercut pocket to gain easier terrain. Continue more easily up rugged rock to the lower-off.

ORAKE IOSI starts as for the previous climb as far as the hollow on the rim of the cave then continues leftwards to a lower-off shared with the next climb. The grade is unknown though the section above the lip of the cave looks pretty tough.

The next four climbs all start at a point below the left rim of the cave and follow lines up the fine but abrasive slab above. Scramble up and left from the foot of the cliff to a point directly under the left edge of the cave. Prospective jug jockeys should note that there are no routes out of the cave as yet. Go to it.

KOTOPAXI ** 5+ (E2 5c) 25m
A good climb though with some rather oddly placed bolts. Climb over the initial bulge by a white paint spot and head up the slab to the edge of the

cave. Climb up left then traverse horizontally to the right (leaning down to clip the bolts and avoiding falling off) until it is possible to trend diagonally rightwards. One short thin section leads to easier climbing and the belays. Stripping the route is problematical so a (brave) second is required.

EN TECHNICOLOR ** 6a (E1) 77m
A long and interesting trip up the full height of the cliff. The first pitch is the crux and it is possible to lower-off from the top of this though the extension is worth doing just to get a look at the amazing cave at the final stance. Start as for the previous climb.
1. 25m   6a   (5b)   Pull over the initial bulges then head straight up the slab on rough rock until the bolt line splits. Trend right following spaced bolts then continue straight up to a stance on good ledges below the impressive impending wall tackled by *HACEROS INOXIDABLES* (see below).
2. 30m   5+   (5b)   Walk rightwards along the ledge then climb straight up the wall, gradually easing as height is gained, until a ledge and belay just below 'the black hole' are reached. Bring up your second then go exploring.
3. 22m   4   (4c)   Traverse horizontally to the right and then continue to the cliff top without too much difficulty.

HACEROS INOXIDABLES *** 6c+ (E5 6b) 30m
A brilliant climb up the wall and bulging crack line above the first stance of the previous wall.
Climb the sustained and technical (and chipped) wall to the roof below the crack. Pull over into the crack and then sprint up this in dramatic position before finishing up the still entertaining wall above. Mega.

EL KALIFA *** 6a (E2 5c) 28m
Although really only a direct finish to the first pitch of *EN TECHNICOLOR* the route is well worth doing. Follow the first pitch of that route until it trends right then continue past a recent scar (crux) to reach the prominent undercut flake that runs across the cliff. Follow this rightwards then pull over its right edge and follow easier rock to the chains.

PINCHITO MORUNO *** 5+ (E1 5b) 28m
To the left of and below the large lower cave is another smaller cave. Start out of this and climb through the bulges onto the slab. Follow the bolt line directly up this on very sharp rock and with the occasional touch of interest to a lower-off below scruffier rock. Excellent sport.

C.C on PINCHITO MORUNO 5+ (E1 5b), Sector Cuevas, Buda

To the left is an open and shrubby corner that would doubtless be a well polished and oft travelled classic in Britain, whereas here it has been ignored. Where did I put that rack of Hexes?

ENTRPINCHO Y EXTRAPLOMO ** 6c+ (E5 6b) 88m
On the other side of the gully is a long and varied route that starts up an open rib. Unfortunately the start of the second pitch is much harder than the rest of the climb.

1. 22m   5+   (5b)   Follow the bolt line up the rib over grey and then orange rock to a belay on top of the pillar below much more impressive terrain. This pitch is worth doing at *(** E1 5b)*.

2. 22m   6c+   (6b)   Climb the tough leaning wall on a series of 'excrescences' to gain entry to the wide leaning crack. Battle up this to a stance on ledges where the angle of the wall starts to fall back.

3. 22m   6a+   (5c)   Climb the wall above the stance trending slightly to the right until it is possible to head left to reach more ledges and a small exposed stance.

4. 22m   5+   (5b)   Again head left until it becomes logical to climb directly up the wall to a belay on the rim of the cliff. Scramble off.

To the left of the second pitch of the previous climb is a bolted line up a leaning wall. This is the impressive-looking *ORGASMATRON*, grade unknown.

Across the previously mentioned gully is a fine high pillar of quality grey rock that is home to seven worthwhile routes. The ledges at the foot of the pillar are reached by an easy scramble from directly below.

BUSCO A JACKS ** 6a & A2 (E2 5c) 78m
This route follows the most right-hand line on the buttress and starts just to the right of the fall line from a small but conspicuous bush about 12m from the ground. An interesting and varied route, with the rather illogical aid pitch being avoidable by climbing *TENDONETES* (see below).

1. 40m   6a   (5c)   Climb the wall on generally good holds passing to the right of the bush, and over the tip of a hanging flake, passing bolts and threads galore to a good stance below the impending buttress above.

2. 20m   A2   Aid up the buttress front until a stance in the groove on the left can be reached. Alternatively do *TENDONETES* (see below) to turn the outing into a *** affair.

3. 18m   5   (5a)   Trend right up the groove passing a couple of bulges to its termination then continue more easily to the cliff top.

TENDONETES ** 6a+ (E3 5c) 20m (78m in total)
The groove to the left of the middle pitch of the previous route is gained via
a left-slanting ramp and followed with sustained interest to a stance where
the angle drops back. Finish as for *BUSCO A JACKS, 18m 5 (5a)*.

The next five climbs are centred around the front of the grey pillar. All
offer fine strenuous climbing on good if occasionally sharp rock. There is a
single bolt belay on the ledges under the centre of the pillar.
Note: The groove line of *TENDONETES 20m ** 6a+ (E3 5c)* is directly above
these routes and makes a logical way onto the cliff top for those who crave
a summit experience.

BOSNIA HERZEGOVINA *** 6a (E2 5c) 30m
Traverse right from the belay and climb the steep juggy bulges passing the
occasional fragile holds until the prominent bush can be reached. Climb
straight past this obstruction then continue slightly leftwards to a good
horizontal break before a finish up the superb rough wall to chains on the
rim. Brill.

The next two routes climb the centre of the pillar to a common lower-
off. Either of them can be extended and made into a *** outing by continuing
up the short and sharp *SA KUPETA* which starts from these chains.

PALESTINA ** 6a (E3 5c) 18m
From the bolt belay on the ledges climb straight up the wall and through a
sizeable bulge. Above this a sustained and intricate groove requires a
forceful approach until a final tricky sequence reaches the chains. If you
intend to continue up *SA KUPETA* clip in and press on, as a rest on them
is most definitely taboo!

KUDISTAN ** 6a+ (E3 5c) 18m
From the bolt belay on the ledges climb up and left to an *in situ* thread then
swing back to the right before climbing straight up the wall then away finally
rightwards until a taxing sequence of moves is required to clip the chains.
Once again the best trip involves pressing on up the head wall.

SA KUPETA ** 6a+ (E3 5c) 12m
Is there a sharper route than this on the planet? From the 'hanging belay'
above the two previous climbs head up the sustained slab on razor blades
and broken glass. Ouch!

NICARAGUA SANDINISTA *** 6b+ (E3 6a) 28m
The left arête of the buttress gives a fine sustained and airy piece of climbing.
From the bolt belay trend left then climb steeply through bulges to gain a

position on the arête. Blast up this direct (though a resting ledge on the left is very tempting) before powering through bulges and making a technical move on some odd holds to easier terrain. Continue up the crest of the arête in a spectacular position.

The final route in this section is something of an unknown quantity. The wall 6m left of the bolt belay is climbed by *TUMBULO 6b*, a route which heads up into the corner that bounds the left side of the upper section of the pillar. From the ground it is difficult to see any bolts in the upper part of the groove; perhaps it had not been completed when we were there, or perhaps (horror of horrors) wires are needed.

SECTOR VIDAS

The final section of cliff is this huge rambling wall to the left of the centre of the cliff. At present there are only three routes on this extensive face, and over to the left it gets ever more impressive. Of the three one is a low grade classic, one is a high grade near classic, and one is an unknown quantity. Choose your poison.

LLAMAMA LLAMALADINGDONG ** 6b+ (E4) 103m

A fine direct line marred only by a patch of soft rock a short way up the crux pitch. The route is a significant pointer to what this cliff has in store for the future.

Scramble up to below the pillar of rock that forms the left edge of the Sector Cuevas then follow the ledge leftwards to its end. No fixed belays.

1. 28m   4   (V Diff) Step right and climb the short wall to easier rock then trend left through the bushes then up a rough slab and large flake to reach a belay in a hollow.

2. 30m   6b+   (6a) Move left round the rib to the foot of the bolt line then follow the groove to the top of a small pillar. Climb the crux wall on disposable holds then trend right into a groove. Up this strenuously until it is possible to move out onto the exposed wall on the left then climb this on surprising holds to a small stance in the base of a groove.

3. 15m   5   (5a) Move right into another groove and climb this to a more comfortable stance.

4. 18m   5+   (5b) Continue up the sustained and interesting groove above to a stance below the overhangs that cap this section of the wall.

5. 12m   4   (Severe) Exit left to gain easy ground and the cliff top. Walk off to the right.

VIDAS EJEMPLARES *** 5+ (E1) 120m
A long and committing expedition that cuts leftwards across the face following a natural weakness. The route has a rather British feel about it, as there is the odd patch of loose rock and although most of the gear is in place much of it is rather antiquated. Despite these shortcomings the route is highly recommended to those who want a break from short, hard, well protected climbs as it is none of these! Carry a rack of medium wires and ten quick-draws.

1. 28m   4   (V Diff) As for the first pitch of *LLAMAMA LLAMALADINGDONG*.

2. 12m   5   (5a)   Step down and move left into a crack (bolt) then traverse left to the second crack line. This leads easily at first then more steeply (peg and old bolt) to a cramped stance and new bolt belays on the edge of the world.

3. 25m   5+   (5b)   Traverse left then cross the tricky slab (two old bolt runners protect this, the crux) and climb up to reach ledges. Move left around the corner to a flaky crack line and follow this past several peg runners to a small but good stance. From here the trap is sprung as descent is no longer an option!

4. 30m   5   (5a)   A serious pitch with little fixed gear. Climb the slab directly above the stance then trend left to below a corner. Pull past a tree into this then trend left again up the continuation slab (rather devious) passing a perched flake with care. At the level of the overhangs traverse 8m left to peg belays behind a tree.

5. 25m   4   (Severe) Step left and then climb rugged ribs and short walls until the angle drops back and scrambling remains. Descend over the top of the hill to the right.

DIEDRO ATLANTIS is the major groove system around to the left of the two previous climbs. Its base is reached by continuing along the bottom of the cliff below the pillar of rock that forms the left edge of the Sector Cuevas. The route is four pitches long, *5+, 6a, 6c+A0, 5*, and at the time of writing it has not be re-equipped. The final stance is shared with *VIDAS EJEMPLARES* and from here the route climbs directly to the cliff top. Perhaps this is that adventure route you have been looking for all holiday!

The final small collection of climbs at Buda is on the enormous boulder that lies some distance to the left of and below the climbs already described. The routes here are generally quite short (up to 15m) and hard, and perhaps the best reason for visiting this spot is the great overview that you get of the rest of the cliffs from here. On the other hand if you want a small collection of tough cookies to throw yourself at, and in an idyllic setting, then look no further.

From right to left the four climbs here are:
MANZANO 6b (E3 5c) 12m
The wall on the far right is the hors d'oeuvres.

LA REFINITIVA * 7c (E6 6c) 15m
The centre of the right-hand face is the main course.

ARISTA CON VISTA * 7b (E5 6b) 15m
The right side of the arête is the dessert.

FESTE HIPPIE 7a (E5 6a) 12m
The left side of the arête is the cheese and biscuits.

OTHER AREAS

Situated on the north coast of the island are three small areas that can effectively be grouped together. Although they are not particularly high or extensive, their pleasant setting makes two of them (Egagropalis Tree and Sol y Sombre) worth a visit. The third area, Penyal de s'Aguila, has seen so little development at the moment it cannot be recommended apart from for an exploration session. There is plenty of scope for new routeing in all three areas, and along extensive sections of the north coast.

EGAGROPALIS TREE

Character
A set of small walls that face south-east, offering superb views over part of the north coast of the island. There are about 20 varied routes here at present with scope for more and the place is worth at least one visit. Some of the rock is a little loose and much of it is very sharp. The names of most of the climbs are still a secret, though the topo and grades here should prove adequate description for a day or two's sport. I have numbered the routes and added the prefix 'E' to stand for Egagropalis. Development here is far from over and there were several sets of chains suspended above unclimbed rock when we made our visit, so expect new climbs to appear between those described here.

Approach
Follow the road from Evissa town northwards towards Sant Miguel de Balansat (15km). On entering the outskirts of the town take the first (or

second) left turn and follow this for 1.3 kilometres to a right fork signed Es Portixol. This is followed for a further 2 kilometres until a left turn on a bend signed 'Cafe Ca n Sulavetas & Supermarket' can be taken. From this point the road is unsurfaced. Drive past the cafe and follow the main track for 0.8 kilometre to a Y-junction, and here take the right fork. Stay with this track for 0.9 kilometre, keeping left at a recently built low wall to arrive at low gate posts and a chain. Once through the chain take the left-hand track past a couple of white houses, up round some S-bends to a flat open area on a col, 0.6. kilometre from the chain. Parking here is recommended though it is possible to turn left and drive up the steep, narrow and stony track for a couple of hundred metres to another parking area on top of the hill. (At this point it is probably worth checking the small print on your car hire paperwork. I think you will find that the hirer is liable for any damage to the underbody of the car, so watch that sump!)

From the top of the hill the cliff is visible to the north and is reached by a pleasant 30 minute walk. The direct approach is blocked by an incised valley so locate a cairned path which initially heads off north-west (half left when facing the cliff) from the parking area. Follow this down across scrubby slabs and into the trees. The path is quite well marked but it is narrow and the start is difficult to locate. The rough nature of the terrain in the area makes the effort in finding and following the track well worthwhile. It undulates through the trees and soon passes a small stone construction and barely discernible charcoal ring. Eventually the trees thin out and the cairns (and occasional arrows) are followed down and across scree and slabs into a gully. At the foot of this turn left past an impressive buttress (with two routes) to reach another gully. Descend this then turn left to pass under more undeveloped rock and arrive at the base of the central section of the best developed middle tier.

Geography

The cliff is divided into three tiers and the majority of the development has taken place on the central and most continuous one of these. The upper tier has some good roof potential, though the lower tier looks less promising. On the left side of the middle tier is a wide gully with routes on both arêtes and to the right is a steep bulging wall rising from a ramp and running rightwards to a steep corner rising above a cave entrance. To the right a square buttress projects with a conspicuous tree on its top and right again is an open slope. Beyond this is a bulging wall with a fine north-east-facing slab forming its right side.

The Climbs

On the descent to the main area a steeply overhanging buttress is passed;

this contains two bolted climbs of unknown difficulty. The left one is the most amenable-looking, a very steep V-groove, while to the right is a much more difficult-looking flat roof.

The left side of the lower tier has a long and, at present, undeveloped wall with a large fir tree standing close to the rock. and to the right of this is a projecting fin of a buttress, containing the first climb described here:

E1 * 5+ (E1 5b) 12m
The sharp arête on the left side of the bay has a steep pull out of a cave to start and then uses massive sharp holds to climb the arête above.

In the very back of the bay is a set of chains above a short steep wall which still awaits the drill.

E2 COMPANIA SENTIMENTAL ** 6c (E4 6b) 12m
The white wall on the right side of the bay has a fierce fingery start to reach the prominent large hole and then is slightly easier up the final wall. Very photogenic.

APPROACH - EGAGROPALIS TREE

Around to the right is a steep wall rising above a slabby ramp and easily reached by a short scramble. The first climb tackles the steep left side of the wall.

E3 **? 7c? 12m
The bulging wall has a few well spaced pockets. It looks both good and tough!

To the right and up the ramp a short distance are two bolt ladders up a less steep section of the wall,

Charcoal Ring

Parking   Parking

Rough

Big House

Chain

Bar

Es Portixol

San Miguel

EGAGROPALIS TREE

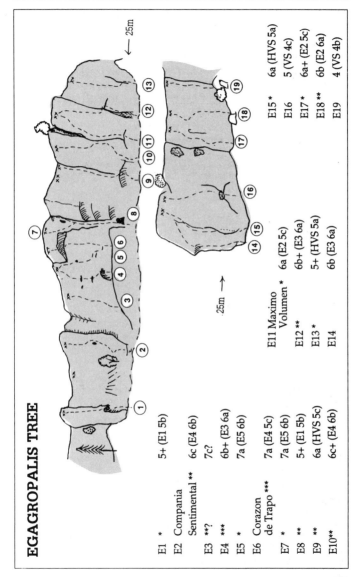

E1 * 5+ (E1 5b)
E2 Compania
   Sentimental ** 6c (E4 6b)
E3 **? 7c?
E4 *** 6b+ (E3 6a)
E5 7a (E5 6b)
E6 Corazon
   de Trapo ***
E7 * 7a (E4 5c)
E8 ** 7a (E5 6b)
E9 ** 5+ (E1 5b)
E10** 6a (HVS 5c)
   6c+ (E4 6b)

E11 Maximo
    Volumen * 6a (E2 5c)
E12 ** 6b+ (E3 6a)
E13 * 5+ (HVS 5a)
E14 6b (E3 6a)

E15 * 6a (HVS 5a)
E16 5 (VS 4c)
E17 * 6a+ (E2 5c)
E18 ** 6b (E2 6a)
E19 4 (VS 4b)

151

just to the left of some large overhangs. The two routes start separately but share a common lower-off. The left one starts from an overhung bay.

E4 *** 6b+ (E3 6a) 15m
A fine varied pitch with some l-o-n-g reaches. Climb out of the hollow and trend left to gain a standing position on the easier angled wall with difficulty. Continue up the wall linking large holds via extending moves until a final tricky sequence leads rightwards up a leaning rib to the chain.

E5 * 7a (E5 6b) 15m
A tougher climb than appearances might initially suggest, with bolts that are rather unsportingly placed! Traverse left along a ledge to the first bolt then climb up and left (via a jig to the right) to enter the groove with great difficulty. Continue up and left with a long reach for a deep hole (beware of *in situ* birds) then press on up the easier groove and reach out left to the lower-off of the previous climb.

E6 CORAZON DE TRAPO *** 7a (E4 5c) 15m
The impressive roof to the right is approached via the pleasant wall and crossed leftwards on (mostly) good holds and a short jump to jugs in a bay. Grapple up the right arête of this to the lower-offs. A spectacular gorilla-thriller.

To the right is a step down in the ledge leading to a cave entrance and above this is a smooth-looking groove protected by a bevy of bulges. Two climbs start up this, either from the cave or by stepping in from the ledge on the left.

E7 * 7a (E5 6b) 15m
Enter the groove and climb it steeply to a deep hole with a rather fragile-feeling thread in it. From here take a big breath then head out leftwards following the lip of the roofs until a final difficult sequence up the headwall reaches the chains.

E8 ** 5+ (E1 5b) 15m
The smooth-looking groove is less of a battle than appearances might suggest. Pull over the initial roofs to enter the groove then follow it by jamming to a final well positioned bit of bridging.

To the right again is a steep open book corner with a good flake crack in its back. The smooth-looking wall to the left of the corner has·a belay installed at its top, but an ascent looks fairly unlikely without a considerable degree of sculpting.

Access to the corner itself is guarded by a sizeable roof.

E9 ** 6a (HVS 5c) 20m
Battle round the roof (the expected hidden jug never materialises) then follow the fine sustained corner to the chains by bridging, jamming and laybacking. Pulling on the initial bolt would lower the grade to *HVS 5a*.

E10 ** 6c+ (E4 6b) 15m
The right wall of the main corner has a tough start using some micro-tufas them moves out to the arête via a prominent flat hold, before swinging back into the centre of the wall to finish.

To the right a square buttress protrudes from the general line of the face. It is topped by a conspicuous tree and bounded by two deep cracks. This is home to two climbs that attempt to climb the front face of the buttress.

E11 MAXIMO VOLUMEN * 6a (E2 5c) 15m
Climb steeply up the right side of the left arête of the tower, using holds round the corner as and when needed, until forced to step right onto the face and slant rightwards towards the chains.

E12 ** 6b+ (E3 6a) 15m
Bridging up the steep right-hand crack system and make a baffling mantelshelf onto the good ledge above. Step out left and climb the sustained face on sharp holds to the lower-off.

Around to the right is an arête and a steep face of good rock bounded on its right side by a deep crack.

E13 * 5+ (HVS 5a) 12m
Climb the crack until it is possible to step onto the face (or do the direct start past the bolt at *(UK 6b)*, then climb the steep face on generous holds apart, for the last couple of moves.

Across the gully and 25m to the right is a rather scruffy-looking buttress that has a clean slab on its right side. There are some worthwhile routes here, though a bit of selectivity is required.

E14 6b (E3 6a) 18m
Start under the prow of the buttress and pull over a roof using temporary-feeling holds to enter a scoop. Continue up and over the beak above by a short jig to the right and then back left to gain a jug on the lip and thus the slab above. Unless the logical finish has been bolted trend right to join and finish as for the next route.

Mike Appleton on an unnamed 6c+ (E4 6b), 'route no. 10' at Egagropalis Tree

E15 * 6a (HVS 5a) 18m
A grotty start leads to greater things. Begin under the right edge of the front of the buttress and grovel leftwards into a constricted groove. Pull out of the top of this into a crack and continue up the fine slab above.

E16 5 (VS 4c) 15m
To the right is a flake with a bush growing on its top. Climb past this up cleaned cracks (no bolts in the lower section so wires are required) then on up better rock to the lower-off of the previous climb.

To the right is a clean and well scarred grey slab. On the extreme left edge of this is:

E17 * 6a+ (E2 5c) 15m
Start just to the right of the bolt line and follow it by sustained moves on sharp holds to flaky jugs at 10m. Easier climbing remains, with a final long reach to the chains.

E18 ** 6b (E2 6a) 15m
A technical gem up the centre of the slab offering sustained and thin climbing. Passing the third bolt is particularly perplexing. Try a sneaky left to right traverse.

E19 4 (VS 4b) 10m
The smooth corner on the right is approached over blocks and bushes. The climbing is OK but the effort in reaching it is not really repaid in full.

SECTOR SOL Y SOMBRE

Character
An area with only limited development at the moment, though in a pleasant setting and worth an afternoon if you enjoy technical face climbing. There are only ten or so routes here at present, two on an east-facing wall (Sector Sol) and the rest on a west-facing wall (Sector Sombre). The names suggest the local climbers get up early because on our visit Sector Sol was in the shade and Sector Sombre was being illuminated by the afternoon sun. Across the bay from the Sector Sol there are some impressive walls beneath a hardly less impressive hotel complex; possibly worth a visit if you are looking for an area to develop.

Approaches
Follow the road from Evissa town northwards towards Sant Miguel de

Balansat (15km). On entering the outskirts of the town take the first left turn and follow this for 1.3 kilometres to a right fork signed 'Es Portixol'. This is followed for 2 kilometres to a left turn on a bend signed 'Cafe Ca n Sulavetas & Supermarket'. Stay on the main road, climbing through a series of hairpin bends, then continue for 1.2 kilometres to where the road bends left and starts to descend steeply. A narrow track goes straight on at this point, and is signed 'No Entry'. Drive down this past a large unfinished building on stilts in the trees on the right and park opposite the large white villa of Casa Alba Mar. On the right here is a surfaced area in the trees, and leaving the centre of the far side of this is a track (cairned) that bends left and heads towards the sea. This is followed for 5 minutes out onto a headland with an impressive inlet on the right; below here is the Sector Sol. Continuing down to the left for a couple of hundred metres is an area of limestone pavement with a large dead tree near the cliff edge, this is directly above the Sector Sombre.

The *SECTOR SOL* only has two routes at the moment though the cliff top is spattered with old bolt sleeves. Both of the routes start from hanging belays on the lip of a substantial roof, reached by abseil, and then make their separate ways back to the cliff top. The grades of these are not known though they do not look too hard.

The *SECTOR SOMBRE* is better developed at present. From the large dead tree on the cliff top a short descent down an open groove should locate chains on the left (looking out). Use these to make a 20m abseil to the base of the face. The routes are described briefly from left to right, though it is worth bearing in mind that, as in other areas on the island, more routes may appear between the ones that already exist.

SS1 6a (E2 5c) 22m
At present the most left-hand route climbs an area of slabby rock around to the left of the landing point from the abseil. Start from flakes and climb the sustained face (harder than it looks) until a pull over a bulge gains the lower-off.

Note: Across the easy open gully to the left of this route is a bulging buttress with lower-off chains on its crest but no other fixed gear as yet.

SS2 6b+ (E3 6a) 22m
This route reclimbs the line of the abseil. From a conglomerate cave pull through the bulges to gain ledges then climb the bulging wall on tiny sharp holds to the easier rib above. Continue up this, cursing the bushes on the way.

SS3 * 7a+ (E4 6b) 22m
The pale hanging groove to the right is entered easily and then climbed with

156

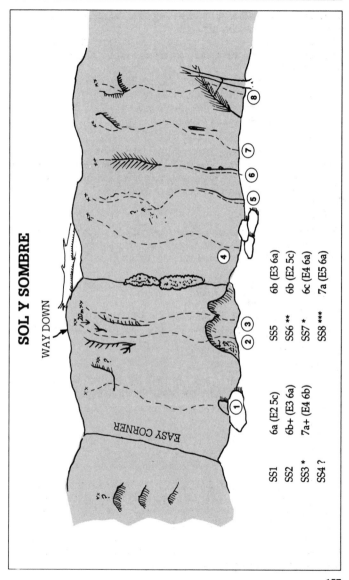

SOL Y SOMBRE

WAY DOWN

EASY CORNER

SS1	6a (E2 5c)	
SS2	6b+ (E3 6a)	
SS3 *	7a+ (E4 6b)	
SS4 ?		
SS5	6b (E3 6a)	
SS6 **	6b (E2 5c)	
SS7 *	6c (E4 6a)	
SS8 ***	7a (E5 6a)	

increasing difficulty to a tough finale up a hanging rib.

To the right is a corner choked with cabbages and other exotic vegetables and just beyond this is a dark slab with bolts up it.

SS4 ? 22m

The line up the slabby wall starts from a pile of blocks and is of unknown difficulty.

To the right are two thin crack systems.

SS5 6b (E3 6a) 22m

The left-hand crack gives good climbing until it is necessary to swing left and pull over a bulge on a rickety hold to easier terrain. From here to the cliff top is straightforward, but there is no fixed gear, and some of the rock is rather suspect. What are the locals playing at?

SS6 ** 6b (E2 5c) 22m

The right-hand crack is altogether a more edifying business. Climb easily to a deep pocket then follow the thinner crack to a deep groove where things ease again. More pleasant climbing leads to the chains.

Just to the right is a fine vertical face with two good climbs on it.

SS7 * 6c (E4 6a) 22m

Climb up and right with difficulty to a tufa then back left onto easier rock. Up this to the left corner of an overhang then make a beefy pull over this final obstacle.

SS8 *** 7a (E5 6a) 22m

Excellent sustained climbing on sharp holds. Start behind the tied-back tree and climb the wall trending slightly leftwards to good holds. Continue up the rib above then swing right and power through the capping bulges to gain a short easy slab.

PENYAL DE S'AGUILA

An area of impressive coastal scenery with a lot of rock, though little of it has been developed. This is the prominent rocky headland that can be seen from both Sector Sol y Sombre and Egagrapolis Tree. At present there are only four bolt lines here and on these much of the fixed gear is rather rusty. There is plenty of scope for new routeing, both traditional and modern, and the area contains many fine crack lines and impressive overhangs in cliffs that rise to at least 100m.

Approaches

Follow the instructions for Sector Sol y Sombre but bear left at the 'No Entry' sign. Follow the road as it weaves downhill until it eventually arrives at an extensive flat open area with some ruined buildings. Leave the car here and follow the road down to the right (looking out to sea), around two more bends until at the final bend before the sea it is possible to descend a short awkward gully. At this point there is a large boulder of conglomerate rock. On the front face of this is *ES VERITAT QUE PAREIX MONTSERRAT 7c*, though at present the bolts do not instil confidence. Traversing to the right (looking out to sea) for a couple of hundred metres there is a series of ledges well above the water line and capped by an impressive series of roofs. Here there are two bolt-protected cracks and a smoother face. One of the cracks is *FRIDAY EVENING FEVER 5* (I guess the right one; what do you think?). The face route is *ROSEGON 6b*.

Tenerife

INTRODUCTION

When I first visited Tenerife in 1991 I was acting on promising information in a Spanish climbing magazine. After two weeks on the island I felt there was enough climbing here for a short visit and so I included brief notes in the back of Andalucian Rock Climbs. In the event, Tenerife has proved far more popular than I could ever have expected, so this expanded information given here should provide enough detailed notes for a week or two's cragging for most normal mortals.

In reality Tenerife is not an ideal climbing venue. The cliffs are generally not of an international quality, and they are well scattered around the island, thus entailing quite a lot of driving. Majorca and mainland Spain have more to offer the inveterate hot rocker, but (and it's a big but) the winter weather on Tenerife is quite superb, whereas in the Mediterranean it can be unsettled. If you come to Tenerife to explore the island's amazing geology, go on a dolphin safari, hike up the 12,000ft El Tiede, try your hand at wind surfing, perhaps do some gorge walking, as well as some cragging you should come away well pleased with your holiday. On the other hand you may spend the whole of your holiday in the Lower Gorge at Arico and still love the place. People's reactions to Tenerife tend to vary considerably, so maybe you will have to go there and make up your own mind.

Tenerife is the largest of the Canary Islands, and the whole group is sometimes known as 'the islands of eternal spring' because of their year round equitable climate. With the north-east trade winds keeping the whole island group warm in the winter and cool in the summer, the temperature varies between 20 and 30°C. As the islands are only 400 miles north of the tropics it is perhaps understandable why they are so pleasant, and swimming in the Atlantic at Christmas can be a lot more enjoyable than you might ever have imagined.

The central feature of the island is the volcanic cone of El Tiede, which rises to over 12,000ft and is the highest peak in all of Spain. In winter it is often snow covered and can present a respectable challenge, though a cable car runs up to over 11,000ft when the summit is free of ice. There is a high altitude refuge close to the normal route up and down the mountain, and a visit to the top is a memorable experience with stunning views in excess of a hundred miles and sulphurous vents belching out scalding steam. The journey up to the base of the volcano is enjoyable in itself as the road rises from sea level to 8000ft, passing through a series of distinctive climatic zones, from tourists at sea level, through bananas, cacti, pine trees, semi-desert and finally the snow line.

By far the busiest time in all of the Canary Islands is the Christmas period so if you intend to go and meet Santa Claus on the beach be sure to book early! Compared to mainland Spain and the Balearics (where winter is the low season) the cost of accommodation in the winter here is expensive, though it is still possible to get a four person apartment for £160 in the high season. Avoid these times and you could save a packet.

It is most likely that any package deal will end up unloading you into one of the concrete complexes that run from the airport all the way round the coast to Los Gigantes. All of these are pleasant enough though Playa de Las Americas is just a bit too 'hip' for most climbers, with discos and bars buzzing well into the early hours. From any of these resorts the two main climbing areas can be reached in about an hour's drive. Because of the amount of driving involved a hire car is an essential; see the notes in the section on Majorca for a UK contact number for Premier Car Hire.

Camping is a possibility though it will by force have to be of the wild variety, and finding water can be a problem. There are a couple of discreet spots at Arico that are used on a regular basis, though if you hire a car, sleeping out is probably as easy an option as any.

The vast majority of the climbing described here are of the 'sport' variety though I have included brief notes on the island's main traditional route area for those who want a bit of adventure thrown in. Enjoy your stay.

LAS CANADAS

Character

Las Canadas remains the premier climbing destination on Tenerife at the present time, and it is well worth a visit, perhaps as much for its truly astounding setting as for the quality of the climbing. The cliffs are a pale pyroclastic rock that looks rather soft and loose from a distance. On closer acquaintance it becomes obvious that nothing could be further from the truth; the raw material is hard and rough with a preponderance of pinch grips, pockets and incut edges. All in all, a marvellous climbing medium.

The altitude of the area (7000+ft) is inclined to cause a bit of puffing and blowing on the first couple of visits, but on the plus side the air is crystal clear, the views are magnificent and you can get a tan in a third of the time it takes on the coast (and if you are blessed with fair northern skin don't forget the sun-block). The area looks rather small from the car park though in reality is extensive with over 100 routes at present and lots of undeveloped rock still to go at.

The locals have developed a strange habit of drilling pockets across the undersides of most of the more impressive roofs which give hard, gymnastic problems that are ideal for chimpanzees who do not value their tendons. For more normal mortals there is plenty to do here.

Access

The cliffs are located inside the caldera, or old crater, that encircles the volcano of El Tiede and which is the central feature of the whole island. The rim of the crater is reached by any one of several access routes from the coast and the approach is well signed; see map in introduction. Pick your route and then join the convoy of small white hire cars and the occasional ultra-slow fruit lorry, and zigzag uphill for approximately an hour to reach the Boca de Tauce at about 6500ft. Follow the road northwards via lava flows, basalt plateaux, volcanic peaks and arid deserts (for about 3 kilometres!) until it rises through an area of strange blue rocks, a product of hydrothermal alteration as the signs inform you. Just past these the road flattens out and there is a sign on the right for Los Roques. Drive down the narrow road on the right just past the sign and park by the small quaint house squeezed between the lava flows. The nearest rocks are 30 seconds away.

Geography

Las Canadas (the canyons) is a complex maze of towers and canyons scattered around a domed hill. The local climbers have divided the area into a series of 'sectors' for ease of identification and I have used the same divisions. Each sector is described briefly with short notes on individual routes. Together with plan views and normal diagrams where appropriate, this should ease the location of your target route or area. The sectors are described in a clockwise manner starting from the car park by the small ICONA (roughly equivalent to our National Trust) house. From the car park (see diagram) the easy slabs that stand in front of the Sector Psiquiatrico are visible just behind the lava piles, and to the left of these is the high tower of the main part of this sector. Left again are the minarets and spires of the Sector Aureola, and hidden behind here is the extensive north-east-facing Sector Sexta Dimension. Up the hill to the right is the isolated tower of Fraggel Rock and above and right of this again is the high red wall of the Sector Rainbow. Down to the right and much nearer the car park are the smaller towers that are the Sectors Chumino on the left and Guira on the right.

Note: I have come across three separate topos to Las Canadas and they show considerable differences in several respects, especially in names and grades of many of the climbs! I have attempted to correlate these topos

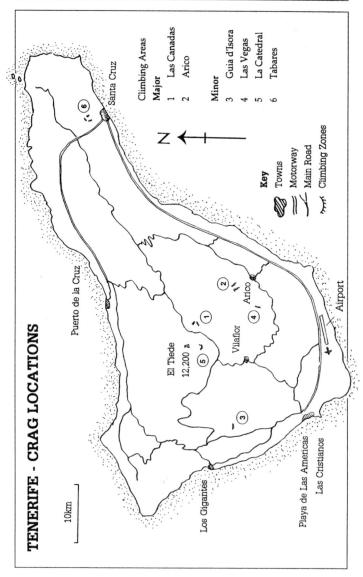

TENERIFE - CRAG LOCATIONS

Climbing Areas

Major

1   Las Canadas
2   Arico

Minor

3   Guia d'Isora
4   Las Vegas
5   La Catedral
6   Tabares

Key

Towns
Motorway
Main Road
Climbing Zones

N

10km

Santa Cruz
Puerto de la Cruz
El Tiede
12,200 a
Vilaflor
Arico
Los Gigantes
Las Cristianos
Playa de Las Americas
Airport

163

LAS CANADAS
The Sectors

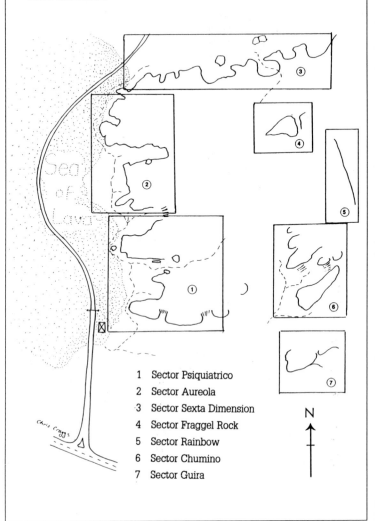

1 Sector Psiquiatrico
2 Sector Aureola
3 Sector Sexta Dimension
4 Sector Fraggel Rock
5 Sector Rainbow
6 Sector Chumino
7 Sector Guira

N

LAS CANADAS : Overview

1 Sector Psiquiatrico
2 Sector Aureola
3 Sector Sexta Dimension
4 Sector Fraggel Rock
5 Sector Rainbow
6 Sector Chumino
7 Sector Guira

along with information from magazines and from local climbers and the present best effort is presented here for your information. Best of luck.

SECTOR PSIQUIATRICO

This is the area closest to the car park and it contains many good climbs across a broad sprectrum of grades. Much of the sector faces south. The area starts with the broad slabs close to the car park, then there are some short but sharp overhangs behind the slabs, and just across the bay is the high south facing wall that is the showpiece of this area.

The extensive slabby area in front of the car park only has two short named routes and these are located in the gully that splits the area neatly in half. The right-hand triangular set of slabs is very easy angled and can be climbed anywhere at *Grade 2* and *3 (V Diff* to *Severe)*. In the gully that separates the two sections there are the previously mentioned pair of minuscule climbs.

GAFITAS 6b (HVS 5c) 8m
On the right wall (looking up) of the gully is this short leaning wall, passing two chain link bolts.

TECHOS DE LOS BRAZOS CRUZADOS 6b+ (E1 6a) 8m
The steep pocketed prow opposite the previous climb passing a solitary bolt.

The left-hand section of the slabs contains little in the way of fixed gear but has a selection of worthwhile lower grade climbs that can easily be done with a small rack of wires and are ideal for beginners or for grabbing a few ticks at the end of the day. None of the lines has a name though I include a short description here for those who want them (at least you will be able to tick them off!). There are twin bolts on the highest point of the slab useful for belaying, top roping or for using as abseil anchors.

From right to left the lines are:

CRACK 2 (Diff) 12m
The straightforward crack and corner which starts 8m up the gully from the right toe of the slab.

CORNER 3 (V Diff) 15m
The crack that starts at the right-hand toe of the slabs leads into a deeper corner then joins the previous line. Finish easily out right or direct with more difficulty.

SECTOR PSIQUIATRICO

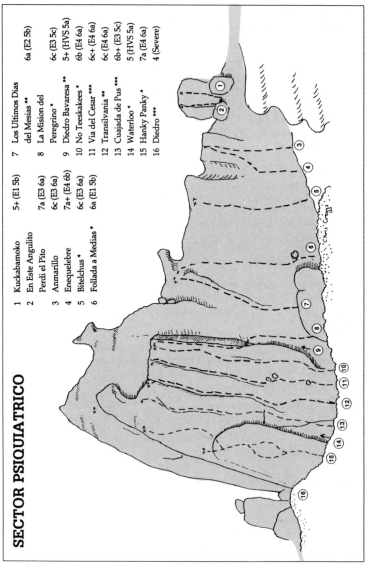

1	Kuckabamoko	5+ (E1 5b)
2	En Este Angulito	
	Perdi el Pito	7a (E3 6a)
3	Anmarillo	6c (E3 6a)
4	Enequelebre	7a+ (E4 6b)
5	Bitelchus *	6c (E3 6a)
6	Follada a Medias *	6a (E1 5b)
7	Los Ultimos Dias	
	del Mesias **	6a (E2 5b)
8	La Mision del	
	Peregrino *	6c (E3 5c)
9	Diedro Bavaresa **	5+ (HVS 5a)
10	No Teeskakees *	6b (E4 6a)
11	Via del Cesar ***	6c+ (E4 6a)
12	Transilvania **	6c (E4 6a)
13	Cuajada de Pus ***	6b+ (E3 5c)
14	Waterloo *	5 (HVS 5a)
15	Hanky Panky *	7a (E4 6a)
16	Diedro ***	4 (Severe)

RIB * 4 (HVS 4c) 15m
The smooth rib has a solitary runner in the form of a hangerless bolt. Hook a wire over and try to avoid falling off!

GROOVE * 3+ (Severe) 15m
The interesting central shallow groove is climbed passing a bulge.

FLAKE 5 (HVS 5a) 15m
In the left wall of the groove is a short curving flake with a bolt runner just above it. This protects the tricky crux sequence, the start and finish being much easier.

CRACK 3 (Severe) 12m
The crack on the right side of the rounded rib that bounds the left side of the face is pleasant enough.

TWIN CRACKS 4 (VS 4b) 12m
The parallel cracks in the front of the rib at the left side of the face have a tricky start but ease as height is gained.

Passing round to the left of the main slabs, a short scramble between the cliff and the encroaching lava reaches another slabby wall, though this one is shorter and is north-facing. There are no recorded routes here though some obvious easy possibilities present themselves to anyone who is interested.

Further to the left, in the back right corner of the bay, is a series of overhangs crossed by five short but tough outings, ideal for bumpy boys and girls who want to escape the sun.

COITUS INTERRUPTUS 7a (E4 6a) 10m
The right-hand line crosses a small roof low down then heads up the tilted pocked wall. Don't lose your concentration at the crucial moment. Small bolts protect.

CARDERO 7a+ (E4 6b) 10m
Starting in the same place, traverse along the lip of the hanging slab on the left to ledges.

To the left a roof runs along the length of the face and passing round the right side of this is

BIOBLAST 7b+ (E5 6b) 10m
Climb round the right side of the roof passing an hourglass-shaped pillar and the overhang above with difficulty.

168

MAXIMUN * 7b+ (E5 6b) 10m
The central line over the roof is the best on the wall. Start to the right of the pocket in the lower wall then pass the roofs by powerful pocket pulling.

The solitary bolt to the left may protect a direct start to the previous route, or an indirect start to the next one.

ANDRES, PRUEBALA OTRA VEZ * 8a (E7 6c) 10m
The series of drilled and 'arrowed' pockets trends left across the widest part of the roof. Not for those with tendon troubles.

The area in the back of the bay is described as a bivouac on the local topo, though from the scattering of 'debris' it looks like Servicio would be a more apt description. Above the right side of the back of the bay and to the right of a large prow is an innocuous looking line that is supposedly 7c, considering its diminutive side it must be a tough one.

The left side of the bay is a fine high wall split by a series of thin diagonal cracks and home to an excellent selection of climbs. Just to make things even better the wall faces just west of south and so is almost always catching the sun. High on the right side of the wall is a large boulder with a prominent sharp arête and this is reached by scrambling up the gully. There are two short offerings here:

KUCABAMOKO 5+ (E1 5b) 7m
The right-hand face of the boulder.

EN ESTE ANGULITO PERDI EL PITO 7a (E3 6b) 7m
The arête of the boulder gives a route that is almost as long as its name.

On the right side of the main face and to the right of a large flake there are two routes protected by rather old bolts and sharing a lower-off.

ANMARILLO 6c (E3 6a) 10m
Straight up the smooth red face on the far right.

ENEQUELEBRE 7a+ (E4 6b) 10m
Climb up the 'blank' lower wall almost into the base of the open gully then trend steeply right to join the previous climb.

BITELCHUS * 6c (E3 6a) 12m
The flat wall just right of the bush gives a sustained and pleasant pitch.

FOLLADA A MEDIAS * 6a (E1 5b) 15m
Left again and just to the right of a large flake is a hole. Climb leftwards out of this then press on straight up the wall.

The next two climbs start from atop the large flake; clip the first bolt before you fall off!

LOS ULTIMOS DIAS DEL MESIAS ** 6a (E2 5b) 22m
The vague slanting crack line gives a pumpy and worthwhile little pitch.

LA MISION DEL PEREGRINO * 6c (E3 5c) 22m
Climb the wall to the right of the flake crack to ledges then step left and climb the more technical upper arête and a final bulge. Good positions, though feeling rather escapable.

DIEDRO BAVARESA ** 5+ (HVS 5a) 30m
The slanting flake and open groove give a good strenuous pitch. From the ledges above the groove move left to a belay then either abseil off or top out and scramble down the back of the tower. Carry a rack of Friends, though several of the bolts on the previous route can be clipped if required.

NO TEESKAKEES * 6b (E4 6a) 22m
The rather hacked face to the left of the arête has a steep lower section past a flake and pockety bulge leading to an easier crack and a final baffling sequence on sloping holds. Escaping right onto the arête is taboo at the grade. Large single bolt lower-off.

To the left is the first of three diagonal cracks. This is:

VIA DEL CESAR *** 6c+ (E4 6a) 22m
An imperial route. Climb the steep lower wall to the prominent large pockets then swing left to a big bolt in the base of the groove. Extemporise up this (crux) then follow the still awkward crack past a poor peg to a lower-off in the left wall of the gully above.

TRANSILVANIA ** 6c (E4 6a) 22m
The groove line to the left is reached up the wall using pockets and followed by good but rather ungainly climbing. The bolts are quite spaced so a couple of small Rocks might not go amiss.

CUAJADA DE PUS *** 6b+ (E3 5c) 22m
The left-hand and least defined crack line is reached by climbing straight up the wall just to the right of a prominent flake crack. Once reached the ragged crack gives excellent sustained climbing; just keep going. The lower-off bolts are on the left at the top.

WATERLOO * 5 (HVS 5a) 12m
The right-facing flake just left of the bushes is followed (no fixed gear) as it

curves over to the left to reach lower-off bolts located just short of the arête.

The smooth face to the left of the flake of *WATERLOO* is climbed by:

HANKY PANKY * 7a (E4 6a) 12m
The crux involves a mild runout to reach the third bolt. Doing this section on the right is worth 7b and stepping out right below the lower-off and climbing the upper section of the face by a short loop is the full tick, being worth ** 7c and 18m long.

Around to the left of the main face is an eye catching slabby groove line, the classical:

DIEDRO *** 4 (Severe) 30m
Follow the crack in the back of the groove (leave it till late in the day if you want to do the route in the sun) to *in situ* belays just below the top of the groove then climb deviously to the top of the tower, absorb the marvellous view and scramble down the back to escape.

In front of the deep groove is a tall square boulder, home to one of the island's shorter offerings, a 7a (6b) boulder problem containing a single bolt just above the crux.

To the left of the deep groove is a wide slabby wall that faces the volcano, and that is home to four climbs.

OJO DEL DIABLO * 7a (E4 6a) 25m
Climb the slab and tough overlap on the right of the face, continue up the slab above and tackle the bulging head wall direct. Pegs and bolts protect.

PLACA DEL OMBRA * 6a 25m
Behind the shallow hanging corner (bolts to the right) and the crack line up the smooth slab. Carry some wires.

AID A1 18m
The wall, roof and slab to the left. Remember the days!

YONONONO ** 5 (HVS 5a) 28m
The crack that bounds the left side of the face gives a pitch that is well worth seeking out if you climb at the grade. Carry a rack of wires. A steep start up the scarred crack leads to bulges. Step left and pull through a bulge (peg) then follow the crack line all the way to the top of the tower. Scramble off the back.

The final route in this sector is located a short distance to the right of the gully that leads up to *FRAGGEL ROCK*.

AL LORO AL LORO QUE VIENE EL MORO 6b+ tackles a bulging wall but had been debolted when I last visited the area.

SECTOR AUREOLA

A complex area of towers and bays to the north of the *SECTOR PSIQUIATRICO*, and easily reached by passing round the left side of the face and scrambling over blocks and lava. Several of the spires would make good objectives for traditional style summit bagging routes; double ropes and a few old slings to abseil from would appear to make sense. The Sector is bound on the right by an open gully that gives an access route up to *FRAGGEL ROCK* and the first four routes are located on the red leaning wall to the left of the gully and above some rather wiry bushes. The area faces south-west and so gets plenty of afternoon sun. The most right-hand route is:

SUICIDETE 7c (E6 6c) 10m
An easy scoop to ledges and then the impressive roof above.

CHAIN BICICLETA * 7b+ (E6 6b) 12m
The fierce hanging corner with bolts in its right wall.

GUSTAVO REPORTERO 7? 12m
The flying arête on the left looks highly improbable.

PONSELO 7a (E5 6a) 12m
The narrow front face of the buttress over a series of bulges.

To the left is a deep narrow ravine with a route on its shady left wall.
DANDO BOTITOS 6c (E4 6a) 12m
Follow the old bolts through the bulges.

The narrow front face to the left of the ravine has an unnamed and ungraded climb over the prow then on up the steep wall on jugs.

Around to the left is a north-facing slabby wall bounded on the left by a corner crack. It is home to a couple of worthwhile and delicate offerings:
PLACA DE BAZOCHI ** 6a (E1 5b) 18m
The right-hand line has good sustained moves up the slab and a tricky roof at the top. Move left to the lower-offs.

SECTOR AUREOLA

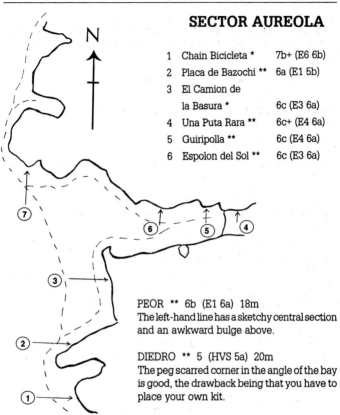

1	Chain Bicicleta *	7b+ (E6 6b)
2	Placa de Bazochi **	6a (E1 5b)
3	El Camion de la Basura *	6c (E3 6a)
4	Una Puta Rara **	6c+ (E4 6a)
5	Guiripolla **	6c (E4 6a)
6	Espolon del Sol **	6c (E3 6a)

PEOR ** 6b (E1 6a) 18m
The left-hand line has a sketchy central section and an awkward bulge above.

DIEDRO ** 5 (HVS 5a) 20m
The peg scarred corner in the angle of the bay is good, the drawback being that you have to place your own kit.

To the left is a wide striated wall with a large perched flake in its centre. This is home to three climbs.

AUREOLA 6c (E3 6a) 12m
The right-hand line follows a thin crack that trends right and is protected by rather ancient bolts.

REY DEL POLLO FRITO * 7a (E4 6a) 12m
Immediately to the left is this route, 'the king of fried chicken', protected by chain-link bolts. It pulls through a stubborn bulge to reach a shiny new lower-off on the prominent ledge system.

EL CAMION DE LA BASURA * 6c (E3 6a) 20m
Climb easy rock to a point just left of the perched flake then follow the green
bolts with a jig to the left at the third clip. Not as rubbishy a route as the name
might suggest.

Just around the arête to the left is a hanging groove tackled by:

LA QUILLA * 6c+ (E4 6a) 15m
Pull into the hanging crack and climb this until it is possible to get out onto
the face on the right. Up this to the top.

TECHO GORDO DE PETETE * 7c (E6 6c) 15m
The orange leaning wall to the left is climbed (surprise, surprise) on a series
of drilled finger pockets.

The rest of the routes in the Sector Aureola are located on the convoluted
west-facing walls across the opposite side of the bush filled bay. The first
of these starts in the back left corner of the bay where a short scramble up
a slab leads to the base of a rounded buttress, with two bolt lines on it. One
of the local climbers has done a girdle traverse of this whole wall
(DECADENCIA FISCAC 6c), and this fact explains the existence of occasional
single bolts in the middle of nowhere. Further up the gully from the rounded
buttress is a solitary route, which presumably climbs the impressive spire
via the scoops and roof: *CONSUMIR PREFERENTEMENTE 6b+*.

LA PUTA RARA Y SU HIJA ** 7a (E4 6a) 12m
The right-hand line on the rounded tower climbs the thin rightward-
trending crack and the wall above on pockets. Also known as *MIERDILLA
DE HISTORIA* on some topos.

UNA PUTA RARA ** 6c+ (E4 6a) 12m
The left-hand line, closely spaced chain link bolts protect this sustained
pitch.

The next two routes start at the very base of the gully used to get to the
previous pair of climbs and climb the tower directly above this point. They
share both the starting moves and the lower-off station.

TAKE A BIT ** 6c (E3 5c) 15m
Bridge the lower crack then tackle the right side of the tower which sports
nice new bolts. Steep and satisfying.

RAYA KAYAC ** 6c (E3 5c) 15m
The hanging crack up the front of the tower; another route worth seeking
out.

To the left is a buttress rising above a large white block. There are three routes here, though the topo only shows two.

An UNNAMED ROUTE trends right up a ramp then climbs the steep left wall of an open groove and over a small overlap to two large rings. It looks about 6a/b and worthwhile.

LA CARA DEL MONO ** 6c (E4 6a) 15m
Start from the block and climb the front of the pillar, via pockets and a final sizeable bulge, to twin bolts.

GUIRIPOLLA ** 6c (E4 6a) 15m
From the block climb the bulging rib heading for the right side of the large overhang near the top of the cliff; exit to the right.

SHIT * 7a (E5 6b) 15m
Despite the name the line through the large notch in the overhang to the left proves both hard and worthwhile.

To the left is a corner that could offer a good traditional climb then the wall swings round and a band of bulges are crossed by two innocuous-looking climbs:

OVERKILL * 7b (E5 6b) 15m
The right-hand line sports some 'odd' holds, and requires some radical moves.

SANITARIUM * 7c (E6 6c) 15m
The left-hand line offers more of the same, only harder.

To the left is a rounded hollow with a route escaping out of its top left corner.

AUREOLA NO ME TOQUES LA PIROLA * 6c+ (E4 6a) 18m
A good route after a rather gripping start. Climb into the scoop then trend left to clip the first (crap) bolt. Pull through the roof, crux, on a discrete chipped hold and clip a good bolt (not before time) then continue more easily and more safely to the top.

ESPOLON DEL SOL ** 6c (E3 6a) 18m
The arête immediately left of an easy gully (low grade trad route there for the taking) gives an intriguing pitch, alternately delicate and strenuous. Just remember, it's not all over until it's over.

Around to the left the lava has run up against the foot of the cliff and there is a broad slabby rib:

PAY LA PENA 6a (E1 5b) 10m
Start from a small flat area and climb the lower section and a short
steepening to a lower-off in an open groove above.

TE QUIERO ZORRA * 6a (E1 5b) 10m
The final route lurks in the back of a bush filled gully and climbs the
enjoyably juggy left wall using a steep crack line.

SECTOR SEXTA DIMENSION

A long sector which has scarcely been developed up to the present day. It
is shady and cool in the winter, requiring track suits and a warm top, but
would make a great summer venue. It can be reached by walking past the
sectors described above and crossing a small col, or more easily walking
along the road from the car park, past the barrier and then around a loop to
arrive at the right edge of the sector. Less than 10 minutes from the car.

The right side of the sector is fronted by a broad flat sandy area with
scattered fire circles. Tucked away in the right corner of this is:
PAULO LAUDELINO CUBINO 7c 8m
A tiny route on the far right side of the sector. Two bolts protect a wild-
looking dyno to easy ground.

Past an area of slabby rock and an isolated block of lava is a bay behind
a huge boulder.
ME HELEN LOS PIES 6a (E1 5b) 12m
An orange pockety wall just to the right of an easy break leads to ledges
below a giant roof.

NO REPERCUTE * 6b (E2 5c) 12m
The striated wall 3m right of the corner, and the bulging arête above. Good.

MIERDA 6a+ (E1 5b) 18m
Start up the gully on the left side of the face and continue up the open
bridging groove above; odd pitch.

Around to the left is the huge projecting beak of an overhang, the Techo
de Madrid, (or Techo de *Mario* on some topos) which is most easily reached
by scrambling up the awkward corner on the right and traversing out to the
left. The flat ledge here would form an ideal bivi-spot as long as you don't
sleep walk. There are three routes over the huge roof and all involve using

176

improved holds to a greater or lesser extent.

HUMAN INSECTICIDE 7c (E6 6b) 10m
The line of neatly drilled finger pockets on the right, protected(?) by the worst set of bolts you are ever likely to meet anywhere!

COMIC * 7c+ (E6 6c) 15m
The central line across the great roof.

SUBWAY ** 8a+ (E7 6c) 18m
Crosses the roof at its widest point, simianly spectacular.

Continuing around to the left there is a small conical tower at the back of the bay, home to two climbs. An easy break on the left gives an access route up from here to Fraggel Rock.

LAS PUTIEDADES DE LULU 6b (E1 5c) 10m
The right trending line.

HAYA O NO HAYA. AQUI ESTA EL RAYA 6b (E1 5c) 10m
The left trending line starting in the same place.

Continuing leftwards past a lot of excellent but undeveloped rock (and three unidentified routes, possibly of traditional style: *CANALON PENETRANTE 5+, AMISTADES PELIGROSES 5+* and *TECHO DE ROSAL 6a*) the cliff increases in size to a spectacular north-east-facing prow capped by a smooth wall:

SABRA-SATILA **** 7a (E5 6a) 45m
The finest route on the island? A majestic pitch started by scrambling up the right and spiralling out on to the spectacular wall on the left, before blasting up the centre of this. Don't forget the double ropes.

Across the gully is a wide wall crying out to be developed and on the far left side, a hundred metres or so up the bank, is the last offering in this area:

LINEA MAGICA * 6a+ (E2 5c) 25m
Climb the pale streak then continue in the same line to ledges and bolt belays.

FRAGGEL ROCK

The conspicuous tower of Fraggel Rock has a good collection of climbs, across a broad range of grades, and offers superlative views and photographic opportunities. Situated a steep 10 minutes from the car, Fraggel is an isolated tower with routes on all sides though, as is usual, the sunny faces have seen the best development. The climbs are described in clockwise fashion starting at the top right corner of the wall that faces the car park.

BANANAS * 7c (E6 6c) 12m
Monkey up the smooth yellow wall on the right edge of the face passing a prominent patch of red rock 'en route'.

DUDO * 7b+ (E6 6b) 12m
Starting under the overlap to the left and following the curving line of bolts left, then right, is this sustained little trip.

MAJESTIX is the bolt line starting in the same place but trending leftwards. The grade is unknown though it looks hard.

To the left the wall is undercut by a series of substantial overhangs and three climbs find their way through these.

MUSSI * 6c (E4 6a) 12m
Straight through the right side of the roofs passing twinned bolts early on, to gain large elongated pockets then following easier rock to the right of the arête.

BOBO * 6a (E1 5b) 12m
Climb the slabby right side of the arête started by trending left through the overhangs. The lower-off is hidden around the corner.

CUSSI * 6b (E2 5b) 12m
The prow of the cliff facing the volcano starts over an overhang with a tricky first clip. Spectacular positions.

INDERCISIONES ** 6a+ (E2 5b) 18m
From the previous route follow ledges around the corner. Pull through the bulges in the centre of the north face then follow the line leftwards to the apex of the tower.

EIGERBAND ** 6b (E2 5c) 18m

The north-east arête of Fraggel is most easily reached by crossing the col behind the tower (to the right of *BANANAS*). Cross the initial large roof rightwards then sprint up the pale wall and steep arête above.

Behind Fraggel is a small wall facing the tower which is home to three quick-ticks.

PUTA PICOLETA 6a (HVS 5b) 10m
The left-hand line has 3 bolt runners.

CERO A LA IZQUIERDA 6a+ (E1 5c) 10m
The central line with 3 bolt runners.

CALLEJON OSCURO 6b (E1 5c) 7m
The minuscule right-hand line with 2 bolt runners.

SECTOR RAINBOW

The highest (in terms of altitude) face in the area is this impressive red wall. At present there are only five routes here, though there is plenty of scope for more. The wall is reached in a steep 15 minutes from the car, though it perhaps makes sense to visit it via one of the other sectors further down the hill.

The cliff is referred to as the Sector Rambo (big muscles required?) on one topo, the Sector Rainbow (multicoloured rock?) on another, and the Sector Raimbow (???) on a third, so your guess is as good as mine as to its real name. The climbing is steep and exhilarating though some of the rock feels a little suspect in places. The routes are described from left to right, and none is equipped with convenient lower-offs at present. From the approach slopes the most conspicuous features of the face are the central double peaked tower, with a bush at its foot, and an open gully on the right, with a large conifer below it.

To the left of and behind the Rainbow Wall is a fine-looking arête climbed by *NO HAY TACTO,* an excellent-looking but rather inaccessible *6c+.*

RABAJAS DE ENERO 6a+ (E2 5b) 12m
The white wall 10m left of the bush and to the left of the fall line from the left-hand summit leads steeply to ledges with bolt belays. Walk off left.

CHAPITA LEJANA * 7a (E4 6a) 24m
The fine arête to the right gives a steep sustained pitch, to a ledge with peg belays. Walk off to the left.

TATOPANI ** 6b+ (E3 5b) 24m
Start just left of the bush and climb straight up the steep wall and continue up a short blunt arête to ledges. The obvious direct finish is crying out to be climbed. Walk off to the left or abseil from bolts on the right.

RAINBOW *** 6a+ (E2 5b) 30m
A great route, well worth the walk up. Start behind the bush and climb straight up the tilted ladder of jugs (sustained 5a) to ledges. Climb the wall behind then either lower-off the last bolt or, better, continue awkwardly to the top of the tower, bring your second up and walk off the back.

BONCHO EN LAS AMERICAS 6b is situated to the right, on the wall behind the large tree. The bolts look rather old and the rock looks a little suspect.

The final two sectors can be seen to the right of the easy slabs by the car park. Although they do not look especially impressive they contain some worthwhile climbs.

SECTOR CHUMINO

A complex tower that appears rather insignificant from the car park but which is home to almost 30 climbs varying in aspect, grade and length. Many of the routes are located in a deep ravine best suited to warmer weather, or to climbers who like to operate in private.

Walk right passing in front of the area of 'easy slabs' towards the tower with a prominent large hollow in the left side of its front face (Sector Guira) then trend up and left to the tower with a prominent high white slab on its south face, bounded on its right edge by a recent rock fall scar. Opposite the white slab are two tiny routes: *GUIR CANTOSA 6a* on the left and *BOGLUNDER 6b* on the right.

The first routes described at the Sector Chumino are on the face around to the right of the fine white slab.

Note: All the climbs are described from right to left, *except* those on the left wall of the central gully.

POR AQUI NO PASAS NI DE GUASA 6b (E2 5c) 12m
Start from ledges 6m right of a small built-up bivi-shelter (not recommended) and climb straight up the bulging wall.

ER GALLEGO NO TIENE PELO 6a+ (E1 5c) 12m
Start in the same place but trend left to a bolt on the lip of the bulges then continue straight up the rib above.

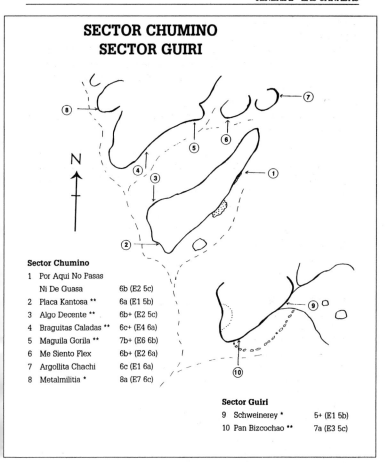

SECTOR CHUMINO
SECTOR GUIRI

N

Sector Chumino

1	Por Aqui No Pasas	
	Ni De Guasa	6b (E2 5c)
2	Placa Kantosa **	6a (E1 5b)
3	Algo Decente **	6b+ (E2 5c)
4	Braguitas Caladas **	6c+ (E4 6a)
5	Maguila Gorila **	7b+ (E6 6b)
6	Me Siento Flex	6b+ (E2 6a)
7	Argollita Chachi	6c (E1 6a)
8	Metalmilitia *	8a (E7 6c)

Sector Guiri

| 9 | Schweinerey * | 5+ (E1 5b) |
| 10 | Pan Bizcochao ** | 7a (E3 5c) |

TOO KISKI LA SOBA 7a (E4 6a) 12m
Start from a pile of boulders and a small battered tree and climb the tough wall above into a hollow near the top of the cliff.

ROCAMADOR 6a (E1 5b) 22m
Near the left edge of the wall climb onto a ledge, up a pillar and then the final groove on slightly suspect rock.

The 'fine white slab' is:

PLACA KANTOSA ** 6a (E1 5b) 26m
Start under an overhang below and left of the fall line from the slab, under a bulging rib. Pull awkwardly out to the right then climb easily to the base of the slab. This is much easier than it looks. Exit to the right or left.

ESA CHAPA SOBRA * 5 (VS 4c) 24m
Around to the left climb the corner and groove following the line of least resistance.

Around to the left again is the canyon that splits the tower in two. There are a dozen or so routes in this secluded setting, a good place to get away from it all. On the right edge of the canyon there are five routes close together on a fine pocketed wall. The two on the far right are new, no grades known, though they look to be about 6c/7a-ish.

The central one of the five is:

ALGO DECENTE ** 6b+ (E2 5c) 22m
Climb straight up the steep pocketed wall to a slab then pass the capping bulge by a tricky pull on a hidden hold.

CHUMINITO PROFUNDO ** 6b+ (E2 5c) 22m
The next line to the left, up the pocket wall again and past another bulge to reach the same belays as the previous climb.

EVA NO QUIERA * 7b (E5 6b) 22m
The left-hand line trends left up steep rock on spaced and poor pockets linked by dynamic moves.

The next seven routes are on the opposite side of the canyon, described from left to right as it rises steeply up the bank.

VAYA TROMPADA 6b 12m
The left arête (or the wall just to its right?) of the canyon is an unknown quantity.

BRAGUITAS CALADAS ** 6c+ (E4 6a) 22m
Up the slope and to the right of a crack line is a line trending left through pocketed bulges to ledges then left again through ever more bulges. Good sport.

MORTALES INGREDIENTES 7? 24m
Starting from the left side of the cave is this very steep line, crossing a bevy

182

of bulges to reach the highest point of the wall.

MAGUILA GORILA ** 7b+ (E6 6b) 22m
The outrageously steep climb just before the wall swings round into a hanging corner. A must for lovers of a swinging time.

MALOS PERROS * 6c (E4 6a) 18m
The line up the left wall of the hanging corner (not a route though it should be) that bounds the right side of the steepest section of the face.

PANZAS DE SANCHO PANZA 6b (E1 5b) 10m
A route up the short brown streak to the right of the corner crack.

BOBERIAS SON SOPAS 6b+ (E2 5c) 10m
The diagonal line close to the right edge of the wall.

To the right across the top of the gully are two separate small towers, both of which are well spattered with bolts. The first (left-hand) tower has three routes, from left to right:

ME SIENTO FLEX 6b+ (E2 6a) 10m
Over a prow and up a thin diagonal crack.

ADONDE MAGARRO 6b (E2 5c) 10m
White bolts protect a climb just left of a brown streaked groove.

UNNAMED 7a (E4 6a) 10m
The smooth bulging rib on the right.

To the right is another small rounded tower with two tiny climbs that are equipped with excellent bolts. This point can also be reached from the front of the sector by walking up the slope to the right of the arrival point.

ARGOLLITA CHUNGA 6b (E1 5c) 7m
The left-hand line.

ARGOLLITA CHACHI 6c (E1 6a) 7m
The line around the arête to the right.

The final three routes in the Sector Chumino are located up the slope to the left of the central gully containing the above climbs. At the top of this is an impressive bulging prow covered in drilled holds (hardly cricket). The stars awarded are for people who enjoy having their tendons stretched to twanging point!

METALMILITIA * 8a (E7 6c) 10m
The right-hand line over the largest part of the roof.

KIM BASINGER * 7c (E6 6b) 10m
The slightly less ridiculous line to the left.

EXTASIS 7c (E6 6b) 10m
Left again.

EL CAPRICHO DEL NENE 6a (E1 5b) 10m
The short arête on the small tower to the left.

SECTOR GUIRI (see diagram p181)

A small tower with half a dozen routes on its south face. The sector is worth a visit for the photogenic nature of these climbs, with the volcano towering in the background, and of course a visit here can easily be combined with routes on the nearby and more extensive Sector Chumino.

Note: The climbs here are described from RIGHT to LEFT.

Walk right passing in front of the area of easy slabs to a tower with a prominent large hollow in the left side of its front face and a low walled sandy area around to the right, 5 minutes from the car. How's the altitude affecting you so far? The first routes start up and right of this area from extensive ledges reached by an easy scramble round to the right.

In the back wall of the bay is another contender for Spain's shortest route, a two bolts in a 4m high red wall, grade unknown. To the left is a higher wall split centrally by a wide chimney gully that starts 7m above the ledge. In the prow to the right of this are two new stainless steel staples, presumably reached from the gully; no grade known.

To the left of the hanging gully is:

SCHWEINEREY * 5+ (El 5b) 15m
A worthwhile pitch but with only two pieces of fixed kit; carry a couple of slings for spikes if you feel the need.

From just left of the central gully trend left across the wall, passing the first bolt (crux), then follow good holds passing another bolt near the top protecting the final steepening. No fixed belays.

Starting from the 'corral' is:

PALIQUE PALICOSO 6a (E1 5c) 18m
Climb the awkward corner (wires?) to a block (or cop out and step in from

*C.C on SCHWEINEREY * 5+ (E1 5b) Sector Guiri, Las Canadas*

185

the right) then step left and clip the first bolt with difficulty. Climb past this (especially thin for the short) then trend left (bolt) and back right to the top of the tower. No fixed belays.

Just to the left is a solitary large bolt in the steep wall that protects either the diagonal groove that leads rightwards into the last route or an unfinished climb directly up the wall.

PAN BIZCOCHAO ** 7a (E3 5c) 15m
A gift at the Spanish grade, especially as it was initially given 7a+. Climb the crack just right of the arête then layback powerfully through the bulges to gain a rest on the left. Climb the arête then swing back right (tricky clip) before powering over the final bulge. Twin bolt belay.

Around to the left the side wall of the arête has a worthwhile-looking slabby pitch with big beefy 'glue-ins' and a reported grade of 7a+.

ARICO

Character
A pleasant open gorge running north-south and with routes on both sides, thus allowing the sun to be enjoyed or avoided. The place is rather dusty but this area of Tenerife is semi-desert, so you will have to grin and bear it! The rock is an ignimbrite or welded ash that was ejected from the volcano and was so hot on landing that it fused together into a solid mass, in a similar manner to Oregon's world famous venue, Smith Rock. Gas cavities were trapped in the ash along with various fragments of solid rock and this has led to the climbs relying heavily on pockets and a remarkable number of 'thread-type' holds. The vast majority of the routes are on smooth open faces, though there are some beetling overhangs and the occasional fine crack line for a touch of variety. Bolt protection is the norm, apart from a very small number of crack lines and the routes rarely exceed 22m in height.

Geography
The gorge is divided into Upper and Lower sections with the car parking just above the top end of the Lower Gorge. The best routes in the Lower Gorge face west and those in the Upper Gorge face east. With a bit of planning it is possible to have a full day on the rock without getting too fried.
NOTE: The terms Left and Right Bank refer to the sectors when seen *from the normal direction of approach.*

ARICO -
LOWER GORGE
SECTORS

Arico: Map Key

P   parking

⊠   buildings

– ▸ – –   access route

🌿   dry stream bed

🌳   prominent trees

☁   impenetrable bushes

·········   water channel

░░   'bamboo' grass

1   Sector Oscuro

2   Sector Techos

3   Sector Tunnel

4   Sector Mirador

5   Sector Pepino

6   Sector Cicatriz

7   Sector 7A

N
↑

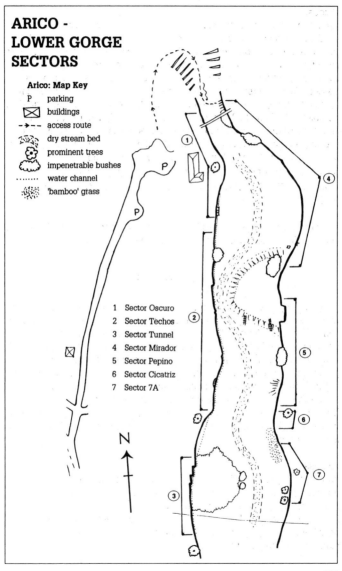

Access

From the coast drive to the small pleasant settlement of Val de Arico (Lomo de Arico on some maps), 35km for Los Cristianos, and turn uphill in the centre of the town on a minor road signed 'Valle de Contador 7km'. Pass round the church, noting the distinctly odd tree, then follow the road steadily uphill for a couple of kilometres until a double hair pin bend is passed. Take the first right turn after this onto a dirt road which immediately splits into three, and follow the central branch. This rises bumpily past a half completed building (at least it looks half completed, despite the fact that it is occupied) then descends to several parking areas by a white building on the edge of the Lower Gorge. This building has been used in the recent past as a (primitive) climbing hut, especially by German climbers.

Note: DO NOT BLOCK ACCESS TO THE CULTIVATED LAND HERE. IF YOU DO YOU MAY FIND YOUR CAR HAS BEEN 'MOVED' ON YOUR RETURN!

The Lower Gorge is directly below and is described first. The Upper Gorge is 5 minutes' walk upstream and is described later.

THE LOWER GORGE

Only developed extensively in recent years the Lower Gorge is home to many steep, hard routes and a small selection of easier fare. Most of the best climbs are on the East Wall and so are in the sun in the afternoon. This may be an important factor if you want to get that all-important 'red point', or if your plane leaves tomorrow and you are determined to go home with a proper tropical tan! In the gorge there is some evidence of mining in the past, in the form of spoil heaps and bits of narrow gauge railways, and it has to be admitted that parts of the gorge do have the atmosphere of a quarry. Despite this much of the climbing is excellent and half an hour facing that glowing orb, high in the southern sky, should make up for any shortcomings in the setting.

Access

From the car parking follow a ramp that runs down into the gorge (heading upstream) then double back and descend a tricky little water chute (care required if damp), cross the stream bed and descend stone steps to the gorge bed. The climbs are described in seven separate sectors, firstly down the right bank (looking downstream) and then down the left bank. See overview plan for the location of the sectors.

THE RIGHT BANK

Note: All routes here are described from right to left.

1. Sector Oscuro
At the bottom of the stone steps is a small collection of climbs on the right side of the gorge, directly under the rickety-looking bridge, a shady setting for cool dudes.

MOSCAS PEGAJOSAS 6c (E3 6a) 7m
The tiny shallow groove at the foot of the steps has two bolt runners and a single bolt lower-off.

ZIPI 6c? 7m
A thin crack rising above a band of bubbly rock also has two bolt runners.

ZAPE 7b? 15m
Just to the left a second thin crack is followed onto the wall above.

ANALYSIS FINAL ** 7a+ (E5 6a) 22m
The first climb of any substance. Skate up the smooth lower section then head leftwards up the leaning wall above to lower-off right under the bridge. A popular pitch that is always well chalked.

Just left is a new route right under the bridge, climbing bubbly rock and pockets, then more steeply to the lower-off of the previous climb. No name is available, though it is *7b*.

BLACK DAY * 6c+ (E4 6a) 12m
The square pillar and bulging wall 5m left of the fall line from the bridge gives an interesting exercise in 'monkey-up-a-stick' climbing style.

Twenty metres further downstream is another new route, up a bubbly wall, crack and prow. No name or grade is known though it looks worthwhile and quite tough, possibly *7b*.

The final two climbs on this sector are situated above three small 'baths' filled with tepid water, perhaps the place to get your laundry done, especially as it's lovely drying weather.

MALDITA SEA MI SEURTE 6c (E3 5c) 18m
From the rim of the 'bath' clip the first bolt on the previous climb then trend to the right through the bulges and up a slab to a lower-off on the top right corner of the wall.

EL SENOR DE LA BESTIAS * 6b (E2 5c) 15m
Make an awkward move to get the first bolt clipped (cheating stone or a shoulder for the short?) then head straight up the steep rib via long reaches. Continue up the arête above with a delicate final move to the belay.

2. Sector Techos
A rather uninspiring set of climbs well spaced down the right side of the ravine. They do, however, have the advantage of being in the shade for most of the day.

Opposite where a scree/spoil slope almost closes the gorge is a bolted groove, of unknown grade and name. It appears dirty and vegetated and looks well worth avoiding.

Fifteen metres further downstream is a slightly more worthwhile offering.

LOS FRIKIS DEL MARTIZEZ 6b (E1 5b) 22m
An open groove leads via some suspect rock to the final tricky corner with the belays in the right wall.

Fifteen metres further downstream two routes exit from a large cave 8m up. This is reached by awkward, dirty climbing. Both routes are a bit of a hassle to strip; a stout second is called for.

ATRAPADO EN LA NOCHE * 7a+ (E5 6b) 18m
Cross the left side of the roof then continue up the impressive stepped prow above.

VACACION EN CASA * 6c+ (E4 6a) 18m
Take a lower line out of the cave to reach a ledge on the left side of the prow then climb the side wall to the lower-offs.

Twenty metres further downstream and opposite the smooth orange wall of the Sector Pepino are two bolt lines:

SIN PATA PALO 6b (E1 5c) 10m
The thin crack gives a short battle with one tricky clip.

TRAVELDEDOS * 7b+ (E6 6b) 15m
To the left is this climb that gets into the prominent cave and exits from this by crossing the large roof.

The only other routes on the right bank of the gorge are on the **3. SECTOR TUNNEL**, which is the blocky wall across the valley from the

SECTOR 7a (see below) rising above the water channel. There are half a dozen hard routes here but on our visit all approaches to the area appeared to be blocked by vicious vegetation of impressive proportions. Perhaps an abseil approach would be a good idea. For completeness the routes here are (from right to left in keeping with the rest of the right bank):

DJ GANLEGO 7a+
ME SOBRAN NEURONAS 7a
CHUMINITO FLAGELOSO 7a
GARIMBA A MEDIAS 6b

and some distance further downstream:

ON THE EDGE 7b+
ESTO ES UN ATRACO ?

THE LEFT BANK

Note: All routes here are described from left to right.

The descriptions now tackle the routes on the left bank (looking downstream) of the gorge. The first area on the left is the ever popular:

4. Sector Mirador
There is a solitary route right under the bridge at the access point for the Lower Gorge.

TORAN 7a (E5 6a) 15m
The thin crack and overhang leads to a lower-off right under the bridge.

Continuing downstream for a hundred metres or so is the main part of this sector, a set of impressive roofs and leaning walls. There are a number of excellent climbs here. The three routes on the far left are reached via a narrow ledge 3m off the ground.

SIN EXCESO DE PESO ** 7b (E5 6b) 15m
On the far left start at two metal plates bolted to the rock and climb the lower rib to a ledge and the tough leaning face above.

JOE PETA * 6c+ (E4 6a) 15m
Climb the crack in a corner, and the continuation crack above, to the belay of the previous route. The bolts are rather spaced so be bold, carry a couple of Friends, or top rope the route!

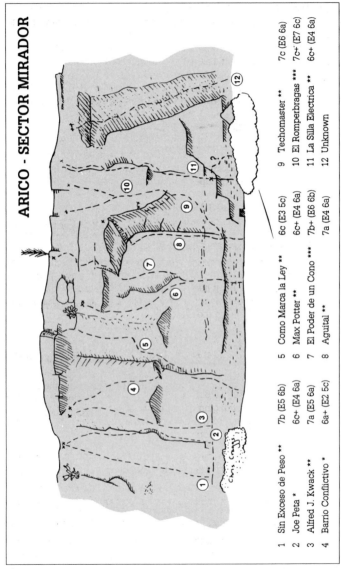

ARICO - SECTOR MIRADOR

1	Sin Exceso de Peso **	7b (E5 6b)	
2	Joe Peta *	6c+ (E4 6a)	
3	Alfred J. Kwack **	7a (E5 6a)	
4	Barrio Conflictivo *	6a+ (E2 5c)	
5	Como Marca la Ley **	6c (E3 5c)	
6	Max Potter **	6c+ (E4 6a)	
7	El Poder de un Cono ***	7b+ (E6 6b)	
8	Aguital **	7a (E4 6a)	
9	Techomaster **	7c (E6 6a)	
10	El Romperbragas ***	7c+ (E7 6c)	
11	La Silla Electrica **	6c+ (E4 6a)	
12	Unknown		

ALFRED J KWACK ** 7a (E5 6a) 15m
Climb the technical lower rib and the tough leaning pocketed wall above.
Worth doing for the name alone!

BARRIO CONFLICTIVO * 6a+ (E2 5c) 22m
The impressive hanging slab is approached up an easy corner crack, and
gained by a tricky pull (oh those pigeons). Head left across the slab to a ledge
then make a baffling final move to the big beefy belay bolt. The final move
was thought to be 7a by one Sheffield hot shot!

COMO MARCA LA LEY ** 6c (E3 5c) 24m
Climb the easy crack as for the previous route then traverse out onto the wall
(crux) before following pockets to a break. Pull leftwards over the roof and
sprint up the final crack on superb finger jams.

MAX POTTER ** 6c+ (E4 6a) 22m
Pull over the roofs on the right with difficulty and trend left up the wall to
a steep hanging slab. Cross this and make a crux lunge round the capping
roof to reach the belay bolts.

EL PODER DE UN CONO *** 7b+ (E6 6b) 24m
Start as for the last climb but head straight up the wall. Pull over the bulge
onto a hanging flake then swing right before powering up to ledges. Reach
the belay by a detour out to the right.

AGUITAL ** 7a (E4 6a) 22m
The impressive hanging roof crack is followed by powerful undercutting to
a lower-off just around the lip.

TECHOMASTER ** 7c (E6 6a) 18m
Start to the right of the hanging roof of the previous climb and head up to
the roofs before trending leftwards below the lip by sustained strenuous
climbing on large but often sloping holds.

EL ROMPEBRAGAS *** 7c+ (E7 6c) 25m
Climb up to the band of roofs as for the previous climb then move right and
pull over to reach rock of a saner angle. Up this trending leftwards to a lower-
off on top of the wall. There is also a more direct finish to the climb at 7b+.

LA SILLA ELECTRICA ** 6c+ (E4 6a) 22m
Use the knotted rope (or follow the new bolts in from the right?) to gain the
impressive groove line and follow it as it cuts through bulges in a most
impressive fashion.

193

To the right is a line starting up the immensely steep side wall and continuing on over roofs galore. It looks very hard!

5. Sector Pepino

An extensive sector with a fine collection of routes, a good number of which are very hard. For normal mortals there is a small number of more reasonable offerings scattered amongst this patch of 'big boys' territory. The first routes are located at the top of a scree/spoil bank by a projecting railway line where a large block is jammed under a roof. Three climbs begin from the square recess behind the jammed boulder, and this is reached by a short awkward scramble.

CHULO DE TURNO * 7a+ (E4 6b) 18m
A bit of a 'one move wonder' but what a move. Climb the face just to the right of the left arête of the recess to reach the thin diagonal crack that splits the roof and extemporise a way past this to the single belay bolt located in a large semi-detached block!!!

The next two climbs start over the roof at the back of the square recess.

LA BASCA ATACA DURO 6c+ (E3 6b) 12m
Pull over the roof and climb the straightforward wall to a perplexing sequence at the change in angle. Try to clip the belay bolt before you grab it!

AGARRAMELA BIEN * 6c (E3 6a) 12m
Pull over the right side of the overhang and climb the pockety wall to a tricky bulge. It is very tempting to bridge to the arête on the right here, though the puritanical will press on smartly to the belay.

PASION POR EL RUDIO * 5+ (E1 5b) 15m
The crack that bounds the recess on the right leads to ledges and the lower-off for the next climb. Gear required.

To the right of and below the large jammed boulder is a bolt belay in a corner to stop your second falling down the unstable slope. Two routes start here:

FANTASAMAGORIA ** 6b+ (E2 5c) 15m
Climb an awkward arête and slab to the cave then pull over the centre of the roof and follow good jugs up the wall until it is possible to get around the left arête. A short steep wall leads to ledges and the lower-off.

ARICO -
SECTOR PEPINO

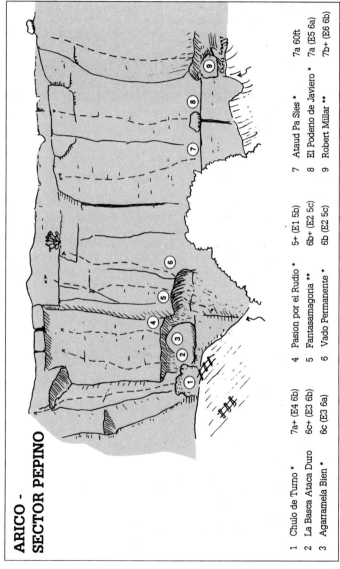

1	Chulo de Turno *	7a+ (E4 6b)
2	La Basca Ataca Duro	6c+ (E3 6b)
3	Agarramela Bien *	6c (E3 6a)

4	Pasion por el Rudio *	5+ (E1 5b)
5	Fantasamagoria **	6b+ (E2 5c)
6	Vado Permanente *	6b (E2 5c)

7	Ataud Pa Sies *	7a 60ft
8	El Poderio de Javiero *	7a (E5 6a)
9	Robert Millar **	7b+ (E6 6b)

VADO PERMANENTE * 6b (E2 5c) 15m
Follow the previous climb to the cave then pull over the right side of the bulges and follow the bolt protected crack (nice idea) to ledges with *in situ* cacti and belay bolts.

To the right is an area of vegetation and then a wall that rises above a horizontal ledge with a conspicuous boulder seated on it. There are two climbs that start off the ledge and they are reached by a short scramble. The left-hand route is:

ATAUD PA SIES * 7a (E5 6a) 18m
Climb the left trending line of pockets.

EL PODERIO DE JAVIERIO * 7a (E5 6a) 18m
Start behind the block and head up the gently leaning wall.

To the right is an impressive red wall rising above a grey scree slope topped by a horizontal cave, whilst around the arête to the right is more impressively steep and smooth rock featuring a prominent curving groove. Further right again is a series of hardly less impressive corners and overhangs. There are many of the island's hardest climbs here and some of the pitches are rather crowded. The descriptions below and the diagram attempt to sort these out and I apologise in advance if you end up on an *8a* instead of a *6b+*!

The leaning wall above the cave has two lines on it:

ROBERT MILLAR ** 7b+ (E6 6b) 18m
The steeply leaning left side of the wall is started from a block and gives a tough pitch.

JALA POR EL RESUELLO ** 7c+ (E7 6c) 18m
The right-hand climb cross the roof of the cave and climbing the centre of the wall. It is a notch harder than Bob.

Two climbs are based around the blunt arête that bounds the right side of the wall.

VUELO DE TRIPI ** 8a+ (E7 7a) 18m
Take the lower arête to the bolt-on hold then trend left to climb the left side of the upper arête.

SENSACION DE PEPINO ** 7b (E5 6b) 18m
Take the lower arête to the bolt-on hold then the right side of the upper section.

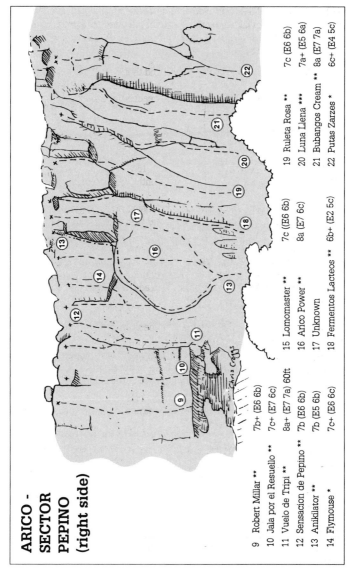

ARICO -
SECTOR
PEPINO
(right side)

9   Robert Millar **   7b+ (E6 6b)
10 Jala por el Resuello **   7c+ (E7 6c)
11 Vuelo de Tripi **   8a+ (E7 7a) 60ft
12 Sensacion de Pepino **   7b (E6 6b)
13 Aniklator **   7b (E5 6b)
14 Flymouse *   7c+ (E6 6c)

15 Lomomaster **   7c ((E6 6b)
16 Anco Power **   8a (E7 6c)
17 Unknown
18 Fermentos Lacteos **   6b+ (E2 5c)

19 Ruleta Rosa **   7c (E6 6b)
20 Luna Llena ***   7a+ (E5 6a)
21 Bubangos Cream **   8a (E7 7a)
22 Putas Zarzes *   6c+ (E4 5c)

The next five climbs start under the smooth orange shield of rock to the right and find their different ways up the impressive rock above.

ANIKILATOR ** 7b (E5 6b) 22m
Trend left following the curving crack up the lower wall then continue up the leaning wall and enter the steep sustained groove above.

FLYMOUSE * 7c+ (E6 6c) 22m
A finish through the bulges to the right of the final corner of the previous route is a tough number.

LOMOMASTER ** 7c (E6 6b) 25m
The natural line of the wall starts as for the previous two climbs then traverses to the right following the curving weakness below the head wall, eventually to enter and climb the hanging corner on the right.

ARICO POWER ** 8a (E7 6c) 22m
Start under the centre of the wall and climb it to the break then press on up the smooth wall to the left of the final corner of the previous route.

Starting in the same place but trending right to climb the smoothest-looking rock in the area and the hanging prow above. An unrecorded route, it looks at least *8b*.

To the right the sheerest section of the face is bounded by a right-facing flake crack followed by the excellent:

FERMENTOS LACTEOS ** 6b+ (E2 5c) 22m
Climb soft grey rock then follow the flake crack around the arête before swinging back left and making a powerful pull into the continuation corner. Finish more easily.

RULETA ROSA ** 7c (E6 6b) 22m
The orange tilted wall and overhanging groove to the right give a bit of a tussle, even for the experienced.

LUNA LLENA *** 7a+ (E5 6a) 22m
To the right is an impressive flake crack trending right below a bevy of bulges. Climb straight up a subsidiary crack to the flake and attack this with conviction. A gem but not a route for people who don't like laybacking.

BUBANGOS CREAM ** 8a (E7 7a) 22m
Starting from a boulder, climb the leaning prow and then press on up the

Graham Parkes laybacking twixt light and shade on
FERMENTOS LACTEOS ** (6b+ E25c), Lower Gorge, Arico

horrendously thin overhanging crack above. Perhaps it's a good idea not to cut your finger nails before trying this one.

PUTAS ZARZES * 6c+ (E4 5c) 22m
The right wall of a deep corner is climbed following a crack system to a deep horizontal break, then power on through the bulges above.

6. Sector Cicatriz

Continuing further downstream away from the crowds, the gorge opens out again to reveal this sector with four climbs, the first of which starts in a red cave.

PONTE EN POSE * 7a+ (E5 6b) 18m
Climb out of the cave and head up the grey leaning wall and final tilted prow.

Further downstream past prickly pears and other exotic scrub are three routes, the first of which climbs the wall left of an obvious central arête.

NUNCA MAS * 7a+ (E5 6b) 18m
Climb the tilted wall left of the hanging bramble bush and continue over a small overhang to twin lower-offs just below some ledges.

MUCHA FIBRA Y POCA TETA * 7b (E6 6b) 18m
The blunt arête is followed to ledges then the wall above leads to a wire cable lower-off, on a level with a giant prickly pear.

LOS CICATRIZ ** 7c+ (E7 6c) 18m
The wall to the right again gives quality face climbing trending to the right to reach a double bolt lower-off.

7. Sector 7A

To the right is an extensive area of tall 'bamboo' type grass and the next climbs are reached by walking around the right side of this, to reach a series of smart grey walls. This is the final sector on the left bank of the gorge and if you operate at the appropriate grade the Sector 7a is well worth a visit to get away from the crowds. The first route climbs the wall at the far left of the area.

BALATE STRON * 7a (E5 6a) 25m
Follow a thin crack up the lower wall then head leftward up the head wall passing a small roof 'en route'.

Five metres to the right is a protruding pillar with a crack running up its centre. There are routes to either side of the crack and any keen traditionalist

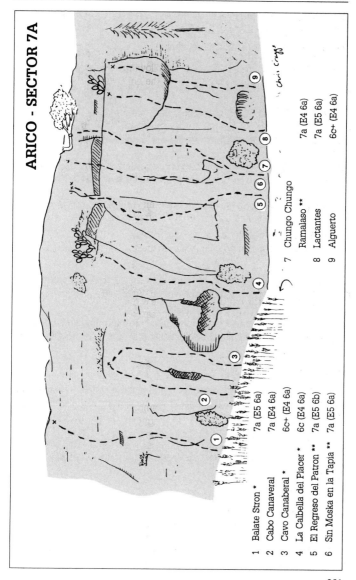

ARICO - SECTOR 7A

Chris Craggs

1   Balate Stron *   7a (E5 6a)
2   Cabo Canaveral   7a (E4 6a)
3   Cavo Canaberal *   6c+ (E4 6a)
4   La Calbella del Placer *   6c (E4 6a)
5   El Regreso del Patron **   7a (E5 6b)
6   Sin Moska en la Tapia **   7a (E5 6a)
7   Chungo Chungo
    Ramalaso **   7a (E4 6a)
8   Lactantes   7a (E5 6a)
9   Alguerto   6c+ (E4 6a)

201

could claim a new route here.

CABO CANAVERAL ** 7a (E4 6a) 18m
The left-hand line gives interesting climbing.

CAVO CANABERAL * 6c+ (E4 6a) 18m
The right-hand line leads to the same lower-off in a similar vein.

To the right is an hourglass-shaped pillar with its left side formed by a cave.
LA CALBELLA DEL PLACER * 6c (E4 6a) 18m
The right arête of the hourglass-shaped pillar leads to a belay right under a giant hanging prickly pear. How did they get to the top of the route to equip it? This is supposed to be the easiest route in the area, but is it?

Right of where the bamboo ends is a red shield split by a thin crack. This is

EL REGRESO DEL PATRON ** 7a (E5 6b) 20m
The excellent steep wall is sustained and thin; the corner above is not.

The next two climbs start on the wall to the right of an open corner, directly below a horizontal roof near the top of the cliff.
SIN MOSKA EN LA TAPIA ** 7a (E5 6a) 20m
Trend left up the lower wall following a thin crack and then do battle with the bottom-shaped overhang above (extension wire cable on bolt) and then the easier wall.

CHUNGO CHUNGO RAMALASO ** 7a (E4 6a) 20m
Start in the same place but swing right and make a couple of perplexing moves up the wall to easier climbing over bulges. Lower-off the *in situ* slings around the horizontal tree.

LACTANTES 7a (E5 6a) 18m
Begin just to the left of a cave/hollow and climb the wall trending right, through a bulging section.

ALGUERTO 6c+ (E4 6a) 18m
The final offering climbs the arête. Trend right up the lower wall, pull through a bulge and continue up the arête above.

In front of this final area are some large boulders with two short climbs on them:

LA LEGIA DE UN LOCO 7b+ (E4 6c) 7m
The short and very sharp right-hand line.

SEMEN RECICLADO 6b+ (E2 6a) 7m
The hardly more worthwhile line facing downstream.

THE UPPER GORGE

The Upper Gorge is more open and less imposing than the Lower Gorge and is home to some more amenable routes. A quick walk through the gorge may leave you 'underwhelmed' but get a few of the climbs under your belt and the place will grow on you. The climbs are described up the left bank looking upstream first, then up the right bank, and again the whole area is divided into sectors; see the overview diagram.

From the car park descend into the stream bed and walk uphill for about 5 minutes. The first small collection of routes is on the right side at the Sector Corazon de Metal (see below). Opposite this is a boulder with a steep face and a bolt belay on top. Don't worry, things get better. Continuing upstream a pipe crosses the valley and the first routes on the left bank are 50m beyond this.

THE LEFT BANK

Note: All routes here are described from left to right.

1. Sector Pena del Lunes
BOULDER 5 (VS 5b) 3m
The first route is a one bolt, one move wonder. Not the best advert for Arico!

NELSON MANDELE 5+ (HVS 5b) 6m
The marginally more worthwhile climb just to the right. A two bolt, two move wonder.

Twenty metres upstream is a much more worthwhile set of routes starting from a flat ledge reached by a short scramble.

ESPOLON DEL RAMPA * 6a+ (E2 5b) 12m
The left edge of the wall gives a pleasant pitch.

PENA DEL LUNES * 6b (E2 5b) 12m
Race up the bulging wall just left of the central thin crack.

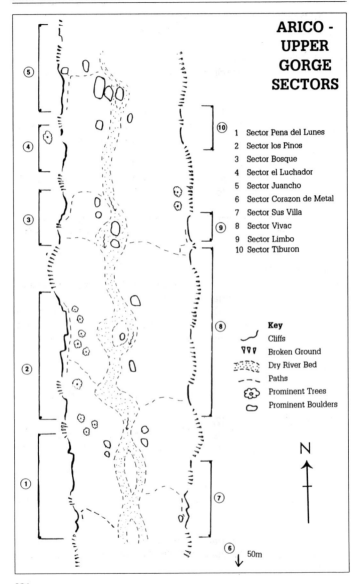

ARICO -
UPPER
GORGE
SECTORS

1 Sector Pena del Lunes
2 Sector los Pinos
3 Sector Bosque
4 Sector el Luchador
5 Sector Juancho
6 Sector Corazon de Metal
7 Sector Sus Villa
8 Sector Vivac
9 Sector Limbo
10 Sector Tiburon

Key

Cliffs
Broken Ground
Dry River Bed
Paths
Prominent Trees
Prominent Boulders

N

50m

FISURA DEL PALIZA 6c+ (E4 6a) 12m
The thin crack requires the placing of gear; strange indeed.

PLACA DEL FRIKI * 6b+ (E2 5c) 12m
The flat wall on the right is climbed past a series of horizontal breaks linked by tricky moves.

NO HAY PIEDA PA LOS GODOS 6c (E4 6a) 15m
Climb the thin crack in the wall to the right then trend left, following a line of pockets with difficulty, to a lower-off on the left arête.

WIRITO SANTO *** 6c (E3 6a) 18m
Around to the right is a grotty corner and in the left wall of this is a line of big bolts. You are unlikely to get lost on this one!

To the right of the corner is a *NEW ROUTE* up a wall and slab, to belay bolts, and then it trends right again up to and over a roof. No grade is known but the climb looks good and not too taxing.

2. Sector Los Pinos
An area well worth a visit with its central section being formed by a series of smart walls behind an attractive stand of tall pine trees. A small terrace in front of these provides the best camping spot in the gorge. However the first three routes in the sector are on an isolated buttress 50m downstream from the pine trees. The buttress is distinguished by a line of overhangs across its base.

NEW ROUTE * 6b (E1 6a) 12m
Pass the first roof with considerable difficulty then trend right to cross the second band of overhangs before moving right again to reach the lower-off.

NEW ROUTE 6a (E1 5b) 12m
Enter the central groove by using a dubious jammed flake, and continue to the roof on more suspect rock. Swing right then pull back left to reach the belay bolt.

ME EMPALO UN PALO 6c+ (E4 6a) 12m
The side wall of the buttress has a small roof and proves to be a tough little cookie.

Fifty metres further upstream and behind the stand of pine trees is the main part of this sector. On the left is a roofed-in cave feature, home to three climbs.

MI ABUELITA LA MALDITA * 6b+ (E2 6a) 10m
The steep sharp pocketed wall to the left of the cave.

UF UF * 6c+ (E4 6a) 10m
The wall just right of the right edge of the cave is even sharper and steeper.

DISTORSION TOTAL * 5+ (E1 5b) 10m
The wall to the right is rather more pleasant; at least the holds are larger.

ACEITUNAS 6c (E4 6a) 10m
The short steep wall around to the right.

Directly behind the three largest pines is a fine steep slab, home to two good routes:

PAPEO CHACHI ** 6a+ (E2 5b) 18m
The left side of the slab and rib above gives excellent sustained climbing.

PAPEO CHUNGO ** 6b (E2 5c) 18m
The crack in the centre of the slab and the rib above gives another worthwhile pitch.

Note: Both previous routes used to share a common lower-off at the top of the slab. I have not done the short extensions up the ribs above the respective bolt ladders, so they may be tougher than the grades given here. *PAPEO CHUNGO* has a fixed maillion attached to the first bolt on the head wall, so it is possible to avoid the final steepening if it proves too much.

To the right and up ledges is a short tilted wall facing in towards the pine trees.

DISTORSION CRANEAL 6c (E3 6a) 7m
The left-hand line using some 'constructed' holds.

McNESIO 6a (E1 5c) 7m
On the right-hand line Mother Nature has been a bit more generous.

A narrow path continues around an arête to reach a fine wall with a prominent bird-limed hole at 5m. This is climbed by:

CONTROL MENTAL ** 6b+ (E3 6a) 18m
Boulder up to the hole then climb the steep wall before trending away to the right to where slabbier moves gain the belay. Well worth seeking out.

PUMIKI EL PRESO * 6c (E3 6a) 12m
Continue around the next arête to find a line of green bolts running up a scooped wall and over a roof.

EL PODER CHICA * 6c (E3 6a) 12m
Further to the right just before the cliff disappears into the brush is a flat wall and sharp arête fully equipped with shiny new bolts.

From here there is no way on through the impenetrable brush, even though the Sector Bosque is not far away, so it is necessary to return to the pines and then to the gorge floor.

3. Sector Bosque
Opposite *SECTOR LIMBO* and to the left of some large blocks in the stream bed is the *SECTOR BOSQUE*, reached by following a narrow path through the trees.

GRADO KENIATA 6b+ (E3 5c) 12m
Starting from ledges up on the left, climb the straightforward lower section then follow the bolts rightwards up the steepening wall above.

MAKI NAVAJA * 6a+ (E2 5b) 15m
Start at the point where the path emerges from the trees. Climb an arête then a curving flake on big holds, and finally the wall above.

The next collection of climbs can be reached by following the vague suggestion of a path along the foot of the cliff, past caves and through trees, though it is easier to use another path that starts a little further upstream. The first three climbs start from a comfortable ledge 7m up, most easily reached from the right.

ANARQUIA EN LA PLANETA 7b (E5 6b) 10m
The left-hand line.

LA VIUDA DEL BOSQUE 6c (E3 6a) 10m
The right-hand line.

LA VIA DEL MEN 7b+ (E6 6c) 10m
The route on the pocketed side wall. It is possible to start as for the previous route and to extend the climb, and claim yourself a *

RELIJATE PRIMO ** 7a+ (E5 6a) 18m
An excellent outing up the arête of the wall. The easy square rib leads to

more dramatic territory (and a gripper clipper) above. From ledges move right to a final tricky move to the lower-off.

To the right, and behind a large tree, are two routes that climb the same piece of rock.

EL ESCUDO DEL GUERRERO * 7a+ (E5 6a) 15m
Plenty of pockets and a bulge thrown in for good measure.

ALUCINA CON MI VERCINA * 6c (E4 6a) 15m
An easier variation on the same theme, just to the right.

ALGUIEN PALMO ** 6b (E2 5b) 15m
At the point where the regular path meets the cliff face is a steep wall. Jug pulling through bulges and thinner moves above combine to make a fine climb.

LA PUTA DEL BOSQUE 6b+ (E2 5c) 12m
The wall on the right is climbed trending leftwards, and just for a change all the holds are pockets.

4. Sector el Luchador
The next sector on the left bank is a set of walls situated under a large pine tree on the cliff top, and reached up a steep dusty path leading to good ledges below the wall.

SUPER LOPEZ * 6b (E2 5c) 12m
On a square-cut tower trending slightly right to begin with, then straight up the centre of the pillar above.

To the right is a grotty corner (any takers) and right again is a slab.

EL CONTRATO DEL ZAPATERO ** 6b+ (E2 5c) 12m
Climb the slab and the sustained rib above.

EL LUCHADOR ** 6c+ (E4 6a) 12m
Climb the lower slab just to the right then step out right onto the face and follow the arête above to the top.

DESEQUILIBRIO GANSO * 7a+ (E5 6a) 12m
Climb the wall, passing the bulging section by strenuous use of a drilled pocket, to a lower-off beneath the rather dangerous-looking block overhang at the top of the cliff.

ELEMENTO BARRIADA * 6b+ (E3 5c) 12m
Climb the wall trending rightwards, crossing a diagonal crack and continuing up the steeper wall above.

SERVA VIRGEN 6b+ (E2 5c) 10m
The steep lower wall leads past three bolts to tape belays on the rim. Abseil off or leave the old karabiner you have been carrying for just such an event.

Further up-stream is a fine red face with a diagonal line of pockets running across it from left to right.

COMPRATE UN FRELAX ** 7a+ (E4 6a) 18m
Climb the uninspiring corner then cross the steep face on spaced pockets to a break and a final tricky move to the chains.

DOS TALEGOS Y MEDIO * 6c+ (E4 6a) 12m
Around the corner to the right climb the bulging wall to the right of a straight crack, passing a pair of 'eyes' to a final slabby section.

5. Sector Juancho
Continuing up the stream bed the way ahead is blocked by a series of huge boulders. A small 'tunnel' leads through these and the Sector Jauncho is located on the left at this point. On the large boulders that effectively block the valley below the centre of the *SECTOR JUANCHO* are two short climbs.

LA CURVA DEL GATO 6b (E1 5c) 6m
The short sharp arête that faces upstream.

LAGARTO JUANCHO 7c (E6 6c) 10m
The drilled pockets up the underside of the biggest boulder.

Once through the 'tunnel' a path leads left behind trees to a block on the ground. At this point there are three routes up a steep wall bounded by clean cut cracks to left and right.

PA LOS POLLOS * 6c (E4 6a) 12m
Start at a bolt belay on a ledge and climb the fine sustained crack to twinned lower-offs on the right. The bad news is you will need a rack of Friends, though for once there is no arguing about the validity of a UK grade.

The wall to the right has three worthwhile climbs for those who enjoy tortuous pocket pulling on 'improved' holds. Good practice for the climbing wall, perhaps!

MOCO LINE ** 7c+ (E6 6c) 12m
The left-hand line proves to be very hard.

PINZATELO BIEN ** 7b+ (E6 6b) 12m
The slightly easier and rather better central line.

COMISARIO ANTIDOPING * 7b+ (E6 6b) 12m
The least worthwhile route right again.

"OYE FRUDIS" * 6a (E2 5b) 12m
Another route to get you ready for back home. Carry a rack. Do you think the idea will ever catch on? Fortunately the lower-offs are in place so there is no need to do battle with the unsavoury territory at the top of the cliff!

ALGUIEN VOLO SOBRE EL CHOZO DEL CUCA ** 8a (E7 6c) 15m
This route climbs the steeply overhanging orange prow above the point where the approach path disappears into the trees, but only by the very talented.

DULCE REVOLUTION * 6b+ (E3 5c) 12m
A worthwhile climb up the lower wall on the right to the base of a corner and then continuing up the right wall above.

To the right is a massive roof 12m up with a good-looking jamming crack (unclimbed) running up to it. In the right wall of the corner is:
NASIO PA' NA' * 7b+ (E6 6b) 12m
Just when you thought it was all over, more harsh pocket pulling.

Right of the roof is an open groove that could do with a wash and brush up (any takers) and right again is a wall peppered with a strange collection of paired holes.
SUELTAME GRIFA * 6b (E2 5c) 10m
Climb the wall by a series of 'poke its eyes out' moves, past four bolts to a lower-off.

Fifty metres further upstream to the left of a small 'penicle', and to either side of a corner are the final two routes.
"AY CHIQUILLA" * 7a+ (E5 6a) 10m
The wall on the left requires gear. In all probability the only gear needed is a top rope!

SUMINISTROS CORONAS 6b (E2 5c) 10m
The bolted wall on the right past a flake to a lower-off on the lip of the roof.

THE RIGHT BANK

Note: All routes here are described from right to left.

6. Sector Corazon de Metal
One hundred and seventy-five metres upstream from the parking area is a small sector on the right at the point where an old path zigzags out of the gorge. It consists of three rounded buttresses separated by two scruffy corners. There are four short routes here.

DERECHO 4 (VS 4b) 7m
The right-hand line has two golden bolts, a covering of dust and creaky holds.

CENTRO 5 (HVS 5a) 10m
The second line follows a tricky shallow crack left of a grotty corner, then trends left to a belay. The lower section is easier away to the right but that's hardly the point!

IZQUIERDA 5 (HVS 5b) 10m
Pull over a bulge on a block and climb the wall rightwards on poor pockets until better holds lead away to the right to the bolt belay of the previous climb.

CORAZON DE METAL 6a+ (E1 5c) 10m
The left-hand route climbs a barrel-shaped buttress via a couple of taxing sequences. Bridging across to the right is most certainly taboo.

7. Sector Sus Villa
A pleasant sunny sector that is always popular. It essentially takes the form of an open bay with a sharp central arête and a large block in front of the wall to the right.

CASCA LA BASCA A LA LASCA ** 6a+ (E2 5b) 15m
The right wall of the recess gives a mildly pumpy pitch on good holds except for the last couple of moves.

BATRIACIO 6b+ (E2 6a) 10m
Climb the smooth wall to the left of the blocky corner, and the bulge above, to a quick 'dyno' for the wire cable belay.

SUS VILLA * 6b (E2 5c) 12m
The right side of the arête is agreeably technical, especially if you like pocket pulling. The slab above is easier.

NO HAY COLEGA SIN TACO 5 (VS 4c) 10m
Around to the left of the central arête the short wall has generous holds.

EL TERROR DE LAS CHIQUILLAS 5 (VS 4c) 10m
The left wall of the corner is once again pleasantly unremarkable.

LA VENGANZA DEL GODO 6b+ (E2 5c) 12m
Fifty metres further upstream and just left of a prominent tree. Climb the leaning wall to a shabby lower-off in the summit block.

8. Sector Vicac
Continuing upstream the next sector consists of a spaced series of discrete buttresses. The first one is an orange wall split by a diagonal crack, and is home to three routes:

HONGUITOS PELIGROSOS * 6b+ (E2 5c) 12m
The wall on the right has some wobbly holds and the bulges above are passed leftwards to easier ground. Limestone climbers will try to avoid the crucial gnarly jam; gritstone climbers will relish it.

FLIPA FLOPA * 6b (E2 6a) 12m
The wall just to the left has a nasty move passing the second bolt and is much easier above.

PETA DE KILO * 6a (E1 5c) 12m
A slippery and reachy lower wall on the left leads to juggy bulges climbed trending rightwards to a belay shared with the previous route.

Fifty metres further upstream is the next route, just to the right of the point where a tall pine tree is growing close to the rock at the foot of the cliff.

NO HAY NIVEL 5+ * (E1 5b) 12m
A pleasant lower wall then bulges lead to the lower-off.

Twenty metres further upstream is another attractive red face (not your partner's sunburnt one), steepening as it rises:

NOCHES DE CORAL * 6b (E2 5c) 12m
Start on the left in a scoop and follow the green bolts up and right to a steep finale.

The final three routes in the Sector Vivac are to be found another 50m or so further upstream. All climb good rock reached in each case by dirty scrambling.

TODOS CON POLI 6a+ (E1 5b) 12m
Start on a ledge and climb a corner crack or the wall immediately to its left to a bulge with the belay on its lip.

TRIPA DE CERDO 6c (E3 6a) 12m
Reached by dirty ledges, climb the flat wall and then the bulges.

EL ENANITO IMPOTENTE 6a+ (E2 5b) 12m
A short distance to the left dirty scrambling leads to a ledge by a block. Climb the left edge of the flat wall to a lower-off below ledges above.

8. Sector Limbo
To the left is a short red wall, with many well chalked pockets and reached by a short scramble up a dusty corner. All the routes are sharp.

DE AQUI PAL LIMBO 7a (E4 6b) 10m
The clean wall and blunt rib above the approach path.

Scramble awkwardly leftwards over some large blocks to reach the rest of the climbs. The foot of the wall here is an excellent sunbathing spot; just watch the spiky plants.

BERBERECHOS AL NATURAL * 6c+ (E4 6a) 10m
A flat wall on small pockets leads to a leaning section and onto a belay shared with the last route.

NO LLEGUES TARDE 7a (E4 6b) 10m
Past a nasty-looking (and unclimbed) off-width is another smooth pocketed wall.

MADIA LA COCODA 6c (E3 6a) 7m
Another (you guessed it) smooth pocketed wall behind the fine tree.

9. Sector Tiburon
Continuing upstream some large boulders block the way. Just past these is an attractive golden wall on the right side of the gorge.

LOS JURONES DE LA OROTAVA 7a+ (E5 6a) 12m
Pass round behind cacti and climb the centre of the leaning wall and then the thin groove.

RAPIDO COMO UN TIBURON 7a (E4 6a) 12m
Twenty metres further left at a prominent hole near the top of the buttress are two routes. This is the right-hand line, climbing diagonally rightwards across the wall with a thin move (best done 'rapidly like a shark') to reach the roof, before moving right again to the lower-off.

TRANKI COMO UN BERBERECHO ** 6b+ (E3 5c) 12m
Tackle the left side of the wall by a crack through bulges and then the wall above, "steady like a cockle!"

The last route on this side of the gorge is some distance further upstream past large boulders and some pine trees.
PICO VENA * 6b (E2 5c) 12m
Start from a ledge and climb a prominent beak, and the wall above.

Anyone who has managed to get this far can consider themselves a true Arico aficionado and head for a couple of days on the beach. You deserve it.

According to the local topo there is one other area at Arico, the *SECTOR DE LOS NARANJOS* and this is supposed to be located 3 kilometers from the town of Arico, along a dirt track that takes a left turn off the road to the Upper and Lower Gorges. I have explored the most obvious of these but failed to locate the cliff. The topo opposite is included for completeness just in case you manage to stumble across the place.

OTHER AREAS

There is a lot of rock on Tenerife and much of it is of climbable quality. Apart from the two main areas of Arico and Las Canadas, I am aware of four other areas that have seen some development, though it is quite possible that there are many more. These four are described in anticlockwise direction starting at '9:00' with Guia d'Isora.

GUIA D'ISORA

An extensive face with only minimal development at the moment. The cliff consists of a high and broad south-facing wall of excellent red rock overlooking one of the many dry ravines, or barrancos, that dissect much of

SECTOR DE LOS NARANJOS

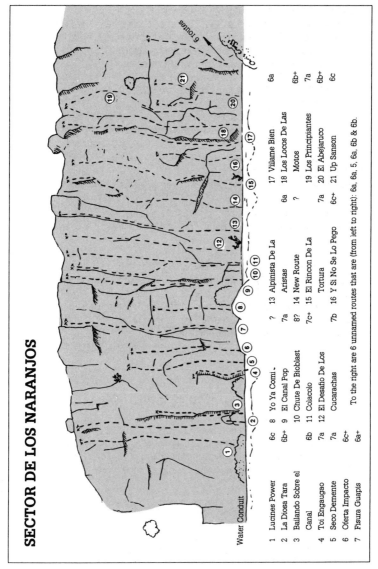

Water Conduit

1	Lucmes Power	6c	
2	La Diosa Tara	6b+	
3	Bailando Sobre el Canal		
4	Toi Engaugao	6b	
5	Seco Demente	7a	
6	Oferta Impacto	7a	
7	Fisura Guapis	6c+	
		6a+	

8	Yo Ya Comi-	?
9	El Canal Pop	7a
10	Chute De Bioblast	8?
11	Colacolo	7c+
12	El Desafio De Los Cucarachas	7a
13	Alpinista De La Aristas	7b
14	New Route	
15	El Rincon De La Tortura	
16	Y Si No Se Lo Pego	

17	Villame Bien	6a
18	Los Locos De Las Motos	6a
		?
19	Los Principiantes	
20	El Abejaruco	7a
21	Up Sanson	6c+
		6b+
		7a
		6b+
		6c

To the right are 6 unnamed routes that are (from left to right): 6a, 6a, 5, 6a, 6b & 6b.

the island. The limited parking for the cliff is reached from the road that runs between Guia d'Isora and Adeje. Two and a half kilometres from Guia, between two tunnels, are two narrow roads both turning inland. The first one is signed El Jara, and the cliff is located up the other one, hidden just round a bend when northbound, opposite a new bus shelter. Follow the road very steeply uphill through the tiny settlement of Acojeja, until stopped by a barrier. Restricted parking is available on the roadside here; have some consideration.

The cliff is visible from the car and is reached in about 20 minutes. Pass through the barrier and after 50m follow an old track that slants down into the dry river bed on the right. From the river bed head straight up the hill opposite to pick up a vague track that slants up to the right through the cacti (occasional cairns) to arrive on the ridge at a stony area about 50m above a prominent 3m high cairn. At this point a well marked mule track heads up the gorge and passes below all of the cliffs.

The first route climbs a deep roofed-in corner with a hand crack in its back.

POLLO A LA BRASA * 6a+ (E2 5b) 22m
Start off a ledge and follow the sustained corner, through a large roof, to a lower-off in the left wall. A good climb if you like fist-cracks and off-widths.

Fifty metres to the right is an attractive slabby rib starting from a ledge above the path:

QUE BANITA SUR MIS NINAS * 5 (E1 5b) 18m
The rib gives a better and harder pitch than initial appearances might otherwise suggest.

Fifty metres right is a steep grey pillar.

VOY PAL MORO * 6c (E4 6a) 15m
A steep start leads to marginally easier terrain above.

Fifty metres further right again and at a higher level is an attractive steep red wall with two prominent cracks splitting it neatly into thirds.
Starting near the left edge of the wall is:

PETER PUNK ** 6c (E4 6a) 22m
The lower wall gives fine sustained climbing, though the runout final section on slightly worrying rock rather spoils the climb.

BAZUKA PUNK *** 7c (E6 6b) 22m
The intricate and sustained central pillar gives a pitch of both high quality

C.C on TIRA DE CADENA *** 6a (E1 5b), Guia d'Isora

and high standard, with gradually escalating difficulty.

TIRA DE CADENA *** 6a (E1 5b) 22m
Tenerife's answer to many a gritstone crack line. Slam in the jams and keep truckin'.

Eighty metres further to the right is an attractive broad pillar with two climbs:
COMANDO 25 *** 7a+ (E5 6b) 25m
The front face of the pillar. Excellent sustained climbing.

EL PODE DEL INVASOR ** 6c (E4 6a) 25m
Just to the right the steep pocketed lower wall leads to an enjoyably intricate slab above.

Forty metres further right is a deep corner, home to a couple of longer climbs, possibly *TORRO P'AL BORO 7a* and the two pitch *AMNESIA TRANSCENDENTAL 6b+, 6c+*. Look for the names on the rock. Right again the cliff becomes much more impressive as a series of majestic smooth walls, possible home to an *8a* and *8a+* reported in Desnivel some time ago. No further details known. The rocks continue rightwards for miles. Can you spare a week or two?

LA CATEDRAL

On the final section of the drive to Las Canadas a series of towers and spires away on the left may catch the attention of any mountain climber worth his salt. The most elegant of these is the 130m high Dru-shaped peak of La Catedral which is home to about a dozen routes in a very traditional mode. Parking is possible on the roadside just before it begins to rise up towards Las Canadas and the west face of the peak can be reached by a 20 minute walk across the shimmering ash desert. It is also possible to descend the steep loose terrain from the Mirador at the Roques de Garcia to reach the east face but there is always the problem of the walk back out.

On close acquaintance much of La Catedral is composed of amazing 'Devil's Causeway' like basalt columns, many of them of impressive proportions. A topo available from the climbing shop in Santa Cruz (see appendix) has some rather sketchy topos of the routes here. For completeness I include diagrams and grades of the best-looking routes on both faces; positions of stances are approximate. Take a full rack, double ropes, possibly hard hats, and definitely some care. Any more detailed descriptions would

LA CATEDRAL - WEST FACE

1 El Pet   5, 3+, 4+, 4
2 Collado Direct   6c, 5, 5+, 6b
3 Via Subirana   5, 5+
4 Via del Techo   5+, A3 & 5, 4+
5 Via la Bella y
   Graciosa Moza   6, 4, 6, 4
6 Via del Viento   4, 5-, 4

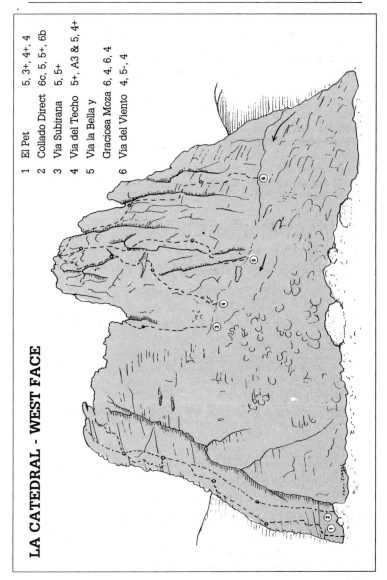

219

be gratefully received. Routes are listed from left to right. Descent from the summit is by two long abseils down the south ridge of the mountain.

The West Face

On the subsidiary tower on the far left side of the face:

EL PET 5,3+,4+,4
Reputedly 'loose but good', leading to the col/shoulder.

COLLADO DIRECT 6c,5,5+,6b
The face just to the right, bolted but rather spartanly so, also leading to the col/shoulder.

And on the main peak starting from a major ramp/ledge reached by a scramble from the right:

VIA SUBIRANA 5,5+
The groove on the far left leading to the col/shoulder.

VIA DEL TECHO 5+,A3&5,4+
A left to right slanting line to the impressive central roof, then the right side of the tower above.

VIA LA BELLA Y GRACIOSA MOZA 6,4,6,4,
The central line on the face and reportedly worthwhile, some bolts.

VIA DEL VIENTO 4,5-,4
The buttress and groove on the right side of the face.

The East Face

VIA BAEZ-ALON 3+,1,4-,3+
Starting from the shoulder between the two faces and following the line of least resistance to the top.

LA PLACA ROJA 5,3
A fine variation finish up the red wall. From its top continue up the arête or traverse right to the regular route.

VIA ORIGINAL 4-,2,4,4
A direct line up the buttress and groove to the right, reportedly "worthwhile and solid".

VIA CUIO-ANGUEL 5,A1&4,4+,3
The groove and buttress right again.

LA CATEDRAL - EAST FACE

1	Via Baez-Alon	3+, 1, 4-, 3+
2	La Placa Roja	5, 3
3	Via Original	4-, 2, 4, 4
4	Via Cuio-Anguel	5, A1 & 4, 4+, 3

LAS VEGAS

The least worthwhile of the developed areas that I have visited. The cliff is a blocky basalt, and is both dusty and somewhat loose in places, though the cliff is home to about 20 routes. The crag is reached by turning uphill in the centre of Chimiche, onto a minor road signed Las Vegas. This is followed for 3 kilometres until it fizzles out just short of Caesar's Palace. A walled track is followed uphill for about 10 minutes until another track branches down to the left across a narrow dry valley, past orange orchards and up to the left side of the cliff behind some shady trees at the Sector Los Pinos. There are ten routes here, generally short and from *6a (E1)* to *6c (E4)* whilst across the cacti fields to the right is a rather higher wall (The Sector Moco) where the routes are of much the same grade. Despite having a local topo the identification of individual climbs has proved difficult. Almost all the climbs contain some bolts but a subsidiary rack is probably a good idea.

TABARES

On the northern side of the island and overlooking the outskirts of Santa Cruz is a valley with a lot of outcropping rock. Unfortunately it is basalt, though there are a good number of worthwhile climbs here. Whether the cliff is worth a visit from the other end of the island depends on how much you enjoy somewhere 'out of the ordinary' also crack climbing. The cliffs are reached from the town of La Cuesta which is reached from the motorway (not well signed) between Santa Cruz and La Laguna. Drive uphill through the centre of La Cuesta past several 'no entry' right turns until a minor road turns north in the middle of the town signed 'Ville Tabares 1.7km & Los Campistos'. This is followed for a couple of kilometres, passing a very red bridge, until the road rounds a bend and the cliffs come into view. The cliffs outcrop in a horseshoe around the head of the valley (see map) and three areas have been developed at present. They are described in order of popularity, which also happens to be in reverse order of quality.

Immediately after the bend (care needed) is a right turn down a dirt track that leads to the parking (in an area that masquerades as the local rubbish dump) for the Sectors Tuberia and Macrocalma. For the Pared de Enfrente it is best to continue on the main track, over a very smelly river, and park by the first buildings. A track leads in front of the first house to the cliff edge. Spanish grades only are given throughout; feel free to add UK equivalents.

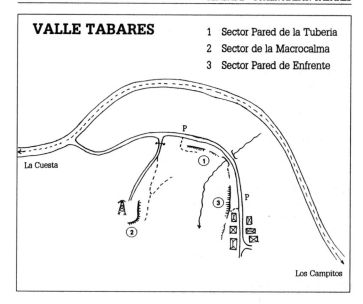

VALLE TABARES

1 Sector Pared de la Tuberia
2 Sector de la Macrocalma
3 Sector Pared de Enfrente

La Cuesta

P

Los Campitos

Pared Tubaria

A short sunny cliff of polished rock containing some desperate pitches. If a 10m high, plumb vertical *8a+* is your idea of heaven, look no further. From the parking descend a short slope to locate the crag, which is characterised by the water pipe running along its foot. The routes here are all short and sharp, the Spanish grades feeling especially tough.

On the far left are several very short lines. The first one of any significance is a crack in the back of a recess; this is immediately to the left of a buttress with three bolt runners in it.

PAULIT 5+ 10m
The slippery crack. Gear required.

PAPAS CON CARNE 6c 10m
The gymnastic buttress just to the right; three bolts protect.

MAPA 6a+ 10m
The slippery finger crack just right again. Gear required.

POTAGE DE BERROS 6c+ 10m
The thin crack to the right, protected by three bolts on its right side.

BUTERFINGERS * 7a 10m
The tenuous finger crack in the groove to the right. Gear required.

MARTIN EL LAJA * 8a+ 12m
The 'impossible' blank wall to the right protected by 4 bolts.

ATOMICA 7b+ 12m
The thin seam to the right has a peg and bolt *in situ*. Other gear required.

ALIEN 8a 12m
Another 'impossible' wall climb protected by 4 bolt runners.

METALLICA 7c 12m
The desperate thin crack line to the right. Three *in situ* pegs protect the most difficult section.

SUICIDAL TENDENCIES 7a 12m
The crack just to the right with three bolt runners finishing at the cliff top agave.

ANDORINA 6b 10m
The more reasonable crack to the right. The trouble is you have to place your own kit.

To the right are two more lines following a bolted crack and arête. No grades known.

Pared Macrocalma
The tall buttress below the power pylon is home to a series of climbs, many of which are worthwhile. They are up to 20m high and north-east-facing, so normally reside in the shade. The cliff is reached down a well made footpath that branches left from the side track forking right off the main track. On the far right is a rather nondescript area of rock, but in the centre of the cliff is a fine clean facing hanging above more broken rock and bounded by two fine grooves. Around to the left are more good groove and crack lines.

On the far right side of the face is the nondescript line of:

VIA DE LA S 4+ 20m
A groove in the lower wall leads past a couple of bolts to a possible stance and easier terrain trending right.

To the left is a huge perched block/flake half way up the cliff. The right side of this is climbed by:

VIA DE LA CHIMENEA * 4+ 20m
Climb the lower groove to a possible stance at the foot of the chimney then follow it and a blocky crack to the cliff top.

There are three short 'eliminates' based around the actual chimney of the last route.

LA VIA HILTI 6a 10m
The wall immediately right of the chimney is climbed via a thin crack to a lower-off.

PASTA GANSA 7a 10m
The wall just left of the chimney to a lower-off.

ESPOLON DE LA FUGA 6a+ 15m
Starts as for *VIA DE LA CHIMENEA* then steps out left to climb the arête on its left side. The best of the trio.

To the left the most obvious feature of the cliff is a fine hanging face, bound on its right by a long twisting groove line. To the right of this is a crack line that runs straight up the cliff to the top of the previously mentioned groove:

VIA DEL CARDON * 6a 22m
Climb easy terrain to a bush at the foot of the crack (possible stance) then follow the crack, past three bolt runners to the cliff top. A supplementary rack is probably a good idea.

The long groove is:
VIAJE CON NOSOTROS ** 5+ 24m
Climb a corner crack into the foot of the groove then follow it rightwards past five bolts to the cliff top.

Above the start of the groove proper is a roof and leaning wall with a bolt ladder up it: *VIA DEL TECHO A1* (it will never catch on).

To the left is the showpiece of the cliff, a fine shield of rock hanging above more broken terrain. I hesitate to suggest that the area is worth a visit for the three of the four routes here, but maybe it is, just.

ESPOLON ASMATICO ** 6b 22m
Start as for the previous climb but trend left to climb the fine wall right of

PARED MACROCALMA

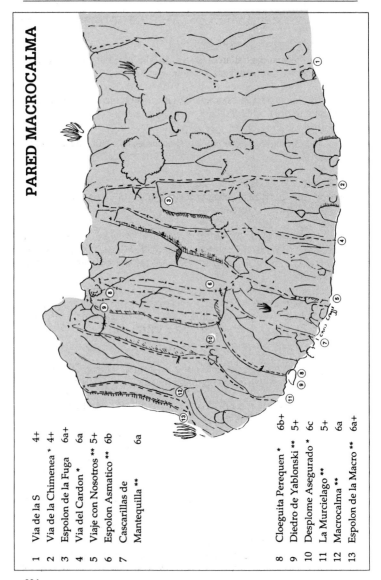

1	Via de la S	4+
2	Via de la Chimenea *	4+
3	Espolon de la Fuga	6a+
4	Via del Cardon *	6a
5	Viaje con Nosotros **	5+
6	Espolon Asmatico **	6b
7	Cascarillas de	
	Mantequilla **	6a

8	Cloeguita Perequen *	6b+
9	Diedro de Yablonski **	5+
10	Desplome Asegurado *	6c
11	La Murcielago **	5+
12	Macrocalma **	6a
13	Espolon de la Macro **	6a+

the blunt central arête. Five bolts protect the main difficulties.

CASCARILLAS DE MANTEQUILLA ** 6a 22m
The left side of the central arête is approached from directly below and climbed passing five more fixed metal Friends.

The left side of the face is bounded by another attractive twisting groove line, *DIEDRO DE YABLONSKI* (see below). Starting up this is:

CLOEGUITA PEREQUEN * 6b+ 22m
Climb the groove then step out right onto the face and follow the bolts (five again) to the cliff top.

DIEDRO DE YABLONSKI ** 5+ 22m
The fine groove gives an excellent sustained pitch. Carry a rack of Friends or (wash my mouth out) top rope it.

DESPLOME ASEGURADO * 6c 22m
The front of the narrow pillar to the left of *DIEDRO DE YABLONSKI* is followed with 'interest' to a final steepening. Three spaced bolts protect the main difficulties.

BUZONES * 5+ 18m
A tricky lower section leads into the base of the steep slab on the left, and this is climbed past a couple of fixed pegs. Carry a rack.

LA MURCIELAGO ** 5+ 20m
The deep groove around to the left is reached from the start of the previous climb. The crack in the back is parallel. Carry a rack of Friends.

The next three routes are most easily accessed from the left, though the first one can be started direct.

SOPA DE TRIPIS * 6b 18m
The steep slab to the left of the deep groove of the previous climb has three bolts protecting the main difficulties. Carry a few wires for the gaps.

MACROCALMA ** 6a 15m
The fine hand crack to the left needs a positive approach and a rack of 'Friendly' devices.

ESPOLON DE LA MACRO ** 6a+ 15m
The arête to the left has five bolt runners and some fine precarious climbing. Enjoy.

DIEDRO DE DESVIRGO 5+ 15m
Starting in the same place and trending left is a crack leading into a groove. Carry a rack, wires for the start and Friends for the wider upper part.

VIA DEL NIDO 5+ 15m
The groove to the left.

LAS PARALELAS 6c+ 6m
The two slim grooves left again. Climb one or both.

Sector Pared Enfrente

This is the imposing set of grooves and pillars on the eastern side of the valley (west-facing). There is limited roadside parking and the routes are approached from above, by abseil, as almost all of the lower section of the face consists of an unsavoury band of soft red rock then a series of dripping overhangs, although four routes ignore this fact and start from the gorge bed. Running along the cliff top, squeezed between spiky plants and a huge drop, is a wire cable installed in the interests of security. Use it; you know it makes sense. The climbs are of two sorts: fine sustained crack lines (a rack of smaller Friends required) and the faces between the cracks that are bolt protected. The routes are generally tough, and this allied to the difficulty of locating specific routes from above means a circumspect approach is sensible. The place may make an ideal top-roping venue if you don't want to get involved with too much of an epic. The climbs are described briefly from left to right (facing the cliff) and their positions can be located using the diagram, in relation to the clusters of fixed bolts spaced along the cliff top, or take a walk round to the other side of the gorge.

MAGNUM 44 * 6a+ 22m
The left-hand route is one of the few to run the full height of the basalt. A fine sustained hand crack. Friends required.

DELICIAS TURCAS * 5+ 18m
The next hand crack to the right, starting from the ledge.

To the right two face routes climb either side of a blunt rib:

BUJERITOS * 6c 18m
The left side of the rib; five bolts and a peg protect.

OVERKILL * 6b 18m
The right side of the rib; five bolts.

PREPARATE 7a 18m

228

The thin hand crack is reached from a stance on the right and has two peg runners. Take wires and Friends.

FISURA TRANSPARENTE * 6b 18m
The wall to the right starting and finishing up thin cracks, three bolts in the centre, wires and Friends for the rest.

ATAUD VACANTE ** 6a+ 18m
The hand and finger crack directly above the belay.

THERMINATOR * 7a 25m
The thin twisting crack contains three peg runners. Carry a rack of wires. An optional pitch from the foot of the cliff is there for those who want it.

AUTOPISTA AL INFERNO ** 7c 18m
The narrow wall and flared arête to the right is tough; six bolt runners protect.

KILLER * 6c 18m
The thin crack just right of the pillar. Keep left at the first fork and right at the second.

EXTASIS TECHNICO * 6c+ 18m
Start as for the previous climb but follow the right fork until it bears away left then leap out onto the face on the right (bolt then peg), then up a crack to the top.

GENOCIDIO ** 6a+ 25m
The long fine hand crack to the right, gained from the bed of the gorge. Carry a rack.

MAD-MAX * 7b 18m
The thin face to the right; four bolts protect.

MOC-MOC * 7c 18m
The thinner face right again; three bolts protect the hard section. Take gear for the rest.

IRON MAIDEN * 6c 25m
The thin hand crack has an optional start from the gorge bed.

BIP-BIP 7a 18m
The face to the right; three bolts protect the hard section.

DOSIS HEAVY METAL ** 6a 18m

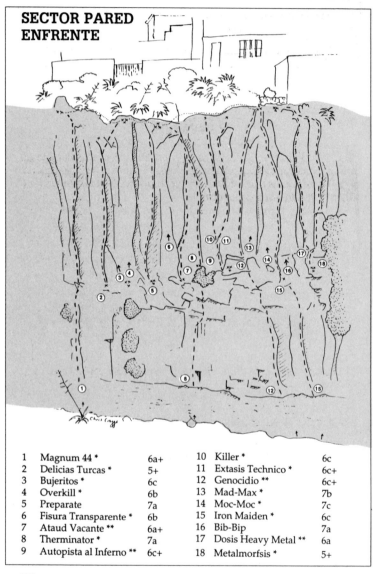

SECTOR PARED ENFRENTE

1	Magnum 44 *	6a+
2	Delicias Turcas *	5+
3	Bujeritos *	6c
4	Overkill *	6b
5	Preparate	7a
6	Fisura Transparente *	6b
7	Ataud Vacante **	6a+
8	Therminator *	7a
9	Autopista al Inferno **	6c+

10	Killer *	6c
11	Extasis Technico *	6c+
12	Genocidio **	6c+
13	Mad-Max *	7b
14	Moc-Moc *	7c
15	Iron Maiden *	6c
16	Bib-Bip	7a
17	Dosis Heavy Metal **	6a
18	Metalmorfsis *	5+